Writing GNU Emacs Extensions

Writing GNU Emacs Extensions

Bob Glickstein

O'REILLY™

Cambridge · Köln · Paris · Sebastopol · Tokyo

Writing GNU Emacs Extensions

by Bob Glickstein

Copyright © 1997 O'Reilly & Associates, Inc. All rights reserved.
Printed in the United States of America.

Editor: Andy Oram

Production Editors: Kismet McDonough-Chan and Ellie Fountain Maden

Printing History:

April 1997:   First Edition.

This book is printed on acid-free paper with 85% recycled content, 15% post-consumer waste. O'Reilly & Associates is committed to using paper with the highest recycled content available consistent with high quality.

ISBN: 1-56592-261-1   [8/97]

For Mom and Dad, without whom...
well, I'd just rather not think about it.

Table of Contents

Preface

Before you even begin to extend Emacs, it's already the highest-function text editor there is. Not only can it do everything you'd normally expect (formatting paragraphs, centering lines, searching for patterns, putting a block in upper case), not only does it have advanced features (matching braces in source code, employing color to highlight syntactic elements in your files, giving online help on every keystroke and other commands), but it also performs a host of functions you'd never dream of finding in a text editor. You can use Emacs to read and compose email and to browse the World Wide Web; you can have it run FTP for you, transparently making remote files editable as if they were local; you can ask it to remind you about upcoming meetings, appointments, and anniversaries. As if that weren't enough, Emacs can also play you in a game of Go-Moku (and win, more than likely); it can tell you today's date in the ancient Mayan calendar; and it can decompose a number into its prime factors.

With all that functionality, it may seem crazy that Emacs users often spend a significant portion of their time extending Emacs. After all, most programmers view their editors as tools for creating *other* software; why spend so much energy modifying the tool itself? A carpenter doesn't tinker with his hammer; a plumber doesn't tinker with his wrench; they use their tools to accomplish the job at hand. So why are Emacs users different?

The answer is that the carpenter and the plumber *would* tinker with their tools to make them better, if they knew how. Who knows exactly what they need better than they do? But they're not toolsmiths. On the other hand, Emacs is a special kind of tool: it's software, which means the tool is the same stuff as what Emacs users use it on. The user of Emacs is often a programmer, and programming Emacs is, after all, just programming. Emacs users are in the happy position of being their own toolsmiths.

This book teaches Emacs Lisp programming using a series of real-life examples progressing from trivial to sophisticated. We'll start with simple configuration tweaks that you can put in your Emacs startup file, and by the end we'll be writing "major modes" and modifying Emacs's own "command loop." Along the way we'll learn about variables, keymaps, interactive commands, buffers, windows, process I/O, and more.

When I refer to Emacs in this book, I specifically mean GNU Emacs. There are many editors that call themselves Emacs. Here's a bit of the history of the name according to the authoritative *On-line Hacker Jargon File*, version 4.0.0, 24-Jul-1996:

> [Emacs] was originally written by Richard Stallman in TECO under ITS at the MIT AI lab; AI Memo 554 described it as "an advanced, self-documenting, customizable, extensible real-time display editor." It has since been re-implemented any number of times, by various hackers, and versions exist that run under most major operating systems. Perhaps the most widely used version, also written by Stallman and now called "GNU EMACS" or GNUMACS, runs principally under UNIX. It includes facilities to run compilation subprocesses and send and receive mail; many hackers spend up to 80% of their tube time inside it. Other variants include GOSMACS, CCA EMACS, UniPress EMACS, Montgomery EMACS, jove, epsilon, and MicroEMACS.

The examples in this book were all developed and tested in GNU Emacs version 19.34 and a pre-release version of Emacs 20.1 under various flavors of UNIX. See Appendix D, *Obtaining and Building Emacs*, for information on where to find the Emacs distribution.

I've let my own progression as an Emacs user be my guide in selecting instructive examples. The sequence of examples in this book essentially retells the story of how my own Emacs usage matured. For instance, from the very first moment I started using Emacs I knew I had to do something about getting that damn **BACK-SPACE** key not to invoke the online help! Maybe you have that problem, too. Solving that problem is the first example we'll cover in the next chapter.

After I'd been using Emacs for a short while, I found myself wanting a number of cursor-motion shortcuts. As I learned, they were easily written in terms of Emacs's existing motion primitives. We'll see several examples of those in Chapter 2, *Simple New Commands*. Later I needed to have some way of undoing one of my most common and maddening typing errors: pressing **CONTROL-v** several times, when I meant to press **CONTROL-b**. Instead of moving the cursor a few spaces to the left, I'd scroll the whole window a few times and lose my place. Fixing this was easily done, too, as you'll see in Chapter 3, *Cooperating Commands*. When I began to manage files full of clever quotations, I needed special tools to handle the specially formatted files. We'll see some of those in Chapter 9, *A Major Mode*.

Except for the first handful of examples, which are simple one- and two-liners, each example has its own chapter. Each chapter illustrates some problem needing an Emacs Lisp solution, then presents a function or set of functions that solves the problem. Then, just as real-life customizations tend to evolve to become more useful and more general, we'll revise the solution once or twice before going on to the next subject.

Each example builds on the concepts of prior examples and introduces a few new ones of its own. By the end of the book, we will have covered most major topics in Emacs Lisp programming and discussed the techniques for quickly finding out how to do anything you might need to do in Emacs Lisp, using on-line documentation and other information. To borrow an old saying: Give a man a new Emacs command and he can hack for a night; teach a man to make new Emacs commands and he can hack for a lifetime.

This book presumes that you're familiar with programming and with Emacs use. It would help if you were acquainted with some variant of the Lisp programming language (of which Emacs Lisp is one dialect), but that's not strictly necessary. The essentials of Lisp programming are pretty simple and should quickly become clear through the examples we'll be using. There's also Appendix A, *Lisp Quick Reference*, which briefly recaps Lisp fundamentals.

If you aren't familiar with the basic concepts in Emacs, refer to *Learning GNU Emacs, 2nd edition* by Debra Cameron, Bill Rosenblatt, and Eric Raymond. Also useful is Emacs's own online documentation, especially the Emacs "info" manual, which is also available in book form as *The GNU Emacs Manual*. If you'd like a more complete understanding of Lisp programming, I recommend *Common Lisp: A Gentle Introduction to Symbolic Computation* by David Touretzky.

This book is not a reference manual for Emacs Lisp; nor, in fact, is it particularly thorough in its coverage of the language. It's a tutorial, covering topics chosen more for good instructional flow than for exhaustiveness. For best effect it should be read from beginning to end. The Free Software Foundation publishes *The GNU Emacs Lisp Reference Manual*, the definitive reference manual on which it would be difficult to improve. It's available in printed and electronic forms from several sources; see Appendix D.

What Is Emacs?

It's missing the point to say that Emacs is just a programmable text editor. It's also, for instance, a C code editor. That may seem like nitpicking, but editing C code and editing text are two very different activities, and Emacs accommodates the differences by being two different editors. When editing code, you don't care about paragraph structure. When editing text, you don't care about indenting each line according to its syntax.

Emacs is also a Lisp code editor. It's also a hexadecimal binary file editor. It's also a structured outline editor. It's also a directory editor, a tar file editor, an email editor, and a hundred others. Each kind of editor is an Emacs *mode*, a chunk of Lisp code that combines Emacs's primitive types and operations in some new way. Each mode is therefore an *extension* of Emacs, which means that when you strip away all those modes—when you remove the extensions and you're left with just the core of Emacs—you don't have any editors at all; you have the raw materials for making editors. You have an editor-builder.

What can you build with an editor-builder? Editors, of course, but what's an editor? An editor is a program for viewing and altering a representation of data of some kind. By "representation" I mean a set of rules for showing the data's structure and content, and for indicating naturally how interactions with the data are supposed to proceed. When editing a text file, the rules are pretty simple: each printable byte gets displayed in sequence, with newline characters causing line breaks; and a cursor indicates where in the byte sequence the next user-invoked operation will occur. When editing a directory, the metaphor is a little less straightforward—data in the directory file must first be translated into a human-readable form—but the resulting interactions still seem natural.

This definition of editor covers nearly the whole range of interactive applications, and that's no accident. Interactive applications are almost always editors for some kind of data or another. Emacs therefore is, in the end, a general-purpose, interactive application builder. It's a user interface toolkit! Like any good toolkit, Emacs supplies a set of user-interface widgets, a set of operations on them, an event loop, a sophisticated I/O regime, and a language for putting them all together. The widget set may not be fancy and graphical like X11, Windows, or Macintosh toolkits are, but as Emacs programmers discover, a full-blown graphical toolkit is often overkill. 99% of most applications is textual, whether it's rows and columns of numbers, lists of menu items, or letters in a crossword puzzle diagram (as in our culminating example in Chapter 10, *A Comprehensive Example*). For such applications, Emacs surpasses other toolkits in power, sophistication, simplicity, and performance.

The real answer to "Why are Emacs users different?" isn't merely that they spend time tinkering with the tools they use. They're using Emacs for its intended purpose: to create a universe of *new* tools.

Conventions Used in This Book

The following conventions are used in this book.

Typographic Conventions

`Constant Willison`
>   Used for Emacs commands and all elements of code.

Italic
>   Used to introduce new terms. Used for filenames, commands entered from a UNIX shell, newsgroups, and Internet addresses.

Bold
>   Used for keystrokes.

Emacs Commands

This book follows the standard Emacs documentation when referring to keys. When you hold down the **CONTROL (CTRL)** key, the syntax **C-** is used. When you hold down the **META** or **ALT** key (or use the **ESCAPE** key for the same effect), the syntax **M-** is used. We also refer to **RET** for the **RETURN** or **ENTER** key, **TAB** for the **TAB** key, **ESC** for the **ESCAPE** key, and **SPC** for the space bar.

Examples

When you see x ⇒ y, it means that the result of computing the expression on the left yields the value on the right.

Organization of This Book

Each chapter in this book builds on the chapters before it. I recommend that you read the chapters in order; that way everything should make sense.

Chapter 1, Customizing Emacs
>   Introduces some basic changes you can make to Emacs. It will familiarize you with Emacs Lisp, how to evaluate Lisp expressions, and how that alters Emacs's behavior.

Chapter 2, Simple New Commands
>   Continues the tutorial by teaching you how to write Lisp functions and install them so they're invoked at the right time. Hooks and the feature called advice are introduced.

Chapter 3, Cooperating Commands

Teaches techniques for saving information between separate function calls and helping groups of functions work together—the first step in writing *systems* instead of mere commands. Symbol properties and markers are among the topics introduced along the way.

Chapter 4, Searching and Modifying Buffers

Shows some of the most common techniques you'll need: those that affect the current buffer and strings within it. Regular expressions are introduced.

Chapter 5, Lisp Files

Discusses loading, autoloading, and packages, which are features you'll need when you start creating large groups of related functions.

Chapter 6, Lists

Fills in some background on this fundamental feature of Lisp.

Chapter 7, Minor Mode

Shows how to assemble related functions and variables into an editing package called a "minor mode." The central example in this chapter deals with making paragraph formatting in Emacs work more like paragraph formatting in a word processor.

Chapter 8, Evaluation and Error Recovery

Shows the flexibility of the Emacs Lisp interpreter, how to control what gets evaluated when, and how to write code that is impervious to run-time errors.

Chapter 9, A Major Mode

Explains the differences between minor and major modes, and offers a simple example of the latter: a mode for treating a file of quotations in a more structured manner than ordinary text.

Chapter 10, A Comprehensive Example

Defines a major mode that drastically alters Emacs's normal behavior. It's a crossword puzzle editor and an illustration of how flexible an environment Emacs is for developing text-oriented applications.

Appendix A, Lisp Quick Reference

Provides a handy guide to Lisp's syntax, data types, and control structures.

Appendix B, Debugging and Profiling

Describes tools you can use to track down problems in your Emacs Lisp code.

Appendix C, Sharing Your Code

Explains the steps you should take when you want to distribute your creations to other people.

Appendix D, Obtaining and Building Emacs

Outlines the steps necessary to get a working version of Emacs running on your system.

Obtaining the Example Programs

If you're using a Web browser, you can get the examples from *ftp://ftp.oreilly.com/published/oreilly/nutshell/emacs_extensions.*

FTP

To use FTP, you need a machine with direct access to the Internet. A sample session is shown, with what you should type in **boldface**.

```
% ftp ftp.oreilly.com
Connected to ftp.oreilly.com.
220 FTP server (Version 6.21 Tue Mar 10 22:09:55 EST 1992) ready.
Name (ftp.oreilly.com:yourname): anonymous
331 Guest login ok, send domain style e-mail address as password.
Password: yourname@yourhost.com (use your user name and host here)
230 Guest login ok, access restrictions apply.
ftp> cd /published/oreilly/nutshell/emacs_extensions
250 CWD command successful.
ftp> binary (Very important! You must specify binary transfer for
gzipped files.)
200 Type set to I.
ftp> get examples.tar.gz
200 PORT command successful.
150 Opening BINARY mode data connection for examples.tar.gz.
226 Transfer complete.
ftp> quit
221 Goodbye.
%
```

The file is a gzipped tar archive; extract the files from the archive by typing:

```
% gzip -dc examples.tar.gz | tar -xvf -
```

System V systems require the following *tar* command instead:

```
% gzip -dc examples.tar.gz | tar -xvof -
```

If *gzip* is not available on your system, use separate *uncompress* and *tar* commands.

```
% uncompress examples.tar.gz
% tar xvf examples.tar
```

Acknowledgments

Thanks to Nathaniel Borenstein, who helped to dispel my chauvinism about C' and taught me an appreciation for the world's amazing variety of programming languages.

Thanks to Richard Stallman for writing Emacs—twice—and who was right about an amazing phenomenon: hackers write better code when it's for their own satisfaction instead of for pay.

Thanks to Mike McInerny, whose stubborn persistence got me started using GNU Emacs—even after several false starts convinced me it wasn't worth my time.

Thanks to Ben Liblit for ideas, code, and bug hunting in my Defer package (which was going to be a chapter in this book until Emacs evolved parallel functionality: the timer package.) Additional help was provided by Simon Marshall, who used and improved on many of the ideas in his `defer-lock`. Hi, Si.

Thanks to Linda Branagan for showing me it's possible for an ordinary person like me to write a book. (Not that *she's* ordinary; not even close.)

Thanks to Emily Cox and Henry Rathvon for some insider information about crossword puzzles.

Thanks to all the folks who reviewed and commented on early drafts of this book: Julie Epelboim, Greg Fox, David Hartmann, Bart Schaefer, Ellen Siever, and Steve Webster.

Thanks to my partners at Zanshin Inc. and the Internet Movie Database for allowing me to divide my energies between those projects and this book.

Thanks to my editor, Andy Oram, for coping flexibly with the aforementioned divided energies.

Thanks to Alex, my dog, for curling happily by my feet for much of the writing of this book.

Most of all, to Andrea Dougherty, who encouraged me, supported me, made innumerable sacrifices, performed uncountable services, provided companionship when I needed it and solitude when I needed *that* (never the other way around), and who in all other respects was good for me and for this book: it must be love.

1

Customizing Emacs

This chapter introduces basic Emacs customizations, and teaches some Emacs Lisp along the way. One of the simplest and most common customizations is to move commands from one key to another. Perhaps you don't like Emacs's two-key sequence for saving files (**C-x C-s**) because you've been using some other editor where save is simply **C-s**. Or perhaps you sometimes accidentally type **C-x C-c**, which exits Emacs, when you mean to press only **C-x**, and you'd like accidental presses of **C-x C-c** to have a less drastic effect. Or perhaps, as in the example that follows, you need to work around an unusual expectation that Emacs has about your keyboard.

Backspace and Delete

Imagine you're typing the word "Lisp" and you accidentally type "List." To correct your typo, do you press the **BACKSPACE** key or the **DELETE** key?

The answer depends on your keyboard, but it's not merely a question of how the key is labeled. Sometimes the key is labeled "Backspace," sometimes it's labeled "Delete," sometimes "Erase," and sometimes it's not labeled with a word but has a left-pointing arrow or some other graphic. To Emacs, what matters isn't the label but the numeric character code that the key generates when pressed. Regardless of the label on the key, the "move left and erase the previous character" key may generate an ASCII "backspace" code (decimal 8, usually denoted **BS**) or an ASCII "delete" code (decimal 127, usually denoted **DEL**).

In its default configuration, Emacs believes only **DEL** is the code meaning "move left and erase the previous character." If you have a **BACKSPACE/DELETE/ERASE** key that generates a **BS**, it won't do what you expect when you press it.

What's worse is what your **BACKSPACE/DELETE/ERASE** key *will* do when you press it, if it's a **BS**-generating key. Emacs presumes that since **BS** isn't used for moving left and erasing the previous character, it's available to perform another function. As it happens, **BS** is also the code sent when you press **C-h**. If you're among those who don't need **C-h** to mean "move left and erase the previous character," then **C-h** is a pretty natural choice for a Help key, and in fact that's what Emacs uses it for by default. Unfortunately, this means that if you have a **BS**-generating **BACKSPACE/DELETE/ERASE** key, then pressing it won't backspace or delete or erase; it will invoke Emacs's online help.

More than one tentative first-time Emacs user has been put off by the surprise that greets them the first time they try to erase a typo. Suddenly a new Emacs window—the Help window—pops up, prompting the hapless user to choose some Help subcommand. The Help window is so verbose and unexpected that it merely exacerbates the user's astonishment. The natural panic reaction—hit **C-g** ("abort the current operation") a bunch of times—is accompanied by a cacophonous ringing of the terminal bell. It's no wonder that intelligent, well-meaning users who might otherwise have helped swell the ranks of fervent Emacs evangelists instead choose to continue struggling with safe, inoffensive vi.

It pains me to think of it, especially when the situation is so easily remedied.

When Emacs starts, it reads and executes the contents of the *.emacs* file in your home directory. Emacs Lisp is the language of this file, and as we will discover in the course of this book, there's almost nothing you can't customize in Emacs by writing some Emacs Lisp and putting it in *.emacs*. The first thing we'll look at is adding some code to *.emacs* to make **BS** and **DEL** *both* do "back up and erase a character," moving the Help command to some other key. First we'll need to take a look at Lisp, the language of the *.emacs* file.

Lisp

Various forms of Lisp have been around since the 1950s. It is traditionally associated with artificial intelligence applications, for which Lisp is well-suited because it permits symbolic computation, can treat code as data, and simplifies building very complicated data structures. But Lisp is much more than just an AI language. It is applicable to a wide range of problems, a fact that is frequently overlooked by computer scientists but which is well known to Emacs users. Among the features that distinguish Lisp from other programming languages are:

Fully-parenthesized prefix notation

All expressions and function calls in Lisp are surrounded by parentheses,[*] and the function name always precedes the arguments to the function. So whereas in other languages you may be able to write:

```
x + y
```

to apply the + function to the arguments x and y, in Lisp you write

```
(+ x y)
```

"Prefix notation" means that the operator precedes the operands. When the operator is between the operands, it's called "infix notation."

Though unfamiliar, prefix notation has some benefits over infix notation. In infix languages, to write the sum of five variables you need four plus signs:

```
a + b + c + d + e
```

Lisp is more concise:

```
(+ a b c d e)
```

Also, questions of operator precedence do not arise. For example, is the value of

```
3 + 4 * 5
```

35 or 23? It depends on whether * has higher precedence than +. But in Lisp, the confusion vanishes:

```
(+ 3 (* 4 5))        ; result is 23
(* (+ 3 4) 5)        ; result is 35
```

(Comments in Lisp are introduced with a semicolon and continue to the end of the line.) Finally, while infix languages need commas to separate the arguments to a function:

```
foo(3 + 4, 5 + 6)
```

Lisp doesn't need that extra bit of syntax:

```
(foo (+ 3 4) (+ 5 6))
```

List data type

Lisp has a built-in data type called a *list*. A list is a Lisp object containing zero or more other Lisp objects, surrounded by parentheses. Here are some lists:

```
(hello there)        ; list containing two "symbols"
(1 2 "xyz")          ; two numbers and a string
(a (b c))            ; a symbol and a sublist (containing two symbols)
()                   ; the empty list
```

---

[*] The proliferation of parentheses in Lisp is a feature that Lisp critics cheerfully decry as a sure sign of its inferiority. According to them, Lisp stands for "Lots of Infernal Stupid Parentheses." (In fact, Lisp stands for "List Processing.") In my view, the much simpler syntax renders Lisp code more readable, not less, than code in other languages, as I hope you will agree.

Lists can be assigned to variables, passed as arguments to functions and returned from them, constructed with such functions as `cons` and `append`, and taken apart with such functions as `car` and `cdr`. We'll be covering all that in plenty of detail later.

Garbage collection

Lisp is a *garbage-collected* language, which means that Lisp itself automatically reclaims the memory used by your program's data structures. By contrast, with languages such as C, one must explicitly allocate memory with `malloc` when it's needed, then explicitly release it with `free`. (The `malloc`/`free` approach and others like it in non-garbage-collecting languages are prone to abuse. Prematurely releasing allocated memory is one of the world's greatest sources of program errors, and forgetting to release allocated memory can cause programs to "bloat" until all available memory is used up.)

For all the convenience that garbage collection affords the programmer, it also has a drawback: periodically, Emacs stops everything it's doing and displays the message "Garbage collecting..." to the user. The user cannot use Emacs until garbage collection is finished.* This usually takes only a second or less, but it may happen very often. Later on we'll learn some programming practices that help to reduce the amount of garbage collection that takes place.

The word *expression* usually means any piece of Lisp code or any Lisp data structure. All Lisp expressions, whether code or data, can be evaluated by the Lisp interpreter built into Emacs to make them yield some computational result. The effect of evaluating a variable is to access the Lisp object previously stored in the variable. Evaluating a list is the way to invoke Lisp functions, as we'll see below.

Since the invention of Lisp, there have been many Lisp dialects, some of which barely resemble the others. MacLisp, Scheme, and Common Lisp are some of the better-known ones. Emacs Lisp is different from all of these. This book focuses only on Emacs Lisp.

Keys and Strings

The goal of this chapter is to make any **BS**-generating key work the same as any **DEL**-generating key. Unfortunately, **C-h** will no longer invoke the Help command.

---

* Emacs uses a mark-and-sweep garbage collection scheme, which is one of the easiest ways to implement garbage collection. There are other approaches to implementing garbage collection that would not be so intrusive from the user's point of view; for instance, so-called "incremental" garbage collection can take place without bringing Emacs to a halt. Unfortunately, Emacs does not employ one of these more advanced approaches.

You'll need to choose some other key to invoke Help; my own choice for the new Help key is **META-question-mark**.

The META Key

The **META** key works like the **CONTROL** key and the **SHIFT** key, which means that you hold it down while pressing some other key. Such keys are called *modifiers*. Not all keyboards have a **META** key, though. Sometimes the **ALT** key will serve the same purpose, but not all keyboards have an **ALT** key, either.

In any case, you don't need to use the **META** key *or* the **ALT** key. The single keystroke **META-*x*** can always be replaced with the two-key sequence **ESC *x***. (Note that **ESC** is *not* a modifier—you press it and release it like a normal key before pressing *x*.)

Binding Keystrokes to Commands

In Emacs, every keystroke invokes a *command* or is part of a multiple-key sequence that invokes a command. Commands are special kinds of Lisp functions, as we will see. Making a keystroke invoke a command such as Help is known as *binding* the keysequence to the command. We'll need to execute some Lisp code to bind keys to commands. One Lisp function for doing this is `global-set-key`.

Here's what a call to `global-set-key` looks like. Remember that a function call in Lisp is simply a parenthesized list. The first element of the list is the name of the function, and any remaining elements are the arguments. The function `global-set-key` takes two arguments: the keysequence to bind, and the command to bind it to.

```
(global-set-key  keysequence  command)
```

One important thing to note about Emacs Lisp is that it is case-sensitive.

The *keysequence* we've chosen is **META-question-mark**. How is this denoted in Emacs Lisp?

Denoting Keys in Strings

There are a few different ways to write a keysequence in Emacs Lisp notation. The simplest is to write the keys as a *string*. In Lisp, a string is a sequence of characters surrounded with double quotes.

```
"xyz"        ; three-character string
```

To get a double quote in the string itself, precede it with a backslash (\):

```
"I said, \"Look out!\""
```

This represents the string containing these characters:

```
I said, "Look out!"
```

To include a backslash in the string, precede it with another backslash.

An ordinary key is denoted by writing the character in a string. For instance, the keystroke q is denoted in Lisp by the string `"q"`. The keystroke \ would be written as `"\\"`.

Special characters such as **META-question-mark** are denoted in strings using a special syntax: `"\M-?"`. Even though there are four characters inside the double quotes, Emacs reads this as a string containing the single character called **META-question-mark**.[*]

In Emacs jargon, **M**-*x* is shorthand for **META**-*x*, and `"\M-`*x*`"` is the string version. **CONTROL**-*x* is abbreviated **C**-*x* in Emacs documentation, and in strings is written as: `"\C-`*x*`"`. You can combine the **CONTROL** and **META** keys, too. **CONTROL-META**-*x* is denoted **C-M**-*x* and is written as `"\C-\M-`*x*`"` in strings. `"\C-\M-`*x*`"`, incidentally, is interchangeable with `"\M-\C-`*x*`"` (**META-CONTROL**-*x*).

(**CONTROL**-*x* is also sometimes abbreviated ^*x* in documentation, corresponding to this alternative string syntax: `"\^`*x*`"`.)

Now we know how to fill in the first argument to our `global-set-key` example:

```
(global-set-key "\M-?" command)
```

(One other way to write the keysequence `"\M-?"` is `"\e?"`. The string `"\e"` denotes the escape character, and **M**-*x* is the same as **ESC** *x*.)

Next we must figure out what belongs in place of *command*. This argument should be the name of the Help function that we want **M**-? to invoke—i.e., the function that **C**-h now invokes. In Lisp, functions are named with *symbols*. Symbols are like function names or variable names in other languages, although Lisp allows a wider variety of characters in symbols than most languages allow in their variable names. For instance, legal Lisp symbols include `let*` and `up&down-p`.

---

[*] You can use the `length` function, which returns the length of a string, to confirm this. If you evaluate (`length "\M-?"`), the result is 1. How to "evaluate" is covered later in this chapter.

To What Is C-h Bound?

In order to find the symbol that names the Help command, we can use **C-h b**, which invokes another command called `describe-bindings`. This is one of the Help system's many subcommands. It presents a window listing all the keybindings in effect. Looking through it for the **C-h** binding, we find this line:

```
C-h          help-command
```

This tells us that `help-command` is the symbol that names the function that invokes Help.

Our Lisp example is almost complete, but we can't just write

```
(global-set-key "\M-?" help-command)          ; almost right!
```

This is wrong because of the way symbols are interpreted when they appear in Lisp expressions. If a symbol appears in the first position of a list, it's the name of a function to execute. If it appears elsewhere, it's a *variable* whose value needs to be retrieved. But when we run `global-set-key` as shown, we don't want the value contained in `help-command`, whatever that may be. The value we want is the symbol `help-command` itself. In short, we wish to *prevent* the symbol from being evaluated before it's passed to `global-set-key`. After all, as far as we know, `help-command` doesn't have a value as a variable.

The way to prevent a symbol (or any Lisp expression) from being evaluated is to *quote* it by preceding it with a single quote (´). It looks like this:

```
(global-set-key "\M-?" 'help-command)
```

Our Lisp example is now complete. If you place this line in your *.emacs* file, then **M-?** will invoke `help-command` the next time you run Emacs, and in all future Emacs sessions. (Soon we'll learn how to make Lisp expressions take effect immediately.) **M-? b** will invoke `describe-bindings` the way **C-h b** did before (and still does—at this point, both **M-?** and **C-h** are bound to `help-command`).

Incidentally, to illustrate the difference between quoting and not quoting, the same effect could be achieved with

```
(setq x 'help-command)               ; setq assigns a variable
(global-set-key "\M-?" x)            ; use x's value
```

The first line sets the variable **x** to hold the symbol `help-command`. The second uses **x**'s value—the symbol `help-command`—as the binding for **M-?**. The only difference between this and the first example is that now you end up with a leftover variable named **x** that didn't exist before.

Symbols aren't the only things that may follow a ´ character; any Lisp expression can be quoted, including lists, numbers, strings, and other kinds of expressions we'll learn about later. Writing ´*expr* is shorthand for

```
(quote expr)
```

which, when evaluated, yields *expr*. You might have noticed that a quote is required before the symbol `help-command` but not before the string argument, `"\M-?"`. This is because in Lisp, strings are *self-evaluating*, which means that when the string is evaluated, the result is the string itself. So quoting it, while harmless, is redundant. Numbers, characters, and vectors are other types of self-evaluating Lisp expressions.

To What Should C-h Be Bound?

Now that we've bound `help-command` to **M-?**, the next thing to do is to change the binding for **C-h**. Using exactly the same process just described—that is, running `describe-bindings` (with *either* **C-h b** or **M-? b** at this point)—we find that the command invoked by **DEL** is `delete-backward-char`.

So we can write

```
(global-set-key "\C-h" ´delete-backward-char)
```

Now **DEL** and **C-h** do the same thing. If you put these lines into your *.emacs* file:

```
(global-set-key "\M-?" ´help-command)
(global-set-key "\C-h" ´delete-backward-char)
```

then in your future Emacs sessions, your **BACKSPACE/DELETE/ERASE** key will do the right thing, whether it sends a **BS** code or a **DEL** code. But how can we cause these changes to take effect in the current session? This requires *explicit evaluation* of these two Lisp expressions.

Evaluating Lisp Expressions

There are several ways to explicitly evaluate Lisp expressions.

1. You can put the Lisp expressions in a file, then *load* the file. Suppose you place the expressions in a file named *rebind.el*. (Emacs Lisp filenames customarily end in *.el*.) You could then type **M-x load-file RET rebind.el RET** to cause Emacs to evaluate the contents of that file.

   If you placed those expressions into your *.emacs* file, you could load *.emacs* in the same way. But after you've been using Emacs for a while, your *.emacs* tends to grow, and if it's very large, loading it could be slow. In that case, you wouldn't want to load the entire file just to get the effect of a couple of small changes. That brings us to our next option.

2. You can use the command `eval-last-sexp`, which is bound to* C-x C-e. (*Sexp*‡ is an abbreviation for *S-expression*, which in turn is short for *symbolic expression*, which is another name for "Lisp expression.") This command evaluates the Lisp expression to the left of the cursor. So what you'd do is position the cursor at the end of the first line:

```
(global-set-key "\M-?" ´help-command)█
(global-set-key "\C-h" ´delete-backward-char)
```

and press **C-x C-e**; then move to the end of the second line:

```
(global-set-key "\M-?" ´help-command)
(global-set-key "\C-h" ´delete-backward-char)█
```

and press **C-x C-e** again. Note that each time you press **C-x C-e**, the result of evaluating `global-set-key`—the special symbol `nil` (which we'll see again later)—is shown in Emacs's message area at the bottom of the screen.

3. You can use the command `eval-expression`, which is bound to **M-:**‡. This command prompts you in the minibuffer (the area at the bottom of the screen) for a Lisp expression, then evaluates it and shows the result.

`eval-expression` is one of a few commands considered by the makers of Emacs to be dangerous for novice users to try. Hogwash, I say; nevertheless, the command is initially *disabled*, so when you try to use it, Emacs tells you "You have typed **M-:**, invoking disabled command `eval-expression`." Then it displays a description of `eval-expression` and prompts you as follows:

```
You can now type
Space to try the command just this once,
        but leave it disabled,
Y to try it and enable it (no questions if you use it again),
N to do nothing (command remains disabled).
```

If you choose **Y**, Emacs adds the following Lisp expression to your *.emacs*:

```
(put 'eval-expression ´disabled nil)
```

(The **put** function relates to *property lists*, which we'll see in the section on "Symbol Properties" in Chapter 3.) My advice is to put this in your *.emacs* yourself before you ever get this message from Emacs, so you'll never have to bother with the "disabled command" warning. As soon as you put the **put**

---

* Technically, one should only speak of keysequences being bound to commands, not commands being bound to keysequences. (To say that a keysequence is "bound" to a command correctly signifies that there's just one thing it can do—invoke that command. To say that a command is "bound" to a keysequence would mean that only one keysequence can invoke the command, but that's never the case.) But this misuse of "bound to" is as common as the correct use, and rarely causes confusion.

† Pronounced "sex pee." Unfortunately.

‡ This keybinding is new in Emacs 19.29. In prior versions, `eval-expression` was bound to **M-ESC** by default.

function in *.emacs*, of course, it's a good idea to evaluate it so it takes effect in the present session, using `eval-last-sexp` as described above.

4. You can use the `*scratch*` buffer. This buffer is automatically created when Emacs starts. The buffer is in *Lisp Interaction* mode. In this mode, pressing C-j invokes `eval-print-last-sexp`, which is like `eval-last-sexp` except that the result of the evaluation is inserted into the buffer at the location of the cursor. Another feature of Lisp Interaction mode is its ability to complete a partially typed Lisp symbol when you press **M-TAB** (which invokes `lisp-complete-symbol`). Lisp Interaction mode is particularly useful for testing and debugging Lisp expressions that are too long to type into the minibuffer, or that yield complicated data structures when evaluated.

Whichever method you use, evaluating the `global-set-key` expression results in the new bindings being used.

Apropos

Before wrapping up this first example, let's discuss Emacs's most important on-line help facility, `apropos`. Suppose you're one of those who have both **BS** *and* **DEL** keys and think it's a good idea for **BS** to erase the character preceding the cursor and **DEL** to erase the character following the cursor. You know that `delete-backward-char` is the command that accomplishes the former, but you don't know which command achieves the latter. You strongly suspect that Emacs must have such a command. How do you find it?

The answer is to use the **apropos** command, which allows you to search all known variables and functions for a pattern you specify. Try this:[*]

```
M-x apropos RET delete RET
```

The result is a buffer listing all the matches for "delete" among Emacs's variables and functions. If we search that buffer for occurrences of the word "character," we narrow the field down to

```
backward-delete-char
Command: Delete the previous N characters (following if N is negative).
backward-delete-char-untabify
Command: Delete characters backward, changing tabs into spaces.
delete-backward-char
Command: Delete the previous N characters (following if N is negative).
delete-char
Command: Delete the following N characters (previous if N is negative).
```

---

[*] All Emacs commands, regardless of which keys (if any) they're bound to, can be invoked with **M-x** *command-name* RET. Naturally, **M-x** is itself just a keybinding for a command, `execute-extended-command`, which prompts for the name of a command to execute.

The function `delete-char` is the one we want.

```
(global-set-key "\C-?" 'delete-char)
```

(For historical reasons, the way to write the **DEL** character is **CONTROL**-question-mark.)

You may invoke `apropos` with a *prefix argument*. In Emacs, pressing **C-u** before executing a command is a way to pass extra information to the command. Frequently, **C-u** is followed by a number; for instance, **C-u 5 C-b** means "move the cursor left 5 characters." Sometimes the extra information is just the fact that you pressed **C-u**.

When `apropos` is invoked with a prefix argument, it not only reports Emacs functions and variables that match the search pattern, it also reports any existing keybindings for each command in the list. (This isn't the default because finding the keybindings can be slow.) Using **C-u M-x apropos RET delete RET** and picking out occurrences of "character" as before, we come up with:

```
backward-delete-char                    (not bound to any keys)
Command: Delete the previous N characters (following if N is negative).
backward-delete-char-untabify           (not bound to any keys)
Command: Delete characters backward, changing tabs into spaces.
delete-backward-char                    C-h, DEL
Command: Delete the previous N characters (following if N is negative).
delete-char                             C-d
Command: Delete the following N characters (previous if N is negative).
```

This confirms that both **C-h** and **DEL** now invoke `delete-backward-char`, and also informs us that `delete-char` already has a binding: **C-d**. After we execute

```
(global-set-key "\C-?" 'delete-char)
```

if we run `apropos` again, we find

```
backward-delete-char                    (not bound to any keys)
Command: Delete the previous N characters (following if N is negative).
backward-delete-char-untabify           (not bound to any keys)
Command: Delete characters backward, changing tabs into spaces.
delete-backward-char                    C-h
Command: Delete the previous N characters (following if N is negative).
delete-char                             C-d, DEL
Command: Delete the following N characters (previous if N is negative).
```

When we know that the target of our search is an Emacs command, as opposed to a variable or function, we can further limit the scope of the search by using command-apropos (**M-?** **a**) instead of apropos. The difference between a command and other Lisp functions is that commands have been written specially to be invoked interactively, i.e., from a keybinding or with **M-x**. Functions that aren't commands can only be invoked as function calls from other Lisp code or by such commands as `eval-expression` and `eval-last-sexp`. We'll look at the roles of functions and commands more in the next chapter.

2

Simple New Commands

In this chapter we'll develop several very small Lisp functions and commands, introducing a wealth of concepts that will serve us when we tackle larger tasks in the chapters to follow.

Traversing Windows

When I started using Emacs, I was dissatisfied with the keybinding **C-x o**, `other-window`. It moves the cursor from one Emacs window into the next. If I wanted to move the cursor to the previous window instead, I had to invoke `other-window` with −1 as an argument by typing **C-u - 1 C-x o**, which is cumbersome. Just as cumbersome was pressing **C-x o** repeatedly until I cycled through all the windows and came back around to what had been the "previous" one.

What I really wanted was one keybinding meaning "next window" and a different keybinding meaning "previous window." I knew I could do this by writing some new Emacs Lisp code and binding my new functions to new keybindings. First I had to choose those keybindings. "Next" and "previous" naturally suggested **C-n** and **C-p**, but those keys are bound to `next-line` and `previous-line` and I didn't want to change them. The next best option was to use some prefix key, followed by **C-n** and **C-p**. Emacs already uses **C-x** as a prefix for many two-keystroke commands (such as **C-x o** itself), so I chose **C-x C-n** for "next window" and **C-x C-p** for "previous window."

I used the Help subcommand `describe-key`[*] to see whether **C-x C-n** and **C-x C-p** were already bound to other commands. I learned that **C-x C-n** was the keybinding

---

[*] The keybinding for `describe-key` is **M-? k** if you've changed the `help-command` binding as described in Chapter 1, *Customizing Emacs*; otherwise it's **C-h k**.

for `set-goal-column`, and **C-x C-p** was the keybinding for `mark-page`. Binding them to commands for "next window" and "previous window" would override their default bindings. But since those aren't commands I use very often, I didn't mind losing the keybindings for them. I can always execute them using **M-x**.

Once I'd decided to use **C-x C-n** for "next window," I had to bind some command to it that would cause "next window" to happen. I wanted a "next window" function that would move the cursor into the next window by default—just like **C-x o**, which invokes `other-window`. So creating the keybinding for **C-x C-n** was a simple matter of putting

```
(global-set-key "\C-x\C-n" 'other-window)
```

into my *.emacs*. Defining a command to bind to **C-x C-p** was trickier. There was no existing Emacs command meaning "move the cursor to the previous window." Time to define one!

Defining other-window-backward

Knowing that `other-window` can move the cursor to the previous window when given an argument of `-1`, we can define a new command, `other-window-backward`, as follows:

```
(defun other-window-backward ()
  "Select the previous window."
  (interactive)
  (other-window -1))
```

Let's look at the parts of this function definition.

1. A Lisp function definition begins with `defun`.

2. Next comes the name of the function being defined; in this case, I've chosen `other-window-backward`.

3. Next comes the function's *parameter list.*[*] This function has no parameters, so we specify an empty parameter list.

4. The string `"Select the previous window."` is the new function's *documentation string*, or *docstring*. Any Lisp function definition may have a docstring. Emacs displays the docstring when showing online help about the function, as with the commands `describe-function` (**M-? f**) or `apropos`.

5. The next line of the function definition, `(interactive)`, is special. It distinguishes this function as an interactive *command*.

---

[*] What's the difference between a "parameter" and an "argument"? The terms are usually used interchangeably, but technically speaking, "parameter" refers to the variable in the function definition, while "argument" is the value that gets passed in when the function is called. The value of the argument is assigned to the parameter.

A command, in Emacs, is a Lisp function that can be invoked *interactively*, which means it can be invoked from a keybinding or by typing **M-x** *command-name*. Not all Lisp functions are commands, but all commands are Lisp functions.

Any Lisp function, including interactive commands, can be invoked from within other Lisp code using the (*function arg . . .*) syntax.

A function is turned into an interactive command by using the special (`interactive`) expression at the beginning of the function definition (after the optional docstring). More about this "interactive declaration" below.

6. Following the name of the function, the parameter list, the docstring, and the `interactive` declaration is the body of the function, which is simply a sequence of Lisp expressions. This function's body is the sole expression (`other-window -1`), which invokes the function `other-window` with an argument of `-1`.

Evaluating the `defun` expression defines the function. It's now possible to call it in Lisp programs by writing (`other-window-backward`); to invoke it by typing **M-x other-window-backward RET**; even to get help on it by typing **M-? f other-window-backward RET**.[*] Now all that's needed is the keybinding:

```
(global-set-key "\C-x\C-p" ´other-window-backward)
```

Parameterizing other-window-backward

This keybinding does what we need, but we can improve on it a bit. When using **C-x o** (or, now, **C-x C-n**) to invoke `other-window`, you can specify a numeric prefix argument n to change its behavior. If n is given, `other-window` skips forward that many windows. For instance, **C-u 2 C-x C-n** means "move to the second window following this one." As we've seen, n may be negative to skip backward some number of windows. It would be natural to give `other-window-backward` the ability to skip backward some number of windows when a prefix argument n is given—skipping *forward* if n is negative. As it is, `other-window-backward` can only move backward one window at a time.

In order to change it, we must parameterize the function to take one argument: the number of windows to skip. Here's how we do that:

```
(defun other-window-backward (n)
  "Select Nth previous window."
  (interactive "p")
  (other-window (- n)))
```

---

[*] Again, it's only **M-? f** if you've changed the keybinding for `help-command` to **M-?**. From here on, I'll assume that you have, or if you haven't you at least know what I mean.

We've given our function a single parameter named n. We've also changed the interactive declaration to (interactive "p"), and we've changed the argument we pass to other-window from -1 to (- n). Let's look at these changes, starting with the interactive declaration.

An interactive command is, as we have observed, a kind of Lisp function. That means that the command may take arguments. Passing arguments to a function from Lisp is easy; they simply get written down in the function call, as in (other-window -1). But what if the function is invoked as an interactive command? Where do the arguments come from then? Answering this question is the purpose of the interactive declaration.

The argument to interactive describes how to obtain arguments for the command that contains it. When the command takes no arguments, then interactive has no arguments, as in our first draft of other-window-backward. When the command does take arguments, then interactive takes one argument: a string of code letters, one code letter per argument being described. The code letter p used in this example means, "if there is a prefix argument, interpret it as a number, and if there is no prefix argument, interpret *that* as the number 1."[*] The parameter n receives the result of this interpretation when the command is invoked. So if the user invokes other-window-backward by typing **C-u 7 C-x C-p**, n will be 7. If the user simply types **C-x C-p**, n will be 1. Meanwhile, other-window-backward can also be called non-interactively from other Lisp code in the normal way: (other-window-backward 4), for example.

The new version of other-window-backward calls other-window with the argument (- n). This computes the negative of n by passing it to the function -. (Note the space between the - and the n.) The function - normally performs subtraction—for instance, (- 5 2) yields 3—but when given only one argument, it negates it.

In the default case, where n is 1, (- n) is -1 and the call to other-window becomes (other-window -1)—precisely as in the first version of this function. If the user specifies a numeric prefix argument—**C-u 3 C-x C-p**, say—then we call (other-window -3), moving three windows backward, which is exactly what we want.

It's important to understand the difference between the two expressions (- n) and -1. The first is a function call. There must be a space between the function name and the argument. The second expression is an integer constant. There may *not* be a space between the minus sign and the 1. It is certainly possible to write (- 1) (though there's no reason to incur the cost of a function call when you

---

[*] To see a description of interactive's code letters, type **M-? f interactive RET**.

can alternatively write -1). It is *not* possible to write -n, because n is not a constant.

Making the Argument Optional

There's one more improvement we can make to other-window-backward, and that's to make the argument n optional when invoked from Lisp code, just as giving a prefix argument is optional when invoking other-window-backward interactively. It should be possible to pass zero arguments (like this: (other-window-backward)) and get the default behavior (as if calling this: (other-window-backward 1)). Here's how that's done:

```
(defun other-window-backward (&optional n)
  "Select Nth previous window."
  (interactive "p")
  (if n
      (other-window (- n))      ; if n is non-nil
      (other-window -1)))       ; if n is nil
```

The keyword &optional appearing in a parameter list means that all subsequent parameters are optional. The function may be called with or without a value for an optional parameter. If no value is given, the optional parameter gets the special value nil.

The symbol nil is special in Lisp for three reasons:

- It designates falsehood. In the Lisp structures that test a true/false condition—if, cond, while, and, or, and not—a value of nil means "false" and any other value means "true." Thus, in the expression

```
(if n
    (other-window (- n))
  (other-window -1))
```

  (which is Lisp's version of an if-then-else statement), first n is evaluated. If the value of n is true (non-nil), then

```
(other-window (- n))
```

  is evaluated, otherwise

```
(other-window -1)
```

  is evaluated.

  There is another symbol, t, that designates truth, but it is less important than nil. See below.

- It is indistinguishable from the empty list. Inside the Lisp interpreter, the symbol nil and the empty list () are the same object. If you call listp, which tests whether its argument is a list, on the symbol nil, you'll get the result t, which means truth. Likewise, if you call **symbolp**, which tests whether its argument is a symbol, on the empty list, you'll get `t` again. However, if you call `symbolp` on any other list, or `listp` on any other symbol, you'll get `nil`—falsehood.

- It is its own value. When you evaluate the symbol `nil`, the result is `nil`. For this reason, unlike other symbols, `nil` doesn't need to be quoted when you want its name instead of its value, because its name is the same as its value. So you can write

```
(setq x nil)        ; assign nil to variable x
```

instead of writing

```
(setq x 'nil)
```

although both will work. For the same reason, you should never *ever* assign a new value to `nil`,[*] even though it looks like a valid variable name.

Another function of `nil` is to distinguish between *proper* and *improper* lists. This use is discussed in Chapter 6, *Lists*.

There is a symbol, `t`, for designating truth. Like `nil`, `t` is its own value and doesn't need to be quoted. Unlike `nil`, `t` isn't mysteriously the same object as something else. And also unlike `nil`, which is the only way to denote falsehood, all other Lisp values denote truth just like `t` does. However, `t` is useful when all you *mean* is truth (as in the result of `symbolp`) and you don't want to choose some arbitrary other Lisp value, like `17` or `"plugh"`, to stand for truth.

Condensing the Code

As mentioned before, the expression

```
(if n                       ; if this...
    (other-window (- n))    ; ...then this
    (other-window -1))      ; ...else this
```

is the Lisp version of an if-then-else statement. The first argument to `if` is a test. It is evaluated to see whether it yields truth (any expression except `nil`) or falsehood (`nil`). If it's truth, the second argument—the "then" clause—is evaluated. If it's falsehood, the third argument—the "else" clause (which is optional)—is evaluated. The result of `if` is always the result of the last thing it evaluates. See Appendix A, *Lisp Quick Reference*, for a summary of `if` and of Lisp's other flow-control functions, such as `cond` and `while`.

In this case, we can make the `if` expression more concise by *factoring out* the common subexpressions. Observe that `other-window` is called in both branches (the "then" and the "else" clauses) of the `if`. The only thing that varies,

---

[*] Actually, Emacs won't let you assign a value to `nil`.

depending on n, is the argument that gets passed to `other-window`. We can therefore rewrite this expression as:

```
(other-window (if n (- n) -1))
```

In general,

```
(if  test
     (a  b)
   (a  c))
```

can be shortened to (*a* (`if` *test* *b* *c*)).

We can factor out common subexpressions again by observing that in both branches of the `if`, we're looking for the negative of something—either the negative of n or the negative of 1. So

```
(if n (- n) -1)
```

can become (- (`if` n n 1)).

Logical Expressions

An old Lisp programmers' trick can now be used to make this expression even more concise:

```
(if n n 1) ≡ (or n 1)
```

The function `or` works like the logical "or" in most languages: if all of its arguments are false, it returns falsehood, otherwise it returns truth. But Lisp's `or` has an extra bit of usefulness: it evaluates each of its arguments in order until it finds one that's non-`nil`, then it returns that value. If it doesn't find one, it returns `nil`. So the return value from `or` isn't merely false or true, it's false or *the first true value in the list*. This means that generally speaking,

```
(if  a  a  b)
```

can be replaced by

```
(or  a  b)
```

In fact, it often should be written that way because if *a* is true, then (`if` *a* *a* *b*) will evaluate it twice whereas (`or` *a* *b*) won't. (On the other hand, if you specifically want *a* evaluated twice, then of course you should use `if`.) In fact,

```
(if  a  a               ; if a is true, return a
   (if  b  b             ; else if b is true, return b
      . . .
         (if  y  y  z)))  ; else if y is true, return y, else z
```

(which might look artificial here but is actually a pretty common pattern in actual programs) can be changed to the following form.

```
(or  a  b  ...  y  z)
```

subject to the warning about evaluating expressions multiple times.

Similarly,

```
(if  a
  (if  b
    ...
      (if  y  z)))
```

(note that none of the `if`s in this example has an "else" clause) can also be written as

```
(and  a  b  ...  y  z)
```

because `and` works by evaluating each of its arguments in order until it finds one that's `nil`. If it finds one, it returns `nil`, and if it doesn't find one, it returns the value of the last argument.

One other shorthand to watch out for: some programmers like to turn

```
(if (and  a  b  ...  y)  z)
```

into

```
(and  a  b  ...  y  z)
```

but not me because, while they're functionally identical, the former has shades of meaning—"do *z* if *a* through *y* are all true"—that the latter doesn't, which could make it easier for a human reader to understand.

The Best other-window-backward

Back to `other-window-backward`. Using our factored-out version of the call to `other-window`, the function definition now looks like this:

```
(defun other-window-backward (&optional n)
  "Select Nth previous window."
  (interactive "p")
  (other-window (- (or n 1))))
```

But the best definition of all—the most Emacs-Lisp-like—turns out to be:

```
(defun other-window-backward (&optional n)
  "Select Nth previous window."
  (interactive "P")
  (other-window (- (prefix-numeric-value n))))
```

In this version, the code letter in the `interactive` declaration is no longer lowercase `p`, it's capital `P`; and the argument to `other-window` is `(- (prefix-numeric-value n))` instead of `(- (or n 1))`.

The capital `P` means "when called interactively, leave the prefix argument in *raw form* and assign it to `n`." The raw form of a prefix argument is a data structure used internally by Emacs to record the prefix information the user gave before invoking a command. (See the section called "Addendum: Raw Prefix Argument" for the details of the raw prefix argument data structure.) The function `prefix-numeric-value` can interpret that data structure as a number in exactly the way (`interactive "p"`) did. What's more, if `other-window-backward` is called non-interactively (and `n` is therefore not a prefix argument in raw form), `prefix-numeric-value` does the right thing—namely, return `n` unchanged if it's a number, and return `1` if it's `nil`.

Arguably, this definition is no more or less functional than the version of `other-window-backward` we had before. But this version is more "Emacs-Lisp-like" because it achieves better code reuse. It uses the built-in function `prefix-numeric-value` rather than duplicating that function's behavior.

Now let's look at another example.

Line-at-a-Time Scrolling

Before I became an Emacs user, I grew accustomed to some functions in other editors that weren't present in Emacs. Naturally I missed having those functions and decided to replace them. One example is the ability to scroll text up and down one line at a time with a single keystroke.

Emacs has two scrolling functions, `scroll-up` and `scroll-down`, which are bound to **C-v** and **M-v**. Each function takes an optional argument telling it how many lines to scroll. By default, they each scroll the text one windowful at a time. (Don't confuse scrolling up and down with moving the cursor up and down as with **C-n** and **C-p**. Cursor motion moves the cursor and scrolls the text only if necessary. Scrolling moves the text in the window and moves the cursor only if necessary.)

Though I could scroll up and down one line at a time with **C-u 1 C-v** and **C-u 1 M-v**, I wanted to be able to do it with a single keystroke. Using the techniques from the previous section, it is easy to write two new commands for scrolling with one keystroke.

First things first, though. I can never remember which function does what. Does `scroll-up` mean that the text moves up, revealing parts of the file that are farther down? Or does it mean that we reveal parts of the file that are farther up, moving the text down? I'd prefer that these functions had less confusing names, like `scroll-ahead` and `scroll-behind`.

We can use `defalias` to refer to any Lisp function by a different name.

```
(defalias 'scroll-ahead 'scroll-up)
(defalias 'scroll-behind 'scroll-down)
```

There. Now we'll never have to deal with those ambiguous names again (although the original names remain in addition to the new aliases).

Now to define two new commands that call `scroll-ahead` and `scroll-behind` with the right arguments. We proceed exactly as we did with `other-window-backward`:

```
(defun scroll-one-line-ahead ()
  "Scroll ahead one line."
  (interactive)
  (scroll-ahead 1))

(defun scroll-one-line-behind ()
  "Scroll behind one line."
  (interactive)
  (scroll-behind 1))
```

As before, we can make the functions more general by giving them an optional argument:

```
(defun scroll-n-lines-ahead (&optional n)
  "Scroll ahead N lines (1 by default)."
  (interactive "P")
  (scroll-ahead (prefix-numeric-value n)))

(defun scroll-n-lines-behind (&optional n)
  "Scroll behind N lines (1 by default)."
  (interactive "P")
  (scroll-behind (prefix-numeric-value n)))
```

Finally, we choose keys to bind to the new commands. I like **C-q** for `scroll-n-lines-behind` and **C-z** for `scroll-n-lines-ahead`:

```
(global-set-key "\C-q" 'scroll-n-lines-behind)
(global-set-key "\C-z" 'scroll-n-lines-ahead)
```

By default, **C-q** is bound to `quoted-insert`. I move that infrequently used function to **C-x C-q**:

```
(global-set-key "\C-x\C-q" 'quoted-insert)
```

The default binding of **C-x C-q** is `vc-toggle-read-only`, which I don't mind losing.

C-z has a default binding of `iconify-or-deiconify-frame` when running under X, and `suspend-emacs` when running in a character terminal. In both cases, the function is also bound to **C-x C-z**, so there's no need to rebind them.

Other Cursor and Text Motion Commands

Here are a few more easy commands with their suggested keybindings.

```
(defun point-to-top ()
  "Put point on top line of window."
  (interactive)
  (move-to-window-line 0))

(global-set-key "\M-," 'point-to-top)
```

"Point" refers to the position of the cursor. This command makes the cursor jump to the top left of the window it's in. The suggested keybinding replaces `tags-loop-continue`, which I like to put on **C-x** ,:

```
(global-set-key "\C-x," 'tags-loop-continue)
```

The next function makes the cursor jump to the bottom left of the window it's in.

```
(defun point-to-bottom ()
  "Put point at beginning of last visible line."
  (interactive)
  (move-to-window-line -1))

(global-set-key "\M-." 'point-to-bottom)
```

The suggested keybinding in this case replaces `find-tag`. I put that on **C-x** . which in turn replaces `set-fill-prefix`, which I don't mind losing.

```
(defun line-to-top ()
  "Move current line to top of window."
  (interactive)
  (recenter 0))

(global-set-key "\M-!" 'line-to-top)
```

This command scrolls the window so that whichever line the cursor is on becomes the top line in the window. The keybinding replaces `shell-command`.

There is one drawback to changing the bindings for keys in Emacs. If you become accustomed to a highly customized Emacs and then try to use an uncustomized Emacs (e.g., on a different computer or using a friend's login account), you'll keep pressing the wrong keys. This happens to me all the time. I've essentially trained myself to be unable to use an uncustomized Emacs without a lot of frustration. But I rarely use an uncustomized Emacs, so the convenience of customizing it the way I like outweighs the occasional drawbacks. Before you move commands from one key to another with wild abandon like I do, you should weigh the costs and benefits of doing so.

Clobbering Symbolic Links

So far, the functions we've written have been very simple. Essentially, they all just rearrange their arguments and then call a single other function to do the real work. Let's look at an example now where more programming is required.

In UNIX, a *symbolic link*, or *symlink*, is a file that refers to another file by name. When you ask for the contents of a symlink, you actually get the contents of the real file named by the symlink.

Suppose you visit a file in Emacs that is really a symlink to some other file. You make some changes and press **C-x C-s** to save the buffer. What should Emacs do?

1. Replace the symbolic link with the edited version of the file, breaking the link but leaving the original link target alone.

2. Overwrite the file pointed to by the symbolic link.

3. Prompt you to choose one of the above actions.

4. Something else altogether.

Different editors handle the symlink situation in different ways, so a user who has grown accustomed to one editor's behavior may be unpleasantly surprised by another's. Plus, I believe that the right answer changes depending on the situation, and that the user should be forced to think about what's right each time this comes up.

Here's what I do: when I visit a file that's really a symlink, I have Emacs automatically make the buffer read-only. This causes a "Buffer is read-only" error as soon as I try to change anything in the buffer. The error acts as a reminder, alerting me to the possibility that I'm visiting a symlink. Then I choose how to proceed using one of two special commands I've designed.

Hooks

For Emacs to make the buffer read-only when I first visit the file, I have to somehow tell Emacs, "execute a certain piece of Lisp code whenever I visit a file." The action of visiting a file should trigger a function I write. This is where *hooks* come in.

A hook is an ordinary Lisp variable whose value is a list of functions that get executed under specific conditions. For instance, the variable `write-file-hooks` is a list of functions that Emacs executes whenever a buffer is saved, and `post-command-hook` is a list of functions to run after every interactive command. The hook that interests us most for this example is `find-file-hooks`, which Emacs runs every time a new file is visited. (There are many more hooks, some of which we'll be looking at later in the book. To discover what hooks are available, try **M-x apropos RET hook RET**.)

The function `add-hook` adds a function to a hook variable. Here's a function to add to `find-file-hooks`:

```
(defun read-only-if-symlink ()
  (if (file-symlink-p buffer-file-name)
      (progn
        (setq buffer-read-only t)
        (message "File is a symlink"))))
```

This function tests whether current buffer's file is a symlink. If it is, the buffer is made read-only and the message "File is a symlink" is displayed. Let's look a little closer at some parts of this function.

- First, notice that the parameter list is empty. Functions that appear in hook variables take no arguments.

- The function `file-symlink-p` tests whether its argument, which is a string naming a file, refers to a symbolic link. It's a Boolean *predicate*, meaning it returns true or false. In Lisp, predicates traditionally have names ending in `p` or `-p`.

- The argument to `file-symlink-p` is `buffer-file-name`. This pre-defined variable has a different value in every buffer, and is therefore known as a *buffer-local* variable. It always refers to the name of the file in the current buffer. The "current buffer," when `find-file-hooks` gets executed, is the newly found file.

- If `buffer-file-name` does refer to a symlink, there are two things we want to do: make the buffer read-only, and display a message. However, Lisp only allows one expression in the "then" part of an if-then-else. If we were to write:

```
(if (file-symlink-p buffer-file-name)
    (setq buffer-read-only t)
    (message "File is a symlink"))
```

it would mean, "if *buffer-file-name* is a symlink, then make the buffer read-only, else print the message, 'File is a symlink'." To get both the call to `setq` and the call to **message** into the "then" part of the `if`, we wrap them in a **progn**, as in the following example.

```
(progn
  (setq buffer-read-only t)
  (message "File is a symlink"))
```

A **progn** expression evaluates each of its subexpressions in order and returns the value of the last one.

- The variable `buffer-read-only` is also buffer-local and controls whether the current buffer is read-only.

Now that we've defined `read-only-if-symlink`, we can call

```
(add-hook 'find-file-hooks 'read-only-if-symlink)
```

to add it to the list of functions that are called whenever a new file is visited.

Anonymous Functions

When you use `defun` to define a function, you give it a name by which the function can be called from anywhere. But what if the function won't ever be called from anywhere else? What if it needs to be available in only one place? Arguably, `read-only-if-symlink` is needed only in the `find-file-hooks` list; in fact, it might even be harmful for it to be called outside of `find-file-hooks`.

It's possible to define a function without giving it a name. Such functions are appropriately known as *anonymous* functions. They're created with the Lisp keyword `lambda`,[*] which works exactly like `defun` except that the name of the function is left out:

```
(lambda ()
  (if (file-symlink-p buffer-file-name)
      (progn
        (setq buffer-read-only t)
        (message "File is a symlink"))))
```

The empty parentheses after the `lambda` are where the anonymous function's parameters would be listed. This function has no parameters.

An anonymous function definition can be used wherever you might use the name of a function:

```
(add-hook 'find-file-hooks
          '(lambda ()
             (if (file-symlink-p buffer-file-name)
                 (progn
                   (setq buffer-read-only t)
                   (message "File is a symlink")))))
```

Now only `find-file-hooks` has access to the function; no other code is able to call it.[†]

---

[*] The "Lambda calculus" is a mathematical formalism having to do with the way functions instantiate their arguments. To some extent it is the theoretical basis for Lisp (and plenty of other computer languages). The word "lambda" has no significance other than being the name of a Greek letter.

[†] That's not exactly true. It is possible for another piece of code to search the contents of the `find-file-hooks` list, pick out any function it finds, and execute it. The point is that the function is hidden, not exposed as with `defun`.

There's one reason not to use anonymous functions in hooks. If you ever wish to remove a function from a hook, you need to refer to it by name in a call to `remove-hook`, like so:

```
(remove-hook 'find-file-hooks 'read-only-if-symlink)
```

This is much harder if the function is anonymous.

Handling the Symlink

When Emacs alerts me that I'm editing a symlink, I may wish to replace the buffer with one visiting the target of the link instead; or I may wish to "clobber" the symlink (replacing the link itself with an actual copy of the real file) and visit that. Here are two commands for these purposes:

```
(defun visit-target-instead ()
  "Replace this buffer with a buffer visiting the link target."
  (interactive)
  (if buffer-file-name
      (let ((target (file-symlink-p buffer-file-name)))
        (if target
            (find-alternate-file target)
          (error "Not visiting a symlink")))
    (error "Not visiting a file")))

(defun clobber-symlink ()
  "Replace symlink with a copy of the file."
  (interactive)
  (if buffer-file-name
      (let ((target (file-symlink-p buffer-file-name)))
        (if target
            (if (yes-or-no-p (format "Replace %s with %s? "
                                     buffer-file-name
                                     target))
                (progn
                  (delete-file buffer-file-name)
                  (write-file buffer-file-name)))
          (error "Not visiting a symlink")))
    (error "Not visiting a file")))
```

Both functions begin with

```
(if buffer-file-name
    ...
  (error "Not visiting a file"))
```

(I've abbreviated the meat of the function as `...` to illustrate the surrounding structure.) This test is necessary because `buffer-file-name` may be `nil` (in the case that the current buffer isn't visiting any file—e.g., it might be the `*scratch*` buffer), and passing `nil` to `file-symlink-p` would generate the error, "Wrong type argument: stringp, nil."[*] The error message means that some

---

[*] Try it yourself: M-: (file-symlink-p nil) RET.

function was called expecting a string—an object satisfying the predicate
`stringp`—but got `nil` instead. The user of `visit-target-instead` or
`clobber-symlink` would be baffled by this error message, so we detect
ourselves whether `buffer-file-name` is `nil`. If it is, then in the "else" clause
of the `if` we issue a more informative error message—"Not visiting a file"—using
`error`. When `error` is called, the current command aborts and Emacs returns to
its *top-level* to await the user's next action.

Why wasn't it necessary to test `buffer-file-name` in `read-only-if-`
`symlink`? Because that function only gets called from `find-file-hooks`, and
`find-file-hooks` only gets executed when visiting a file.

In the "then" part of the `buffer-file-name` test, both functions next have

```
(let ((target (file-symlink-p buffer-file-name))) ...)
```

Most languages have a way to create *temporary* variables (also called local variables) that exist only in a certain region of code, called the variable's *scope*. In
Lisp, temporary variables are created with `let`, whose syntax is

```
(let ((var₁ value₁)
      (var₂ value₂)
      ...
      (varₙ valueₙ))
   body₁ body₂ ... bodyₙ)
```

This gives var_1 the value $value_1$, var_2 the value $value_2$, and so on; and var_1 and
var_2 can be used only within the $body_i$ expressions. Among other things, using
temporary variables helps to avoid conflicts between regions of code that happen
to use identical variable names.

So the expression

```
(let ((target (file-symlink-p buffer-file-name))) ...)
```

creates a temporary variable named `target` whose value is the result of calling

```
(file-symlink-p buffer-file-name)
```

As mentioned earlier, `file-symlink-p` is a predicate, which means it returns
truth or falsehood. But because "truth" in Lisp can be represented by any expression except `nil`, `file-symlink-p` isn't constrained to returning `t` if its
argument really is a symlink. In fact, it returns the name of the file to which the
symlink refers. So if `buffer-file-name` is the name of a symlink, `target` will
be the name of the symlink's target.

With the temporary variable `target` in effect, the body of the `let` looks like this
in both functions:

```
(if target
    ...
  (error "Not visiting a symlink"))
```

After executing the body of the let, the variable target no longer exists.

Within the let, if target is nil (because file-symlink-p returned nil, because buffer-file-name must not be the name of a symlink), then in the "else" clause we issue an informative error message, "Not visiting a symlink." Otherwise we do something else that depends on which function we're talking about. Finally we reach a point where the two functions differ.

At this point, visit-target-instead does

```
(find-alternate-file target)
```

which replaces the current buffer with one visiting target, prompting the user first in case there are unsaved changes in the original buffer. It even reruns the find-file-hooks when the new file is visited, which is good because it, too, may be a symlink!

At the point where visit-target-instead calls find-alternate-file, clobber-symlink does this instead:

```
(if (yes-or-no-p ...) ...)
```

The function yes-or-no-p asks the user a yes or no question and returns true if the answer was "yes," false otherwise. The question, in this case, is:

```
(format "Replace %s with %s? "
        buffer-file-name
        target)
```

This constructs a string in a fashion similar to C's printf. The first argument is a pattern. Each %s gets replaced with the string representation of a subsequent argument. The first %s gets replaced with the value of buffer-file-name and the second gets replaced with the value of target. So if buffer-file-name is the string "foo" and target is "bar", the prompt will read, "Replace foo with bar?" (The format function understands other %-sequences in the pattern string. For instance, %c prints a single character if the corresponding argument is an ASCII value. See the online help for format—by typing M-? f format RET—for a complete list.)

After testing the return value of yes-or-no-p to make sure the user answered "yes," clobber-symlink does this:

```
(progn
  (delete-file buffer-file-name)
  (write-file buffer-file-name))
```

As we've seen, the progn is for grouping two or more Lisp expressions where only one is expected. The call to delete-file deletes the file (which is really just a symlink), and the call to write-file saves the contents of the current buffer right back to the same filename, but this time as a plain file.

I like to put these functions on **C-x t** for `visit-target-instead` (unused by default) and **C-x l** for `clobber-symlink` (by default bound to `count-lines-page`).

Advised Buffer Switching

Let's conclude this chapter with an example that introduces a very useful Lisp tool called *advice*.

It frequently happens that I'm editing many similarly named files at the same time; for instance, *foobar.c* and *foobar.h*. When I want to switch from one buffer to the other, I use **C-x b**, `switch-to-buffer`, which prompts me for a buffer name. Since I like to keep my keystrokes to a minimum, I depend on **TAB** completion of the buffer name. I'll type

```
C-x b fo TAB
```

expecting that the **TAB** will complete "fo" to "foobar.c", then I'll press **RET** to accept the completed input. Ninety percent of the time, this works great. Other times, such as in this example, pressing **fo TAB** will only expand as far as "foobar.", requiring me to disambiguate between "foobar.c" and "foobar.h". Out of habit, though, I often press **RET** and accept the buffer name "foobar.".

At this point, Emacs creates a brand-new empty buffer named *foobar.*, which of course isn't what I wanted at all. Now I've got to kill the brand-new buffer (with **C-x k**, `kill-buffer`) and start all over again. Though I do occasionally need the ability to switch to a nonexistent buffer, that need is very rare compared with the number of times I commit this error. What I'd like is for Emacs to catch my error before letting me commit it, by only accepting the names of existing buffers when it prompts me for one.

To achieve this, we'll use advice. A piece of advice attached to a Lisp function is code that gets executed before or after the function each time the function is invoked. *Before advice* can affect the arguments before they're passed to the advised function. *After advice* can affect the return value that comes out of the advised function. Advice is a little bit like hook variables, but whereas Emacs defines only a few dozen hook variables for very particular circumstances, *you* get to choose which functions get "advised."

Here's a first try at advising `switch-to-buffer`:

```
(defadvice switch-to-buffer (before existing-buffer
                             activate compile)
  "When interactive, switch to existing buffers only."
  (interactive "b"))
```

Let's look at this closely. The function `defadvice` creates a new piece of advice. Its first argument is the (unquoted) name of the existing function being advised—in this case, `switch-to-buffer`. Next comes a specially formatted list. Its first element—in this case, `before`—tells whether this is "before" or "after" advice. (Another type of advice, called "around," lets you embed a call to the advised function inside the advice code.) Next comes the name of this piece of advice; I named it `existing-buffer`. The name can be used later if you want to remove or modify the advice. Next come some keywords: `activate` means that this advice should be active as soon as it's defined (it's possible to define advice but leave it inactive); and `compile` means that the advice code should be "byte-compiled" for speed (see Chapter 5, *Lisp Files*).

After the specially formatted list, a piece of advice has an optional docstring.

The only thing in the body of this advice is its own `interactive` declaration, which *replaces* the `interactive` declaration of `switch-to-buffer`. Whereas `switch-to-buffer` accepts any string as the buffer-name argument, the code letter b in an `interactive` declaration means "accept only names of existing buffers." By using the `interactive` declaration to make this change, we've managed to not affect any Lisp code that wants to call `switch-to-buffer` non-interactively. So this tiny piece of advice effectively does the whole job: it changes `switch-to-buffer` to accept only the names of existing buffers.

Unfortunately, that's too restrictive. It should still be possible to switch to nonexistent buffers, but only when some special indication is given that the restriction should be lifted—say, when a prefix argument is given. Thus, **C-x b** should refuse to switch to nonexistent buffers, but **C-u C-x b** should permit it.

Here's how this is done:

```
(defadvice switch-to-buffer (before existing-buffer
                              activate compile)
   "When interactive, switch to existing buffers only,
unless given a prefix argument."
   (interactive
    (list (read-buffer "Switch to buffer: "
                       (other-buffer)
                       (null current-prefix-arg)))))
```

Once again, we're overriding the `interactive` declaration of `switch-to-buffer` using "before" advice. But this time, we're using `interactive` in a way we haven't seen before: we're passing a list as its argument, rather than a string of code letters.

When the argument to `interactive` is some expression other than a string, that expression is evaluated to get a list of arguments that should be passed to the function. So in this case we call `list`, which constructs a list out of its arguments, with the result of

```
(read-buffer "Switch to buffer: "
             (other-buffer)
             (null current-prefix-arg))
```

The function `read-buffer` is the low-level Lisp function that prompts the user for a buffer name. It's "low-level" in the sense that all other functions that prompt for buffer names ultimately call `read-buffer`. It's called with a prompt string and two optional arguments: a default buffer to switch to, and a Boolean stating whether input should be restricted to existing buffers only.

For the default buffer, we pass the result of calling `other-buffer`, which computes a useful default buffer for this very purpose. (Usually it chooses the most recently used buffer that isn't presently visible in a window.) For the Boolean stating whether to restrict input, we use

```
(null current-prefix-arg)
```

This tests whether `current-prefix-arg` is `nil`. If it is, the result will be `t`; if it's not, the result will be `nil`. Thus, if there is no prefix argument (i.e., `current-prefix-arg` is `nil`), then we call

```
(read-buffer "Switch to buffer: "
             (other-buffer)
             t)
```

meaning "read a buffer name, restricting input to existing buffers only." If there *is* a prefix argument, then we call

```
(read-buffer "Switch to buffer: "
             (other-buffer)
             nil)
```

meaning "read a buffer name with no restrictions" (allowing non-existent buffer names to be entered). The result of `read-buffer` is then passed to `list`, and the resulting list (containing one element, the buffer name) is used as the argument list for `switch-to-buffer`.

With `switch-to-buffer` thus advised, Emacs won't let me respond to the prompt with a nonexistent buffer name unless I asked for that ability by pressing **C-u** first.

For completeness, you should similarly advise the functions `switch-to-buffer-other-window` and `switch-to-buffer-other-frame`.

Addendum: Raw Prefix Argument

The variable `current-prefix-arg` always contains the latest "raw" prefix argument, which is the same thing you get from

```
(interactive "P")
```

The function `prefix-numeric-value` can be applied to a "raw" prefix argument to get its *numeric value*, which is the same thing you get from

```
(interactive "p")
```

What does a raw prefix argument look like? Table 2-1 shows possible raw values along with their corresponding numeric values.

Table 2-1: Prefix arguments

If the User Types	Raw Value	Numeric Value
C-u followed by a (possibly negative) number	The number itself	The number itself
C-u - (with no following number)	The symbol –	-1
C-u *n* times in a row (with no following number or minus sign)	A list containing the number 4^n	4^n itself
No prefix argument	`nil`	1

3

In this chapter:
- *The Symptom*
- *A Cure*
- *Generalizing the Solution*

Cooperating Commands

This chapter shows how to get different commands to work together by saving information in one command and retrieving it in another. The simplest way to share information is to create a variable and store a value in it. We'll certainly do that in this chapter. For instance, we'll store the current buffer position and reuse it in a later command. But we'll also learn some more sophisticated ways to preserve state, notably markers and symbol properties. We'll combine these techniques with information about buffers and windows to write a set of functions that allow you to "undo" scrolling.

The Symptom

You're deep into editing some complicated Lisp code. You're concentrating, juggling the tenuous connections between the conceptual structures in your brain and the glyphs that represent them on the screen. You're in a particularly tricky part when you notice a typo a few characters to the left. You mean to press **C-b C-b C-b** to back up and correct it, but instead—horrors!—you press **C-v C-v C-v**, paging the Emacs window three times, ending up light years away from the code you were editing. Your mental context is ruined as you try to figure out where the cursor was before your mistake, and why, and what you were doing there. As you scroll, or search, or cycle through the mark-ring or the undo-list trying to get back to where you were, you forget about that original typo you were trying to correct, and much later it turns into a bug in your code that takes hours to find.

Emacs hasn't helped in this instance, it has hindered. It has made it too easy to get lost in your document and too hard to find your way back. Although Emacs has an extensive undo facility, it only allows you to undo *changes*. You can't undo simple navigation.

A Cure

Suppose we could alter **C-v** (the `scroll-up` command[*]) in such a way that when you press it, Emacs thinks, "Maybe the user is pressing **C-v** in error, so I'll record some 'undo' information in case it's needed." Then we could write another function, `unscroll`, which undoes the effects of the latest scroll. Getting lost should therefore cause no more disruption to your mental context than it takes to remember the keybinding for `unscroll`.

Actually, that's not quite good enough. If you press several **C-v**s in a row, one call to `unscroll` should undo them all, not only the last one. This means that only the first **C-v** in a sequence should memorize the starting location. How can we arrange for this to happen? Somewhere in our **C-v** code, before we memorize the starting location, we have to test either (a) that the next command will be a call to `scroll-up`, or (b) that the previous command *wasn't* a call to `scroll-up`. Obviously, (a) is impossible: we can't know the future. Fortunately, (b) is easy: Emacs maintains a variable for this purpose called `last-command`. This variable is the first mechanism we'll use to communicate information from one command to a later one.

Now the only question remaining is: how can we attach this extra code to the `scroll-up` command? The advice facility is ideal for this purpose. Recall that a piece of advice can run before or after the advised function. In this case, we'll need before advice, because it's only before `scroll-up` runs that we know the starting location.

Declaring Variables

We'll start by setting up a global variable, `unscroll-to`, which will hold the "undo" information, which is simply the position in the buffer to which `unscroll` should move the cursor. We'll use `defvar` to declare the variable.

```
(defvar unscroll-to nil
  "Text position for next call to 'unscroll'.")
```

Global variables don't need to be declared. But there are some advantages to declaring variables with `defvar`:

- Using `defvar` allows a docstring to be associated with the variable, in the same way that `defun` allows a docstring to be associated with a function.

---

[*] Although in Chapter 2, *Simple New Commands*, we used `defalias` to make `scroll-ahead` and `scroll-behind` synonyms for `scroll-up` and `scroll-down`, in this chapter we'll refer to `scroll-up` and `scroll-down` by their original names.

- A *default value* for the variable can be given. In this case, the default value for `unscroll-to` is `nil`.

  Setting a variable's default value with `defvar` is different from setting a variable's value with `setq`. Instead of unconditionally assigning the value to the variable like `setq` does, `defvar` assigns the value only if the variable does not yet have any value.

  Why is this important? Suppose your *.emacs* file contains the line

  ```
  (setq mail-signature t)
  ```

  meaning that when you send a mail message from within Emacs, you wish to append your *.signature* file to it. When you start Emacs, `mail-signature` gets set to `t`, but the Lisp file that defines the mail-sending code, *sendmail*, has not yet been loaded. It's loaded on demand when you first invoke the `mail` command. When you do, Emacs executes this line from the *sendmail* Lisp file:

  ```
  (defvar mail-signature nil ...)
  ```

  This says that `nil` is a default initial value for `mail-signature`. But you've already given `mail-signature` a value, and you wouldn't want loading *sendmail* to override your setting. On the other hand, if your *.emacs* didn't specify any value for `mail-signature`, you would want this value to be in effect.

- A variable declaration using `defvar` can be found by the various tag-related commands. Tags are a way to quickly find variable and function definitions in a programming project. Emacs's tag facilities, such as the `find-tag` command, can find anything created with the `def...` functions (`defun`, `defalias`, `defmacro`, `defvar`, `defsubst`, `defconst`, `defadvice`).

- When you byte-compile the code (see Chapter 5, *Lisp Files*), the byte-compiler emits a warning for each variable it encounters that hasn't been declared with `defvar`. If all your variables are declared, then you can use the warnings to find places where you've mistyped the name of a variable.

Saving and Restoring Point

Let's define the value of `unscroll-to` to be the position in the text where the cursor was before the latest sequence of `scroll-ups`. The position of the cursor in the text is the number of characters from the beginning of the buffer (counting from 1) and is called *point* or *the point*. The value of point at any moment is given by the function `point`.

```
(defadvice scroll-up (before remember-for-unscroll
                     activate compile)
  "Remember where we started from, for `unscroll'."
```

```
(if (not (eq last-command 'scroll-up))
    (setq unscroll-to (point)))))
```

The body of this advice works as follows:

1. The function `eq` takes two arguments and tells whether they are identical. In this case, the arguments are the value of the `last-command` variable, and the literal symbol `scroll-up`. The value of `last-command` is the symbol naming the last command that the user invoked (usually—see the section on "Using `this-command`" later in this chapter).

2. The result of the call to `eq` is passed to `not`, which inverts the truth value of its argument. If `nil` is passed to `not`, the result is `t`. If anything else is passed to `not`, the result is `nil`.[*]

3. If the result of the call to `not` is true—i.e., if `last-command` is *not* the symbol `scroll-up`—then the variable `unscroll-to` is set to the current value of point by calling the function `point` with no arguments.

Now it should be easy to define `unscroll`:

```
(defun unscroll ()
  "Jump to location specified by 'unscroll-to'."
  (interactive)
  (goto-char unscroll-to))
```

The function `goto-char` moves the cursor to the given position.

Window Appearance

There's something unsatisfactory about this solution. After an `unscroll`, the cursor is restored to its correct location, true, but the screen may look very different from the way it appeared before the C-v excursion. For example, I may be editing a line of code that is near the bottom of the Emacs window when I mistakenly press C-v C-v C-v. I'll immediately invoke `unscroll`, but even though the cursor goes back where it belongs, the line in question may now appear in the middle of the window.

Since our goal is to minimize the disruption caused by unintended scrolling, we'd really like to restore not only the location of the cursor, but also the appearance of the window with respect to which lines are visible where.

Saving the value of point is no longer sufficient, therefore. We must also save a value representing what's visible in the current window. Emacs provides several functions describing what's visible in a window, such as `window-edges`,

---

[*] If you think the way `not` works sounds like the way `null` works, you're right—they're exactly the same function. One is simply an alias for the other. Which one you use is a readability issue. Use `null` when testing to see whether an object is the empty list. Use `not` when inverting truth values.

`window-height`, and `current-window-configuration`. For now we'll only use `window-start` which, for a given window, yields the buffer position that is the first visible character (i.e., the upper-left corner) in the window. We're just adding a little more information to be preserved between commands.

Updating our example is straightforward. First we replace our declaration of the variable `unscroll-to` with two new variables: one containing the saved value of point, and one containing the saved position of the first visible character in the window.

```
(defvar unscroll-point nil
  "Cursor position for next call to 'unscroll'.")
(defvar unscroll-window-start nil
  "Window start for next call to 'unscroll'.")
```

Next we update the advice on **scroll-up** and **unscroll** to set and use these two values.

```
(defadvice scroll-up (before remember-for-unscroll
                      activate compile)
  "Remember where we started from, for 'unscroll'."
  (if (not (eq last-command 'scroll-up))
      (progn
        (setq unscroll-point (point))
        (setq unscroll-window-start (window-start)))))

(defun unscroll ()
  "Revert to 'unscroll-point' and 'unscroll-window-start'."
  (interactive)
  (goto-char unscroll-point)
  (set-window-start nil unscroll-window-start))
```

Since the advice is still named **remember-for-unscroll**, this advice *replaces* the previous advice, which was identically named.

The function **set-window-start** sets the window-start position in the same way that **goto-char** sets the position of the cursor. However, **set-window-start** takes two arguments. The first argument is the window whose start position is being set. If **nil** is passed as the first argument (as in this example), **set-window-start** defaults to the currently selected window. (Window objects for passing to **set-window-start** can be obtained from such functions as **get-buffer-window** and **previous-window**.)

There's one more piece of information we might like to save for unscrolling purposes, and that's the window's *hscroll,* the number of columns by which the window is scrolled horizontally, normally zero. We'll add yet another variable for storing it:

```
(defvar unscroll-hscroll nil
  "Hscroll for next call to 'unscroll'.")
```

then we'll update `unscroll` and the `scroll-up` advice again to include calls to `window-hscroll` (which reports the window's current hscroll) and `set-window-hscroll` (which sets it):

```
(defadvice scroll-up (before remember-for-unscroll
                      activate compile)
  "Remember where we started from, for 'unscroll'."
  (if (not (eq last-command 'scroll-up))
      (setq unscroll-point (point)
            unscroll-window-start (window-start)
            unscroll-hscroll (window-hscroll))))

(defun unscroll ()
  "Revert to 'unscroll-point' and 'unscroll-window-start'."
  (interactive)
  (goto-char unscroll-point)
  (set-window-start nil unscroll-window-start)
  (set-window-hscroll nil unscroll-hscroll))
```

Notice that in this version of the `scroll-up` advice, the `progn` call:

```
(progn
  (setq ...)
  (setq ...))
```

has been turned into a single `setq` call with multiple variable-value pairs. For conciseness, `setq` can set any number of variables.

Detecting Errors

What happens if the user invokes `unscroll` before any call to `scroll-up`? The variables `unscroll-point`, `unscroll-window-start`, and `unscroll-hscroll` will all contain their default value, `nil`. This value is unsuitable for passing to the functions `goto-char`, `set-window-start`, and `set-window-hscroll`. As soon as the call to `goto-char` is reached, execution of the `unscroll` command will abort with this error: "Wrong type argument: integer-or-marker-p, nil." This means a function expecting an integer or a marker (to satisfy the predicate `integer-or-marker-p`) was passed `nil` instead. (Markers are explained in an earlier section of this chapter.)

To keep the user from being baffled by this cryptic error message, it's a good idea to precede the call to `goto-char` with a simple check and a more informative error message:

```
(if (not unscroll-point)        ; i.e., if unscroll-point is nil
    (error "Cannot unscroll yet"))
```

When `error` is invoked, execution of `unscroll` aborts and the message "Cannot unscroll yet" is displayed.

Generalizing the Solution

It's easy to press **C-v** when meaning to press **C-b**. That's what led us to devise the unscroll function. Now observe that it's just as easy to press **M-v** (scroll-down) when meaning to press **M-b** (backward-word). It's the same problem, but in the other direction, sort of. It would be nice if we could generalize unscroll to undo scrolling in any direction.

The obvious way to generalize unscroll is to advise scroll-down in the same way that we advised scroll-up:

```
(defadvice scroll-down (before remember-for-unscroll
                        activate compile)
  "Remember where we started from, for `unscroll'."
  (if (not (eq last-command 'scroll-down))
      (setq unscroll-point (point)
            unscroll-window-start (window-start)
            unscroll-hscroll (window-hscroll))))
```

(Note that two functions, such as scroll-up and scroll-down, may have identically named pieces of advice, such as remember-for-unscroll, without conflict.)

Now we must decide how we want unscroll to behave in the case where we mingle erroneous **C-v**s with erroneous **M-v**s. In other words, suppose you mistakenly press **C-v C-v M-v**. Should unscroll revert to the position before the **M-v**, or should it revert all the way back to the position before the first **C-v**?

I prefer the latter behavior. But this means that in the advice for scroll-up, where we now test whether the last command was scroll-up, we must now test whether it was *either* scroll-up or scroll-down, and do the same in scroll-down.

```
(defadvice scroll-up (before remember-for-unscroll
                      activate compile)
  "Remember where we started from, for `unscroll'."
  (if (not (or (eq last-command 'scroll-up)
               (eq last-command 'scroll-down)))
      (setq unscroll-point (point)
            unscroll-window-start (window-start)
            unscroll-hscroll (window-hscroll))))

(defadvice scroll-down (before remember-for-unscroll
                        activate compile)
  "Remember where we started from, for `unscroll'."
  (if (not (or (eq last-command 'scroll-up)
               (eq last-command 'scroll-down)))
      (setq unscroll-point (point)
            unscroll-window-start (window-start)
            unscroll-hscroll (window-hscroll))))
```

Take a moment to make sure you understand the expression

```
(if (not (or (eq last-command 'scroll-up)
             (eq last-command 'scroll-down)))
    (setq ...))
```

It's best to read such expressions by moving inward one level of subexpression at a time. Start with

```
(if (not ...)
    (setq ...))
```

"If something's not true, set some variable(s)." Next, peer a little deeper:

```
(if (not (or ...))
    (setq ...))
```

"If none of a set of conditions is true, set some variable(s)." Finally,

```
(if (not (or (eq last-command 'scroll-up)
             (eq last-command 'scroll-down)))
    (setq ...))
```

means, "If neither 'last-command is scroll-up' nor 'last-command is scroll-down' is true, set some variable(s)."

Suppose somewhere down the line, you come up with more commands you'd like to advise this way; let's say scroll-left and scroll-right:

```
(defadvice scroll-up (before remember-for-unscroll
                       activate compile)
  "Remember where we started from, for 'unscroll'."
  (if (not (or (eq last-command 'scroll-up)
               (eq last-command 'scroll-down)
               (eq last-command 'scroll-left)      ; new
               (eq last-command 'scroll-right)))   ; new
      (setq unscroll-point (point)
            unscroll-window-start (window-start)
            unscroll-hscroll (window-hscroll))))

(defadvice scroll-down (before remember-for-unscroll
                         activate compile)
  "Remember where we started from, for 'unscroll'."
  (if (not (or (eq last-command 'scroll-up)
               (eq last-command 'scroll-down)
               (eq last-command 'scroll-left)      ; new
               (eq last-command 'scroll-right)))   ; new
      (setq unscroll-point (point)
            unscroll-window-start (window-start)
            unscroll-hscroll (window-hscroll))))

(defadvice scroll-left (before remember-for-unscroll
                         activate compile)
  "Remember where we started from, for 'unscroll'."
  (if (not (or (eq last-command 'scroll-up)
               (eq last-command 'scroll-down)
```

```
                        (eq last-command 'scroll-left)
                        (eq last-command 'scroll-right)))
            (setq unscroll-point (point)
                  unscroll-window-start (window-start)
                  unscroll-hscroll (window-hscroll))))

(defadvice scroll-right (before remember-for-unscroll
                         activate compile)
  "Remember where we started from, for `unscroll'."
  (if (not (or (eq last-command 'scroll-up)
               (eq last-command 'scroll-down)
               (eq last-command 'scroll-left)
               (eq last-command 'scroll-right)))
      (setq unscroll-point (point)
            unscroll-window-start (window-start)
            unscroll-hscroll (window-hscroll))))
```

Not only is this very repetitive and error-prone, but for each new command that we wish to make "unscrollable," the advice for each existing unscrollable command must have its `last-command` test modified to include the new one.

Using this-command

Two things can be done to improve this situation. First, since the advice is identical in each case, it can be factored out into a shared function:

```
(defun unscroll-maybe-remember ()
  (if (not (or (eq last-command 'scroll-up)
               (eq last-command 'scroll-down)
               (eq last-command 'scroll-left)
               (eq last-command 'scroll-right)))
      (setq unscroll-point (point)
            unscroll-window-start (window-start)
            unscroll-hscroll (window-hscroll))))

(defadvice scroll-up (before remember-for-unscroll
                      activate compile)
  "Remember where we started from, for `unscroll'."
  (unscroll-maybe-remember))

(defadvice scroll-down (before remember-for-unscroll
                        activate compile)
  "Remember where we started from, for `unscroll'."
  (unscroll-maybe-remember))

(defadvice scroll-left (before remember-for-unscroll
                        activate compile)
  "Remember where we started from, for `unscroll'."
  (unscroll-maybe-remember))

(defadvice scroll-right (before remember-for-unscroll
                         activate compile)
  "Remember where we started from, for `unscroll'."
  (unscroll-maybe-remember))
```

Second, instead of having to test for *n* possible values of `last-command`, all meaning "the last command was unscrollable," it would be nice if there were a single such value, and if all the unscrollable commands could somehow set `last-command` to that value.

Enter `this-command`, the variable that contains the name of the *current* command invoked by the user. In fact, the way `last-command` gets set is this: while Emacs is executing a command, `this-command` contains the name of the command; then when it is finished, Emacs puts the value of `this-command` into `last-command`.

While a command is executing, it can change the value of `this-command`. When the *next* command runs, the value will be available in `last-command`.

Let's choose a symbol to represent all unscrollable commands: say, `unscrollable`. Now we can change `unscroll-maybe-remember` as follows:

```
(defun unscroll-maybe-remember ()
  (setq this-command 'unscrollable)
  (if (not (eq last-command 'unscrollable))
      (setq unscroll-point (point)
            unscroll-window-start (window-start)
            unscroll-hscroll (window-hscroll))))
```

Any command that calls `unscroll-maybe-remember` now causes `this-command` to contain `unscrollable`. And instead of checking `last-command` for four different values (more if we add new unscrollable commands), we only need to check for one value (even if we define new unscrollable commands).

Symbol Properties

Our improved `unscroll-maybe-remember` works great, but (as perhaps you've come to expect by now) there are still some refinements we can make. The first is to address this problem: the variables `this-command` and `last-command` aren't exclusively ours to do with as we please. They're central to the Emacs Lisp interpreter, and other components of Emacs depend on them, too. For all we know, there exists an Emacs component that depends on the various scroll functions *not* overriding the settings of `this-command` and `last-command`. Still, we would like a single, distinguished value in `last-command` to identify all unscrollable commands.

Here's where *symbol properties* come in handy. In addition to having a variable value and/or a function definition, every Emacs Lisp symbol may also have associated with it a *property list*. A property list is a mapping from names to values. Each name is yet another Lisp symbol, while each value may be any Lisp expression.

Properties are stored with the `put` function and retrieved with the `get` function. Thus, if we give the value 17 to the property named `some-property` belonging to the symbol `a-symbol`:

```
(put 'a-symbol 'some-property 17)
```

then

```
(get 'a-symbol 'some-property)
```

returns 17. If we try to `get` a property from a symbol that doesn't have that property, the result is `nil`.

Instead of using `unscrollable` as a value for `this-command` and `last-command`, we can instead use an `unscrollable` *property*. We'll set it up so that commands that are unscrollable have the `unscrollable` property of their names set to `t`, like so:

```
(put 'scroll-up 'unscrollable t)
(put 'scroll-down 'unscrollable t)
(put 'scroll-left 'unscrollable t)
(put 'scroll-right 'unscrollable t)
```

This only has to be done once, before any calls to `unscroll-maybe-remember`.

Now `(get x 'unscrollable)` will be true only when *x* is one of the symbols `scroll-up`, `scroll-down`, `scroll-left`, and `scroll-right`. For all other symbols, since the `unscrollable` property is (presumably) undefined, the result will be `nil`.

We can now change

```
(if (not (eq last-command 'unscrollable)) ...)
```

in `unscroll-maybe-remember` to

```
(if (not (get last-command 'unscrollable)) ...)
```

and we can also stop assigning `unscrollable` to `this-command`:

```
(defun unscroll-maybe-remember ()
  (if (not (get last-command 'unscrollable))
      (setq unscroll-point (point)
            unscroll-window-start (window-start)
            unscroll-hscroll (window-hscroll))))
```

Markers

How can we make this code even better? Suppose you inadvertently `scroll-down` a few times and you want to `unscroll`. But before you do, you happen to see a bit of text you'd like to change, and you change it. Then you `unscroll`. The screen hasn't been correctly restored!

The reason is that editing text earlier in the buffer changes all the subsequent buffer positions. An edit involving a net addition or removal of n characters adds or subtracts n to or from all subsequent positions. Therefore the saved buffer positions in the variables `unscroll-point` and `unscroll-window-start` will be off by n. (If n is zero, you got lucky.)

Instead of using absolute positions as the values of `unscroll-point` and `unscroll-window-start`, it would be a good idea to use *markers*. A marker is a special object that specifies a buffer position just like an integer does. But if the buffer position moves because of insertions or deletions, the marker "moves" too so that it keeps pointing to the same spot in the text.

Since we're changing `unscroll-point` and `unscroll-window-start` to be markers, we no longer initialize them with `nil`. We instead initialize them as new, empty marker objects using the function `make-marker`:

```
(defvar unscroll-point (make-marker)
  "Cursor position for next call to 'unscroll'.")
(defvar unscroll-window-start (make-marker)
  "Window start for next call to 'unscroll'.")
```

The function `set-marker` is used to set the position of a marker.

```
(defun unscroll-maybe-remember ()
  (if (not (get last-command 'unscrollable))
      (progn
        (set-marker unscroll-point (point))
        (set-marker unscroll-window-start (window-start))
        (setq unscroll-hscroll (window-hscroll)))))
```

The call to `progn` is back because the single call to `setq` has been split up into several function calls. We don't use a marker for `unscroll-hscroll` because its value isn't a buffer position.

We don't need to rewrite `unscroll`, because `goto-char` and `set-window-start` can both handle arguments that are markers as well as arguments that are integers. So the previous definition (reprinted here for convenience) will continue to work:

```
(defun unscroll ()
  "Revert to 'unscroll-point' and 'unscroll-window-start'."
  (interactive)
  (goto-char unscroll-point)
  (set-window-start nil unscroll-window-start)
  (set-window-hscroll nil unscroll-hscroll))
```

Addendum: Efficiency Consideration

When we declare `unscroll-point` and `unscroll-marker`, we create "empty" marker objects and reuse them in each call to `unscroll-remember`, rather than creating new marker objects in each call to `unscroll-remember` and discarding the old objects. This is an optimization. Not only is it better, in general, to avoid very prolific object creation when possible, but markers happen to be more expensive than other objects to create. Each marker that points into some buffer somewhere has to be updated every time text is inserted or deleted in that buffer. A discarded marker object will eventually be reclaimed by the garbage collector, but until it is, it'll slow down editing in its buffer.

In general, when you intend to discard a marker object *m* (meaning that you no longer intend to refer to its value), it's a good idea to first make it point "nowhere" by doing this:

```
(set-marker m nil)
```

4

Searching and Modifying Buffers

There will be lots of times when you want to search through a buffer for a string, perhaps replacing it with something else. In this chapter we'll show a lot of powerful ways to do this. We'll cover the functions that perform searches and also show you how to form regular expressions, which add great flexibility to the kinds of searches you can do.

Inserting the Current Time

It is sometimes useful to insert the current date or time into a file as you edit it. For instance, right now, as I'm writing this, it's 10:30pm on Friday, 18 August, 1996. A few days ago, I was editing a file of Emacs Lisp code and I changed a comment that read

```
;; Each element of ENTRIES has the form
;; (NAME (VALUE-HIGH . VALUE-LOW))
```

to

```
;; Each element of ENTRIES has the form
;; (NAME (VALUE-HIGH . VALUE-LOW))
;; [14 Aug 96] I changed this so NAME can now be a symbol,
;; a string, or a list of the form (NAME . PREFIX) [bg]
```

I placed a *timestamp* in the comment because it could be useful when editing that code in the future to look back and see when this change was made.

A command that merely inserts the current time is simple, once you know that the function **current-time-string** yields today's date and time as a string.[*]

---

[*] How do you find this out in the first place? Using **M-x apropos RET time RET**, of course.

```
(defun insert-current-time ()
  "Insert the current time"
  (interactive "*")
  (insert (current-time-string)))
```

The section "More Asterisk Magic" later in this chapter explains the meaning of
(interactive "*") and insert.

The simple function above is pretty inflexible, as it always results in inserting a
string of the form "Sun Aug 18 22:34:53 1996" (in the style of the standard C
library functions ctime and asctime). That's cumbersome if all you want is the
date, or just the time, or if you prefer 12-hour time instead of 24-hour time, or
dates in the form "18 Aug 1996" or "8/18/96" or "18/8/96".

Happily, we can get finer control if we're willing to do a little extra work. Emacs
includes a few other time-related functions, notably current-time, which
yields the current time in a raw form, and format-time-string, which can
take such a time and format it in a wide variety of ways (in the style of C's strf-
time). For instance,

```
(format-time-string "%l.%M %p" (current-time))
```

returns "10.38 PM". (The format codes used here are %l, "hour from 1-12," %M,
"minute from 00-59," and %p, "the string 'AM' or 'PM'." For a complete list of
format codes, use describe-function on format-time-string.)

From here it's a short leap to providing two commands, one for inserting the
current time and one for inserting the current date. We can also easily permit the
format used by each to be user-configurable, based on a configuration variable
the user can set. Let's call the two functions insert-time and insert-date.
The corresponding configuration variables will be insert-time-format and
insert-date-format.

User Options and Docstrings

First we'll define the variables.

```
(defvar insert-time-format "%X"
  "*Format for \\[insert-time] (c.f. 'format-time-string').")

(defvar insert-date-format "%x"
  "*Format for \\[insert-date] (c.f. 'format-time-string').")
```

There are two new things to note about these docstrings.

- First, each begins with an asterisk (*). A leading asterisk has special meaning
  in defvar docstrings. It means that the variable in question is a *user option*.
  A user option is just like any other Lisp variable except that it's treated specially in two cases:

— User options can be set interactively using `set-variable`, which prompts the user for a variable name (with completion of partially typed names) and a value. In some cases, the value can be entered in an intuitive way without having to dress it up in Lisp syntax; e.g., strings can be entered without their surrounding double-quotes.

To set variables interactively when they aren't user options, you must do something like

```
M-: (setq variable value) RET
```

(using Lisp syntax for *value*).

— User options, but not other variables, can be edited *en masse* using the option-editing mode available as **M-x edit-options RET**.[*]

• The second new thing about these docstrings is that each contains the special construct `\[`*command*`]`. (Yes, it's `\[...]`, but since it's written inside a Lisp string, the backslash has to be doubled: `\\[...]`.) This syntax is magic. When the docstring is displayed to the user—such as when the user uses `apropos` or `describe-variable`—`\[`*command*`]` is replaced with a representation of a keybinding that invokes *command*. For example, if **C-x t** invokes `insert-time`, then the docstring

```
"*Format for \\[insert-time] (c.f. `format-time-string')."
```

is displayed as

```
*Format for C-x t (c.f. `format-time-string').
```

If there is no keybinding for `insert-time`, then **M-x insert-time** is used. If there are two or more keybindings for `insert-time`, Emacs chooses one.

Suppose you want the string `\[insert-time]` to appear literally in a docstring. How could you prevent its keybinding being substituted? For this purpose there is a special escape sequence: `\=`. When `\=` precedes `\[...]`, the magic replacement of `\[...]` doesn't happen. Of course, Lisp string syntax dictates that this be written as `"...\\=\\[...]..."`.

`\=` is also useful for escaping the asterisk at the beginning of a `defvar` docstring, if you don't want the variable to be a user option but you absolutely *must* have a docstring that begins with an asterisk.

All variables that are shared between two or more functions should be declared with `defvar`. Which of those should be user options? A rule of thumb is that if the variable directly controls a user-visible feature that a user might want to change, and if setting that variable is straightforward (i.e., no complex data structures or specially coded values), then it should be a user option.

---

[*] Emacs 20.1, which was not yet released when this book went to press, will introduce a major new system for editing user options called "customize." Hooking user options into the "customize" system requires using special functions called `defgroup` and `defcustom`.

More Asterisk Magic

Now that we've defined the variables that control `insert-time` and `insert-date`, here are the definitions of those simple functions.

```
(defun insert-time ()
  "Insert the current time according to insert-time-format."
  (interactive "*")
  (insert (format-time-string insert-time-format
                              (current-time))))

(defun insert-date ()
  "Insert the current date according to insert-date-format."
  (interactive "*")
  (insert (format-time-string insert-date-format
                              (current-time))))
```

The two functions are identical except that one uses `insert-time-format` where the other uses `insert-date-format`. The `insert` function takes any number of arguments (which must all be strings or characters) and inserts them one after another in the current buffer at the present location of point, moving point forward.

The main thing to notice about these functions is that each begins with

```
(interactive "*")
```

By now you know that `interactive` turns a function into a command and specifies how to obtain the function's arguments when invoked interactively. But we haven't seen `*` in the argument of `interactive` before, and besides, these functions take no arguments, so why does `interactive` have one?

The asterisk, when it is the first character in an `interactive` argument, means "abort this function if the current buffer is read-only." It is better to detect a read-only buffer before a function begins its work than to let it get halfway through then die from a "Buffer is read-only" error. In this case, if we omitted to check for read-onlyness, the call to `insert` would trigger its own "Buffer is read-only" error almost right away and no harm done. A more complicated function, though, might cause irreversible side effects (such as changing global variables), expecting to be able to finish, before discovering that it can't.

Writestamps

Inserting the current date and time automatically and in such a configurable format is pretty neat and probably beyond the ken of most text editors, but its usefulness is limited. Undoubtedly more useful would be the ability to store a *writestamp* in a file; that is, the date and/or time the file was last written to disk. A writestamp updates itself each time the file is saved anew.

Updating Writestamps

The first thing we'll need is a way to run our writestamp-updating code each time the file is saved. As we discovered in the section "Hooks" in Chapter 2, the best way to associate some code with a common action (such as saving a file) is by adding a function to a hook variable, provided that a suitable hook variable exists. Using **M-x apropos RET hook RET**, we discover four promising hook variables: `after-save-hook`, `local-write-file-hooks`, `write-contents-hooks`, and `write-file-hooks`.

We can discard `after-save-hook` right away. We don't want our code executed, modifying writestamps, *after* the file is saved, because then it will be impossible to save an up-to-date version of the file!

The differences between the remaining candidates are subtle:

`write-file-hooks`
> Code to execute for any buffer each time it is saved.

`local-write-file-hooks`
> A buffer-local version of `write-file-hooks`. Recall from the "Hooks" section of Chapter 2 that a buffer-local variable is one that can have different values in different buffers. Whereas `write-file-hooks` pertains to every buffer, `local-write-file-hooks` can pertain to individual buffers. Thus, if you want to run one function while saving a Lisp file and another one when saving a text file, `local-write-file-hooks` is the one to use.

`write-contents-hooks`
> Like `local-write-file-hooks` in that it's buffer-local and it contains functions to execute each time the buffer is saved to a file. However—and I warned you this was subtle—the functions in `write-contents-hooks` pertain to the buffer's *contents*, while the functions in the other two hooks pertain to the *files* being edited. In practice, this means that if you change the major mode of the buffer, you're changing the way the *contents* should be considered, and therefore `write-contents-hooks` reverts to `nil` but `local-write-file-hooks` doesn't. On the other hand, if you change Emacs's idea of which file is being edited, e.g. by invoking `set-visited-file-name`, then `local-write-file-hooks` reverts to `nil` and `write-contents-hooks` doesn't.

We'll rule out `write-file-hooks` because we'll want to invoke our writestamp-updater only in buffers that have writestamps, not every time any buffer is saved. And, hair-splitting semantics aside, we'll rule out `write-contents-hooks` because we want our chosen hook variable to be immune to changes in the buffer's major mode. That leaves `local-write-file-hooks`.

Now, what should the writestamp updater that we'll put in `local-write-file-hooks` do? It must locate each writestamp, delete it, and replace it with an updated one. The most straightforward approach is to surround each writestamp with a distinguishing string of characters that we can search for. Let's say that each writestamp is surrounded by the strings "WRITESTAMP((" on the left and "))" on the right, so that in a file it looks something like this:

```
...
went into the castle and lived happily ever after.
The end. WRITESTAMP((12:19pm 7 Jul 96))
```

Let's say that the stuff inside the **WRITESTAMP((...))** is put there by `insert-date` (which we defined earlier) and so its format can be controlled with `insert-date-format`.

Now, supposing we have some writestamps in the file to begin with,[*] we can update it at file-writing time like so:

```
(add-hook 'local-write-file-hooks 'update-writestamps)

(defun update-writestamps ()
  "Find writestamps and replace them with the current time."
  (save-excursion
    (save-restriction
      (save-match-data
        (widen)
        (goto-char (point-min))
        (while (search-forward "WRITESTAMP((" nil t)
          (let ((start (point)))
            (search-forward "))")
            (delete-region start (- (point) 2))
            (goto-char start)
            (insert-date))))))))
  nil)
```

There's a lot here that's new. Let's go through this function a line at a time.

First we notice that the body of the function is wrapped inside a call to **save-excursion**. What **save-excursion** does is memorize the position of the cursor, execute the subexpressions it's given as arguments, then restore the cursor to its original position. It's useful in this case because the body of the function is going to move the cursor all over the buffer, but by the time the function finishes we'd like the caller of this function to perceive no cursor motion. There'll be much more about **save-excursion** in Chapter 8, *Evaluation and Error Recovery*.

---

[*] Inserting writestamps is similar to inserting the date or the time. A function for doing so is left as an exercise for the reader.

Next is a call to `save-restriction`. This is like `save-excursion` in that it memorizes some information, then executes its arguments, then restores the information. The information in this case is the buffer's *restriction*, which is the result of *narrowing*. Narrowing is covered in Chapter 9. For now let's just say that narrowing refers to Emacs's ability to show only a portion of a buffer. Since `update-writestamps` is going to call `widen`, which undoes the effect of any narrowing, we need `save-restriction` in order to clean up after ourselves.

Next is a call to `save-match-data` that, like `save-excursion` and `save-restriction`, memorizes some information, executes its arguments, then restores the information. This time the information in question is the result of the latest search. Each time a search occurs, information about the result of the search is stored in some global variables (as we will see shortly). Each search wipes out the result of the previous search. Our function will perform a search, but for the sake of other functions that might be calling ours, we don't want to disrupt the global match data.

Next is a call to `widen`. As previously mentioned, this undoes any narrowing in effect. It makes the entire buffer accessible, which is necessary if every writestamp is to be found and updated.

Next we move the cursor to the beginning of the buffer with `(goto-char (point-min))` in preparation for the function's main loop, which is going to search for each successive writestamp and rewrite it in place. The function `point-min` returns the minimum value for point, normally `1`. (The only time `(point-min)` might not be `1` is when there's narrowing in effect. Since we've called `widen`, we know narrowing is *not* in effect, so we could write `(goto-char 1)` instead. But it's good practice to use `point-min` where appropriate.)

The main loop looks like this:

```
(while (search-forward "WRITESTAMP((" nil t)
  ...)
```

This is a `while` loop, which works very much like while loops in other languages. Its first argument is an expression that is tested each time around the loop. If the expression evaluates to true, the remaining arguments are executed and the whole cycle repeats.

The expression `(search-forward "WRITESTAMP((" nil t)` searches for the first occurrence of the given string, starting from the current location of point. The `nil` means the search is not bounded except by the end of the buffer. This is explained in more detail later. The `t` means that if no match is found, `search-forward` should simply return `nil`. (Without the `t`, `search-forward` signals an error, aborting the current command, if no match is found.) If the search is successful, point is moved to the first character after the matched text, and `search-forward` returns that position. (It's possible to find where the match began using `match-beginning`, which is shown in Figure 4-1.)

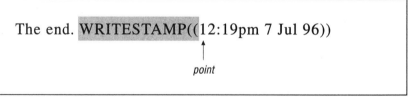

Figure 4-1. After searching for the string WRITESTAMP((

The body of the `while` loop is

```
(let ((start (point)))
  ...)
```

This creates a temporary variable, `start`, that holds the location of point, which is the beginning of the date string inside the `WRITESTAMP((...))` delimiters.

With `start` defined, the body of the `let` contains:

```
(search-forward "))")
(delete-region start (- (point) 2))
(goto-char start)
(insert-date)
```

This call to `search-forward` places point after the two closing parentheses. We still know the beginning of the timestamp, because this location is in `start`, as shown in Figure 4-2.

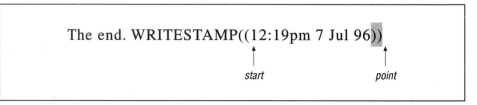

Figure 4-2. After searching for ")) "

This time, only the first argument to `search-forward`, the search string, is given. Earlier we saw two additional arguments: the search bound, and whether to signal an error. When omitted, they default to `nil` (unbounded search) and `nil` (signal an error if the search fails).

After `search-forward` succeeds—and if it fails, an error is signaled and execution of the function never gets past `search-forward`—`delete-region` deletes the text region that is the date in the writestamp, starting at position start and ending before position (- (point) 2) (two characters to the left of point), leaving the results shown in Figure 4-3.

Figure 4-3. After deleting the region between start *and* (- (point) 2)

Next, (goto-char start) positions the cursor inside the writestamp delimiters and, finally, (insert-date) inserts the current date.

The while loop executes as many times as there are matches for the search string. It's important that each time a match is found, the cursor remains "to the right" of the place where the match began. Otherwise, the next iteration of the loop will find the same match for the search string!

When the while loop is done, save-match-data returns, restoring the match data; then save-restriction returns, restoring any narrowing that was in effect; then save-excursion returns, restoring point to its original location.

The final expression of **update-writestamps**, after the call to **save-excursion**, is

```
nil
```

This is the function's *return value*. The return value of a Lisp function is simply the value of the last expression in the function's body. (All Lisp functions return a value, but so far every function we've written has done its job via "side effects" instead of by returning meaningful values.) In this case we force it to be nil. The reason is that functions in local-write-file-hooks are treated specially. Normally, the return value of a function in a hook variable doesn't matter. But for functions in local-write-file-hooks (also in write-file-hooks and write-contents-hooks), a non-nil return value means, "This hook function has taken over the job of writing the buffer to a file." If the hook function returns a non-nil value, the remaining functions in the hook variables are not called, and Emacs does not write the buffer to a file itself after the hook functions run. Since **update-writestamps** is *not* taking over the job of writing the buffer to a file, we want to be sure it returns nil.

Generalizing Writestamps

This approach to implementing writestamps works, but there are a few problems. First, by hardwiring the strings `"WRITESTAMP(("` and `"))"` we've doomed the user to an unaesthetic and inflexible way to distinguish writestamps in text. Second, the user's preference might not be to use `insert-date` for writestamps.

These problems are simple to fix. We can introduce three new variables: one that, like `insert-date-format` and `insert-time-format`, describes a time format to use; and two that describe the delimiters surrounding a writestamp.

```
(defvar writestamp-format "%C"
  "*Format for writestamps (c.f. 'format-time-string').")

(defvar writestamp-prefix "WRITESTAMP(("
  "*Unique string identifying start of writestamp.")

(defvar writestamp-suffix "))"
  "*String that terminates a writestamp.")
```

Now we can modify **update-writestamps** to be more configurable.

```
(defun update-writestamps ()
  "Find writestamps and replace them with the current time."
  (save-excursion
    (save-restriction
      (save-match-data
        (widen)
        (goto-char (point-min))
        (while (search-forward writestamp-prefix nil t)
          (let ((start (point)))
            (search-forward writestamp-suffix)
            (delete-region start (match-beginning 0))
            (goto-char start)
            (insert (format-time-string writestamp-format
                                        (current-time)))))))))
  nil)
```

In this version of **update-writestamps**, we've replaced occurrences of `"WRITESTAMP(("` and `"))"` with **writestamp-prefix** and **writestamp-suffix**, and we've replaced **insert-date** with

```
(insert (format-time-string writestamp-format
                            (current-time)))
```

We also changed the call to **delete-region**. Previously it looked like this:

```
(delete-region start (- (point) 2))
```

That was when we had the writestamp suffix hardwired to be `"))"`, which is two characters long. But now that the writestamp suffix is stored in a variable, we don't know in advance how many characters long it is. We could certainly find out, by calling `length`:

```
(delete-region start (- (point)
                        (length writestamp-suffix)))
```

but a better solution is to use `match-beginning`. Remember that before the call to `delete-region` is

```
(search-forward writestamp-suffix)
```

No matter what `writestamp-suffix` is, `search-forward` finds the first occurrence of it, if one exists, and returns the first position after the match. But extra data about the match, notably the position where the match begins, is stored in Emacs's global match-data variables. The way to access this data is with the functions `match-beginning` and `match-end`. For reasons that will become clear shortly, `match-beginning` needs an argument of 0 to tell you the position of the beginning of the match for the latest search. In this case, that happens to be the beginning of the writestamp suffix, which also happens to be the end of the date inside the writestamp, and therefore the end of the region to delete:

```
(delete-region start (match-beginning 0))
```

Regular Expressions

Suppose the user chooses "Written: " and "." as the `writestamp-prefix` and `writestamp-suffix`, so that writestamps appear like so: "Written: 19 Aug 1996." This is a perfectly reasonable preference, but the string "Written: " is less likely than "WRITESTAMP((" to be completely unique. In other words, the file may contain occurrences of "Written: " that aren't writestamps. When `update-writestamps` searches for `writestamp-prefix`, it might find one of these occurrences, then search for the next occurrence of a period and delete everything in between. Worse, this unwanted deletion takes place almost undetectably, just as the file is being saved, with the cursor location and other appearances preserved.

One way to solve this problem is to impose tighter constraints on how the writestamp may appear, making mismatches less likely. One natural restriction might be to require writestamps to appear alone on a line: in other words, a string is a writestamp only if `writestamp-prefix` is the first thing on the line and `writestamp-suffix` is the last thing on the line.

Now it won't suffice to use

```
(search-forward writestamp-prefix ...)
```

to find writestamps, because this search isn't constrained to find matches only at the beginnings of lines.

This is where *regular expressions* come in handy. A regular expression—called a *regexp* or *regex* for short—is a search pattern just like the first argument to `search-forward`. Unlike a normal search pattern, regular expressions have certain syntactic rules that allow more powerful kinds of searches. For example, in the regular expression '^Written: ', the caret (^) is a special character that means, "this pattern must match at the beginning of a line." The remaining characters in the regexp '^Written: ' don't have any special meaning in regexp syntax, so they match the same way ordinary search patterns do. Special characters are sometimes called *metacharacters* or (more poetically) *magic*.

Many UNIX programs use regular expressions, among them *sed, grep, awk,* and *perl.* The syntax of regular expressions tends to vary slightly from one application to another, unfortunately; but in all cases, most characters are non-"magic" (particularly letters and numbers) and can be used to search for occurrences of themselves; and longer regexps can be built up from shorter ones simply by stringing them together. Here is the syntax of regular expressions in Emacs.

1. Period (.) matches any single character except newline.

2. Backslash, followed by a magic character, matches that character literally. So, for example, \. matches a period. Since backslash itself is magic, \\ matches \ itself.

3. A set of characters inside square brackets matches any one of the enclosed characters. So [aeiou] matches any occurrence of a or e or i or o or u. There are some exceptions to this rule—the syntax of square brackets in regular expressions has its own "subsyntax," as follows:

   (a) A range of consecutive characters, such as abcd, can be abbreviated a-d. Any number of such ranges can be included, and ranges can be intermixed with single characters. So [a-dmx-z] matches any a, b, c, d, m, x, y, or z.

   (b) If the first character is a caret (^), then the expression matches any character *not* appearing inside the square brackets. So [^a-d] matches any character *except* a, b, c, or d.

   (c) To include a right-square-bracket, it must be the first character in the set. So []a] matches] or a. Similarly, [^]a] matches any character *except*] and a.

   (d) To include a hyphen, it must appear where it can't be interpreted as part of a range; for example, as the first or last character in the set, or following the end of a range. So [a-e-z] matches a, b, c, d, e, -, or z.

   (e) To include a caret, it must appear someplace other than as the first character in the set.

   (f) Other characters that are normally "magic" in regexps, such as * and ., are not magic inside square brackets.

4. A regexp *x* may have one of the following suffixes:

(a) An asterisk, matching zero or more occurrences of *x*

(b) A plus sign, matching one or more occurrences of *x*

(c) A question mark, matching zero or one occurrence of *x*

So a* matches a, aa, aaa, and even an empty string (zero a s);[*] a+ matches a, aa, aaa, but not an empty string; and a? matches an empty string and a. Note that *x+* is equivalent to *xx**.

5. The regexp ^*x* matches whatever *x* matches, but only at the beginning of a line.

The regexp *x*$ matches whatever *x* matches, but only at the end of a line.

This means that ^*x*$ matches a line containing nothing but a match for *x*. In this case, you could leave out *x* altogether; ^$ matches a line containing no characters.

6. Two regular expressions *x* and *y* separated by \| match whatever *x* matches *or* whatever *y* matches. So hello\|goodbye matches hello or goodbye.

7. A regular expression *x* enclosed in escaped parentheses— \(and \)— matches whatever *x* matches. This can be used for grouping complicated expressions. So \(ab\)+ matches ab, abab, ababab, and so on. Also, \(ab\|cd\)ef matches abef or cdef.

As a side effect, any text matched by a parenthesized subexpression is called a *submatch* and is memorized in a numbered register. Submatches are numbered from 1 through 9 by counting occurrences of \(in a regexp from left to right. So if the regexp ab\(cd*e\) matches the text abcddde, then the one and only submatch is the string cddde. If the regexp ab\(cd\|ef\(g+h\)\)j\(k*\) matches the text abefgghjkk, then the first submatch is efggh, the second submatch is ggh, and the third submatch is kk.

8. Backslash followed by a digit *n* matches the same text matched by the *n*th parenthesized subexpression from earlier in the same regexp. So the expression \(a+b\)\1 matches abab, aabaab, and aaabaaab, but not abaab (because ab isn't the same as aab).

9. The empty string can be matched in a wide variety of ways.

(a) \` matches the empty string that's at the beginning of the buffer. So \`hello matches the string hello at the beginning of the buffer, but no other occurrence of hello.

(b) \' matches the empty string that's at the end of the buffer.

---

[*] The * regular expression operator is known among computer scientists as a "Kleene closure."

(c) \= matches the empty string that's at the current location of point.

(d) \b matches the empty string that's at the beginning or end of a word. So \bgnu\b matches the word "gnu" but not the occurrence of "gnu" inside the word "interregnum".

(e) \B matches the empty string that's anywhere *but* at the beginning or end of a word. So \Bword matches the occurrence of "word" in "sword" but not in "words".

(f) \< matches the empty string at the beginning of a word only.

(g) \> matches the empty string at the end of a word only.

As you can see, regular expression syntax uses backslashes for many purposes. So does Emacs Lisp string syntax. Since regexps are written as Lisp strings when programming Emacs, the two sets of rules for using backslashes can cause some confusing results. For example, the regexp ab\|cd, when expressed as a Lisp string, must be written as "ab\\|cd". Even stranger is when you want to match a single \ using the regexp \\ : you must write the string "\\\\". Emacs commands that prompt for regular expressions (such as **apropos** and **keep-lines**) allow you to type them *as* regular expressions (not Lisp strings) when used interactively.

Regexp Quoting

Now that we know how to assemble regular expressions, it might seem obvious that the way to search for **writestamp-prefix** at the beginning of a line is to prepend a caret onto **writestamp-prefix** and append a dollar sign onto **writestamp-suffix**, like so:

```
(re-search-forward (concat "^"
                           writestamp-prefix) ...)        ; wrong!

(re-search-forward (concat writestamp-suffix
                           "$") ...)                       ; wrong!
```

The function **concat** concatenates its string arguments into a single string. The function **re-search-forward** is the regular expression version of **search-forward**.

This is almost right. However, it contains a common and subtle error: either **writestamp-prefix** or **writestamp-suffix** may contain "magic" characters. In fact, **writestamp-suffix** does, in our example: it's ".". Since . matches any character (except newline), this expression:

```
(re-search-forward (concat writestamp-suffix
                           "$") ...)
```

which is equivalent to this expression:

```
(re-search-forward ".$" ...)
```

matches any character at the end of a line, whereas we only *want* to match a period (.).

When building up a regular expression as in this example, using pieces such as `writestamp-prefix` whose content is beyond the programmer's control, it is necessary to "remove the magic" from strings that are meant to be taken literally. Emacs provides a function for this purpose called `regexp-quote`, which understands regexp syntax and can turn a possibly-magic string into the corresponding non-magic one. For example, `(regexp-quote ".")` yields `"\\."` as a string. You should always use `regexp-quote` to remove the magic from variable strings that are used to build up regular expressions.

We now know how to begin a new version of `update-writestamps`:

```
(defun update-writestamps ()
  "Find writestamps and replace them with the current time."
  (save-excursion
    (save-restriction
      (save-match-data
        (widen)
        (goto-char (point-min))
        (while (re-search-forward
                 (concat "^"
                         (regexp-quote writestamp-prefix))
                 nil t)
          ...)))))
  nil)
```

Limited Searching

Let's finish our new version of `update-writestamps` by filling in the body of the `while` loop. Just after `re-search-forward` succeeds, we need to know whether the current line ends with `writestamp-suffix`. But we can't simply write

```
(re-search-forward (concat (regexp-quote writestamp-suffix)
                           "$"))
```

because that could find a match several lines away. We're only interested in knowing whether the match is on the current line.

One solution is to limit the search to the current line. The optional second argument to `search-forward` and `re-search-forward`, if non-`nil`, is a buffer position beyond which the search may not go. If we plug in the buffer position corresponding to the end of the current line like so:

```
(re-search-forward (concat (regexp-quote writestamp-suffix)
                           "$")
                   end-of-line-position)
```

then the search is limited to the current line, and we'll have the answer we need. So how do we come up with *end-of-line-position?* We simply put the cursor at the end of the current line using `end-of-line`, then query the value of point. But after we do that and before `re-search-forward` begins, we must make sure to return the cursor to its original location since the search must start from there. Moving the cursor then restoring it is exactly what `save-excursion` is designed to do. So we could write:

```
(let ((end-of-line-position (save-excursion
                              (end-of-line)
                              (point))))
  (re-search-forward (concat (regexp-quote writestamp-suffix)
                             "$")
                     end-of-line-position))
```

which creates a temporary variable, `end-of-line-position`, that is used to limit `re-search-forward`; but it's simpler not to use a temporary variable if we don't really need it:

```
(re-search-forward (concat (regexp-quote writestamp-suffix)
                           "$")
                   (save-excursion
                     (end-of-line)
                     (point)))
```

Observe that the value of the `save-excursion` expression is, like so many other Lisp constructs, the value of its last subexpression (`point`).

So `update-writestamps` can be written like this:

```
(defun update-writestamps ()
  "Find writestamps and replace them with the current time."
  (save-excursion
    (save-restriction
      (save-match-data
        (widen)
        (goto-char (point-min))
        (while (re-search-forward
                (concat "^"
                        (regexp-quote writestamp-prefix))
                nil t)
          (let ((start (point)))
            (if (re-search-forward (concat (regexp-quote
                                            writestamp-suffix)
                                           "$")
                                   (save-excursion
                                     (end-of-line)
                                     (point))
                                   t)
                (progn
                  (delete-region start (match-beginning 0))
                  (goto-char start)
                  (insert (format-time-string writestamp-format
                                              (current-time)))))))))
  nil)
```

Notice that both calls to `re-search-forward` have `t` as the optional third argument, meaning "if the search fails, return `nil` (as opposed to signaling an error)."

More Regexp Power

We have created a more or less straightforward translation of `update-writestamps` from its original form to use regular expressions, but it doesn't really exploit the power of regexps. In particular, the entire sequence of finding a writestamp prefix, checking for a matching writestamp suffix on the same line, and replacing the text in between can be reduced to just these two expressions:

```
(re-search-forward (concat "^"
                           (regexp-quote writestamp-prefix)
                           "\\(.*\\)"
                           (regexp-quote writestamp-suffix)
                           "$"))
(replace-match (format-time-string writestamp-format
                                   (current-time))
               t t nil 1)
```

The first expression, the call to `re-search-forward`, constructs a regexp that looks like this:

^prefix\ (.*\) *suffix*$

where *prefix* and *suffix* are `regexp-quote`d versions of `writestamp-prefix` and `writestamp-suffix`. This regexp matches one entire line, beginning with the writestamp prefix, followed by any string (which is made a submatch by the use of \(...\)), and ending with the writestamp suffix.

The second expression is a call to `replace-match`, which replaces some or all of the matched text from a previous search. It's used like this:

```
(replace-match   new-string
                 preserve-case
                 literal
                 base-string
                 subexpression)
```

The first argument is the new string to insert, which in this example is the result of `format-time-string`. The remaining arguments, which are all optional, have the following meanings:

preserve-case

> We set this to `t`, which tells `replace-match` to preserve alphabetic case in *new-string*. If it's `nil`, `replace-match` tries to intelligently match the case of the text being replaced.

literal

> We use t, which means "treat *new-string* literally." If it's `nil`, then `replace-match` interprets `new-string` according to some special syntax rules (for which see `describe-function` on `replace-match`).

base-string

> We use `nil`, which means "Modify the current buffer." If this were a string, then `replace-match` would perform the replacement in the string instead of in a buffer.

subexpression

> We use 1, which means "Replace submatch 1, not the entire matched string" (which would include the prefix and the suffix).

So after finding the writestamp with `re-search-forward` and "submatching" the text between the delimiters, our call to `replace-match` snips out the text between the delimiters and inserts a fresh new string formatted according to `writestamp-format`.

As a final improvement to **update-writestamps**, we can observe that if we write

```
(while (re-search-forward (concat ...) ...)
  (replace-match ...))
```

then the `concat` function is called each time through the loop, constructing a new string each time even though its arguments never change. This is inefficient. It would be better to compute the desired string once, before the loop, and store it in a temporary variable. The best way to write **update-writestamps** is therefore:

```
(defun update-writestamps ()
  "Find writestamps and replace them with the current time."
  (save-excursion
    (save-restriction
      (save-match-data
        (widen)
        (goto-char (point-min))
        (let ((regexp (concat "^"
                              (regexp-quote writestamp-prefix)
                              "\\(.*\\)"
                              (regexp-quote writestamp-suffix)
                              "$")))
          (while (re-search-forward regexp nil t)
            (replace-match (format-time-string writestamp-format
                                               (current-time))
                           t t nil 1))))))
  nil)
```

Modifystamps

Well, timestamps were marginally useful, and writestamps were somewhat more so, but *modifystamps* may be even better. A modifystamp is a writestamp that records the time the file was last modified, which may not be the same as the last time it was saved to disk. For instance, if you visit a file and save it under a new name without making any changes to it, you shouldn't cause the modifystamp to change.

In this section we'll briefly explore two very simple approaches to implementing modifystamps, and one clever one.

Simple Approach #1

Emacs has a hook variable called `first-change-hook`. Whenever a buffer is changed for the first time since it was last saved, the functions in `first-change-hook` get executed. Implementing modifystamps by using this hook merely entails moving our old `update-writestamps` function from `local-write-file-hooks` to `first-change-hook`. Of course, we'll also want to change its name to `update-modifystamps`, and introduce new variables—`modifystamp-format`, `modifystamp-prefix`, and `modifystamp-suffix`—that work like their writestamp counterparts without overloading the writestamp variables. Then `update-modifystamps` should be changed to use the new variables.

Before any of this happens, `first-change-hook`, which is normally global, should be made buffer-local. If we add `update-modifystamps` to `first-change-hook` while it is still global, `update-modifystamps` will be called every time any buffer is saved. Making it buffer-local in the current buffer causes changes to the variable to be invisible outside that buffer. Other buffers continue to use the default global value.

```
(make-local-hook 'first-change-hook)
```

Although ordinary variables are made buffer-local with either `make-local-variable` or `make-variable-buffer-local` (see below), hook variables must be made buffer-local with `make-local-hook`.

```
(defvar modifystamp-format "%C"
  "*Format for modifystamps (c.f. 'format-time-string').")

(defvar modifystamp-prefix "MODIFYSTAMP(("
  "*String identifying start of modifystamp.")

(defvar modifystamp-suffix "))"
  "*String that terminates a modifystamp.")
```

```
(defun update-modifystamps ()
 "Find modifystamps and replace them with the current time."
 (save-excursion
   (save-restriction
     (save-match-data
       (widen)
       (goto-char (point-min))
       (let ((regexp (concat "^"
                             (regexp-quote modifystamp-prefix)
                             "\\(.*\\)"
                             (regexp-quote modifystamp-suffix)
                             "$")))
         (while (re-search-forward regexp nil t)
           (replace-match (format-time-string modifystamp-format
                                              (current-time))
                          t t nil 1))))))
 nil)
```

```
(add-hook 'first-change-hook 'update-modifystamps nil t)
```

The `nil` argument to **add-hook** is just a place holder. We care only about the last
argument, `t`, which means "change only the buffer-local copy of **first-change-
hook**."

The problem with this approach is that if you make ten changes to the file before
saving it, the modifystamps will contain the time of the first change, not the last
change. Close enough for some purposes, but we can do better.

Simple Approach #2

This time we'll go back to using **local-write-file-hooks**, but we'll call
update-modifystamps from it only if **buffer-modified-p** returns true,
which tells us that the current buffer has been modified since it was last saved:

```
(defun maybe-update-modifystamps ()
 "Call 'update-modifystamps' if the buffer has been modified."
 (if (buffer-modified-p)
     (update-modifystamps)))
```

```
(add-hook 'local-write-file-hooks 'maybe-update-modifystamps)
```

Now we have the opposite problem from simple approach #1: the last-modified
time isn't computed until the file is saved, which may be much later than the
actual time of the last modification. If you make a change to the file at 2:00 and
save at 3:00, the modifystamps will record 3:00 as the last-modified time. This is a
closer approximation, but it's still not perfect.

Clever Approach

Theoretically, we could call **update-modifystamps** after every change to the
buffer, but in practice it's prohibitively expensive to scan through the whole file
and rewrite parts of it after every keystroke. But it's not too expensive to memo-

rize the current time after each buffer change. Then, when the buffer is saved to a file, the memorized time can be used for computing the time in the modifystamps.

The hook variable `after-change-functions` contains functions to call after each buffer change. First let's make it buffer-local:

```
(make-local-hook 'after-change-functions)
```

Now we define a buffer-local variable to hold this buffer's latest modification time:

```
(defvar last-change-time nil
  "Time of last buffer modification.")
(make-variable-buffer-local 'last-change-time)
```

The function `make-variable-buffer-local` causes the named variable to have a separate, buffer-local value in every buffer. This is subtly different from `make-local-variable`, which makes a variable have a buffer-local value in the *current* buffer while allowing other buffers to share the same *global* value. In this case, we use `make-variable-buffer-local` because there is no meaningful global value of `last-change-time` for other buffers to share.

Now we need a function to set `last-change-time` each time the buffer changes. Let's call it `remember-change-time` and add it to `after-change-functions`:

```
(add-hook 'after-change-functions 'remember-change-time nil t)
```

Functions in `after-change-functions` are passed three arguments describing the change that just took place (see the section called "Mode Meat" in Chapter 7). But `remember-change-time` doesn't care *what* the change was; only that there *was* a change. So we'll allow `remember-change-time` to take arguments, but we'll ignore them.

```
(defun remember-change-time (&rest unused)
  "Store the current time in 'last-change-time'."
  (setq last-change-time (current-time)))
```

The keyword `&rest`, followed by a parameter name, must appear last in a function's parameter list. It means "collect up any remaining arguments into a list and assign it to the last parameter" (`unused` in this case). The function may have other parameters, including `&optional` ones, but these must precede the `&rest` parameter. After all the other parameters are assigned in the normal fashion, the `&rest` parameter gets a list of whatever's left. So if a function is defined as

```
(defun foo (a b &rest c)
  ...)
```

and is called with `(foo 1 2 3 4)`, then a will be 1, b will be 2, and c will be the list `(3 4)`.

In some situations, &rest is very useful, even necessary; but right now we're only using it out of laziness (or economy, if you prefer), to avoid having to name three separate parameters that we don't plan to use.

Now we must revise update-modifystamps: it must use the time stored in last-change-time instead of using (current-time). For efficiency, it should also reset last-change-time to nil when it is done, so if the file is subsequently saved without being modified, we can avoid the overhead of calling update-modifystamps.

```
(defun update-modifystamps ()
  "Find modifystamps and replace them with the saved time."
  (save-excursion
    (save-restriction
      (save-match-data
        (widen)
        (goto-char (point-min))
        (let ((regexp (concat "^"
                              (regexp-quote modifystamp-prefix)
                              "\\(.*\\)"
                              (regexp-quote modifystamp-suffix)
                              "$")))
          (while (re-search-forward regexp nil t)
            (replace-match (format-time-string modifystamp-format
                                               last-change-time)
                           t t nil 1))))))
  (setq last-change-time nil)
  nil)
```

Finally, we wish not to call update-modifystamps when last-change-time is nil:

```
(defun maybe-update-modifystamps ()
  "Call `update-modifystamps' if the buffer has been modified."
  (if last-change-time        ; instead of testing (buffer-modified-p)
      (update-modifystamps)))
```

There's still one important thing missing from maybe-update-modifystamps. Before reading ahead to the next section, can you figure out what it is?

A Subtle Bug

The problem is that every time a modifystamp gets rewritten by update-modifystamps, the buffer changes, causing last-change-time to change! Only the first modifystamp will be correctly rewritten. Subsequent ones will contain a time much closer to when the file was saved than when the last modification was made.

One way around this problem is to temporarily set the value of after-change-functions to nil while executing update-modifystamps as shown below.

```
(add-hook 'local-write-file-hooks
          '(lambda ()
             (if last-change-time
                 (let ((after-change-functions nil))
                   (update-modifystamps)))))
```

This use of `let` creates a temporary variable, `after-change-functions`, that supersedes the global `after-change-functions` during the call to `update-modifystamps` in the body of the `let`. After the `let` exits, the temporary `after-change-functions` disappears and the global one is again in effect.

This solution has a drawback: if there are other functions in `after-change-functions`, they'll also be disabled during the call to `update-modifystamps`, though you might not intend for them to be.

A better solution would be to "capture" the value of `last-change-time` before any modifystamps are updated. That way, when updating the first modifystamp causes `last-change-time` to change, the new value of `last-change-time` won't affect any remaining modifystamps because `update-modifystamps` won't be referring to `last-change-time`.

The simplest way to "capture" the value of `last-change-time` is to pass it as an argument to `update-modifystamps`:

```
(add-hook 'local-write-file-hooks
          '(lambda ()
             (if last-change-time
                 (update-modifystamps last-change-time))))
```

This requires changing `update-modifystamps` to take one argument and use it in the call to `format-time-string`:

```
(defun update-modifystamps (time)
  "Find modifystamps and replace them with the given time."
  (save-excursion
    (save-restriction
      (save-match-data
        (widen)
        (goto-char (point-min))
        (let ((regexp (concat "^"
                              (regexp-quote modifystamp-prefix)
                              "\\(.*\\)"
                              (regexp-quote modifystamp-suffix)
                              "$")))
          (while (re-search-forward regexp nil t)
            (replace-match (format-time-string modifystamp-format
                                               time)
                           t t nil 1))))))
  (setq last-change-time nil)
  nil)
```

You might be thinking that setting up a buffer to use modifystamps involves evaluating a lot of expressions and setting up a lot of variables, and that it seems hard to keep track of what's needed to make modifystamps work. If so, you're right. So in the next chapter, we'll look at how you can encapsulate a collection of related functions and variables in a Lisp file.

5

Lisp Files

Up to now, most of the Emacs Lisp we've written has been suitable for inclusion in your *.emacs* file. The alternative is to put Emacs Lisp code into files separated by functionality. This requires a little more effort to set up, but has some benefits over putting everything into *.emacs*:

- Code in *.emacs* is always executed when Emacs starts up, even if it is never needed in a given session. This makes startup time longer and consumes memory. By contrast, a separate file of Lisp code can be loaded only when and if needed.

- Code in *.emacs* typically isn't *byte-compiled*. Byte-compiling is the process of turning Emacs Lisp into a more efficient form that loads faster, runs faster, and uses less memory (but which, like compiled programs in other languages, contains unreadable codes that are not meant for human eyes). Byte-compiled Lisp files usually have names ending in *.elc* ("Emacs Lisp, compiled"), while their non-compiled counterparts usually have names ending in *.el* ("Emacs Lisp").

- Putting everything into *.emacs* can cause that file to balloon over time into an impossible-to-manage jumble.

The previous chapter is a good example of a set of related functions and variables that can be encapsulated in a separate Lisp file that should only be loaded when and if needed, and that calls for byte-compilation for very efficient execution.

Creating a Lisp File

Emacs Lisp files have names ending in *.el*, so to begin, let's create *timestamp.el* and put in it the finished forms of the last chapter's code, as shown below.

```
(defvar insert-time-format ...)
(defvar insert-date-format ...)
(defun insert-time () ...)
(defun insert-date () ...)

(defvar writestamp-format ...)
(defvar writestamp-prefix ...)
(defvar writestamp-suffix ...)
(defun update-writestamps () ...)

(defvar last-change-time ...)
(make-variable-buffer-local 'last-change-time)
(defun remember-change-time ...)
(defvar modifystamp-format ...)
(defvar modifystamp-prefix ...)
(defvar modifystamp-suffix ...)
(defun maybe-update-modifystamps () ...)
(defun update-modifystamps (time) ...)
```

Don't include the calls to **add-hook** or **make-local-hook** yet. We'll get to those later. For now, observe that Lisp files should be written such that they can be loaded at any time, even multiple times, without unwanted side-effects. One such side-effect would be including (**make-local-hook** **'after-change-functions**) in *timestamp.el*, then loading *timestamp.el* while the current buffer is not the one whose **after-change-functions** you want to make local.

Loading the File

Once the code is in *timestamp.el*, we must arrange for its definitions to be available when we need them. This is done by *loading* the file, which causes Emacs to read and execute its contents. There are many ways to load Lisp files in Emacs: interactively, non-interactively, explicitly, implicitly, and with and without path-searching.

Finding Lisp Files

Emacs can load files based on full path names such as */usr/local/share/emacs/ site-lisp/foo.el*, but it is usually more convenient to use only a file's base name, *foo.el*, and let Emacs find it among the directories in the *load path*. The load path is simply a list of directories that Emacs searches for files to load, very much like the way the UNIX shell uses the environment variable **PATH** to find programs to execute. Emacs's load path is stored as a list of strings in the Lisp variable **load-path**.

When Emacs starts, **load-path** has an initial setting that looks something like the following example.

```
("/usr/local/share/emacs/19.34/site-lisp"
 "/usr/local/share/emacs/site-lisp"
 "/usr/local/share/emacs/19.34/lisp")
```

Directories in `load-path` are searched in the order they appear. To add a directory to the beginning of `load-path`, use

```
(setq load-path
      (cons "/your/directory/here"
            load-path))
```

in your *.emacs* file. To add a directory to the end, use

```
(setq load-path
      (append load-path
              '("/your/directory/here")))
```

Notice that in the first example, `"/your/directory/here"` appears as an ordinary
string, but in the second example, it appears inside a quoted list. Chapter 6, *Lists*,
explains these and other ways to manipulate lists in Lisp.

If you ask Emacs to find a Lisp file in the load path and you omit the suffix of the
file for which you're looking—e.g., you specify *foo* instead of *foo.el*—Emacs first
looks for *foo.elc*, the byte-compiled form of *foo.el*. If that's not found in the load
path, then *foo.el* is tried, followed by plain *foo*. It's usually best to omit the suffix
when specifying a file to load. Not only does it get you that useful search
behavior, but it helps `eval-after-load` to work properly (see the section
about `eval-after-load` later in this chapter).

Interactive Loading

Two Emacs commands exist for interactively loading a Lisp file: `load-file` and
`load-library`. When you type **M-x load-file RET**, Emacs prompts you for the
full pathname of a Lisp file (e.g., */home/bobg/emacs/foo.el*) and does not search
`load-path`. It uses the normal filename-prompting mechanisms, so filename
completion is available. On the other hand, when you type **M-x load-library RET**,
Emacs prompts you for just the base name of the library (e.g, *foo*) and attempts to
find it in `load-path`. It does *not* use filename-prompting and completion is not
available.

Programmatic Loading

When loading files from Lisp code, you may choose explicit loading, conditional
loading, or autoloading.

Explicit loading

Files are loaded explicitly by calling `load` (which works like the interactive `load-library`) or `load-file`.

```
(load "lazy-lock")
```

searches `load-path` for *lazy-lock.elc*, *lazy-lock.el*, or *lazy-lock*.

```
(load-file "/home/bobg/emacs/lazy-lock.elc")
```

doesn't use `load-path`.

Explicit loading should be used when you definitely need the file to be loaded immediately, and you either know that the file hasn't already been loaded or you don't care. As it turns out, given the alternatives below, it is rarely the case that you need to explicitly load a Lisp file.

Conditional loading

When *n* different pieces of Lisp code want to load a particular file, two Emacs Lisp functions, `require` and `provide`, give a way to make sure it only gets loaded once instead of *n* times.

A Lisp file usually contains a collection of related functions. The collection can be thought of abstractly as a single *feature*. Loading the file makes available the feature it contains.

Emacs makes the feature concept explicit. Features are named by Lisp symbols, declared with `provide`, and requested by `require`.

Here's how it works. First, we'll choose a symbol to stand for the feature provided by the file *timestamp.el*. Let's use the obvious one, `timestamp`. We indicate that *timestamp.el* provides the feature `timestamp` by writing

```
(provide 'timestamp)
```

in *timestamp.el*. Normally this appears at the very end of the file, so that the feature isn't "provided" unless everything preceding it worked correctly. (If something fails, then loading of the file aborts before reaching the call to `provide`.)

Now suppose that somewhere, there's some code that needs the timestamp functionality. Using `require` like this:

```
(require 'timestamp "timestamp")
```

means, "if the `timestamp` feature is not yet present, load *timestamp*" (using `load`, which searches `load-path`). If the `timestamp` feature has already been provided (presumably because *timestamp* has already been loaded), nothing happens.

Usually, all the necessary calls to `require` are collected together at the beginning of a Lisp file—something like the way C programs usually begin with lots of `#includes`. But some programmers like to place `require` calls deep in the code that actually depends on the required feature. There may be many such places, and if each such place actually caused the file to load, the program would slow to a crawl, loading Lisp files possibly dozens of times each. Using "features" to make sure files only get loaded once can be a real timesaver!

In the call to `require`, if the filename is the "string equivalent" of the feature name, then the filename can be omitted and will be inferred from the feature name. The "string equivalent" of a symbol is simply the symbol's name as a string. The string equivalent of the feature symbol `timestamp` is `"timestamp"`, so we can write

```
(require 'timestamp)
```

instead of `(require 'timestamp "timestamp")`. (The function `symbol-name` called on a symbol yields its string equivalent.)

If `require` causes the associated file to be loaded (because the feature hasn't yet been provided), that file should `provide` the requested feature. Otherwise, `require` reports that loading the requested file failed to provide the desired feature.

Autoloading

With *autoloading,* you can arrange to defer loading a file until it's needed—that is, until you call one of its functions. Setting up autoloads is very inexpensive, and therefore is usually done in the *.emacs* file.

The function `autoload` connects a function name with the file that defines it. When Emacs tries to invoke a function that is not yet defined, it loads the file that, according to `autoload`, supposedly defines it. Without an `autoload`, attempting to invoke an undefined function is an error.

Here's how it's used:

```
(autoload 'insert-time "timestamp")
(autoload 'insert-date "timestamp")
(autoload 'update-writestamps "timestamp")
(autoload 'update-modifystamps "timestamp")
```

The first time any of the functions `insert-time`, `insert-date`, `update-writestamps`, or `update-modifystamps` is called, Emacs loads *timestamp.* Not only will this cause the invoked function to get defined, but it will define the other three as well, so subsequent calls to these functions *won't* reload *timestamp.*

The `autoload` function has several optional parameters. The first one is a docstring for the not-yet-defined function. Including a docstring allows the user to get help on the function (via `describe-function` and `apropos`) even before its definition has been loaded from the file.

```
(autoload 'insert-time "timestamp"
  "Insert the current time according to insert-time-format.")
(autoload 'insert-date "timestamp"
  "Insert the current date according to insert-date-format.")
(autoload 'update-writestamps "timestamp"
  "Find writestamps and replace them with the current time.")
(autoload 'update-modifystamps "timestamp"
  "Find modifystamps and replace them with the given time.")
```

The next optional parameter describes whether the function, once loaded, will be an interactive command or a mere function. If omitted or `nil`, the function is expected to be non-interactive; otherwise it's expected to be a command. When this information exists prior to loading the actual function definition, it can be used by such functions as `command-apropos` that need to distinguish interactive from non-interactive functions.

```
(autoload 'insert-time "timestamp"
  "Insert the current time according to insert-time-format."
  t)
(autoload 'insert-date "timestamp"
  "Insert the current date according to insert-date-format."
  t)
(autoload 'update-writestamps "timestamp"
  "Find writestamps and replace them with the current time."
  nil)
(autoload 'update-modifystamps "timestamp"
  "Find modifystamps and replace them with the given time."
  nil)
```

If you mistakenly label a non-interactive function interactive or vice versa in the `autoload` call, it won't matter once the real definition is loaded. The real definition replaces all information given in the `autoload` call.

The last optional parameter is one we won't cover for now. It specifies the *type* of the autoloadable object, if not a function. As it turns out, keymaps and macros (which we'll cover in coming chapters) may also be autoloaded.

Compiling the File

As mentioned at the beginning of this chapter, once we have our Lisp code in a file of its own, we can *byte-compile* it. Byte-compiling converts Emacs Lisp into a more compact, faster-running format. Like compilation in other programming languages, the result of byte-compilation is essentially unreadable to humans. *Unlike* other kinds of compilation, the result of byte-compilation is still portable among different hardware platforms and operating systems (but may not be portable to older versions of Emacs).

Byte-compiled Lisp code executes *substantially* faster than uncompiled Lisp code.

Byte-compiled Emacs Lisp files have names ending in *.elc*. As mentioned earlier, `load` and `load-library`, when given no file suffix, will preferentially load a *.elc* file over a *.el* file.

There are several ways to byte-compile files. The most straightforward ways are

> *From within Emacs*: Execute **M-x byte-compile-file RET file.el RET**.
>
> *From the UNIX shell*: Run *emacs -batch -f batch-byte-compile file.el*.

You can byte-compile an entire directory full of Lisp files with `byte-recompile-directory`.

When Emacs loads a *.elc* file, it compares the date of the file with the date of the corresponding *.el* file. If the *.elc* is out of date with respect to the *.el*, Emacs will still load it but it will issue a warning.

eval-after-load

If you'd like to defer the execution of some code until a particular file has been loaded, `eval-after-load` is the way to do it. For example, suppose you came up with a better definition for `dired-sort-toggle` than the one that's in *dired* (Emacs's directory-editing module). You couldn't simply put your version into your *.emacs*, because the first time you edit a directory, *dired* will be autoloaded, complete with its definition for `dired-sort-toggle`, which will wipe out your definition.

What you could do instead is:

```
(eval-after-load
 "dired"
 '(defun dired-sort-toggle ()
    ...))
```

This will execute the `defun` immediately after *dired* is loaded, clobbering *dired*'s version of `dired-sort-toggle` instead of the other way around. Note, however, that this will work only if *dired* is loaded under precisely the name *dired*. It won't work if *dired* is loaded under the name *dired.elc* or */usr/local/share/emacs/19.34/lisp/dired*. The `load` or `autoload` or `require` that causes *dired* to be loaded must refer to it by exactly the same name used in `eval-after-load`. This is why, as mentioned earlier, it's best always to load files by just their base name.

Another use for `eval-after-load` is when you need to refer to a variable, function, or keymap in a package that's not loaded yet, and you don't want to force the package to be loaded:

```
(eval-after-load
 "font-lock"
 '(setq lisp-font-lock-keywords lisp-font-lock-keywords-2))
```

This refers to the value of `lisp-font-lock-keywords-2`, a variable defined in *font-lock*. If you try to refer to `lisp-font-lock-keywords-2` before *font-lock* is loaded, you'll get a "Symbol's value as variable is void" error. But there's no hurry to load *font-lock*, because this `setq` only uses `lisp-font-lock-keywords-2` in order to set `lisp-font-lock-keywords`, another *font-lock* variable that's not needed until *font-lock* gets loaded for some other reason. So we use `eval-after-load` to make sure that the `setq` doesn't happen too early and cause an error.

What happens if you call `eval-after-load` and the named file has already been loaded? Then the given Lisp expression is executed immediately. What if there's more than one `eval-after-load` for the same file? They all execute, one after another, when the file is finally loaded.

You may have observed that `eval-after-load` works very much like hook variables. It's true, they do, but one important difference is that hooks only execute Lisp functions (frequently in the form of anonymous `lambda` expressions), whereas `eval-after-load` can execute any Lisp expression.

Local Variables Lists

What we've described in this chapter so far is enough to set up a file of Lisp code and have it loaded on demand. But in the case of *timestamp*, things are a little different. We've already arranged for calling `update-writestamps` to autoload *timestamp*, but who or what is going to call `update-writestamps` and force *timestamp* to load? Recall that `update-writestamps` is supposed to get called from `local-write-file-hooks`. So how does `update-writestamps` get into `local-write-file-hooks`? Loading the file mustn't do that for the reasons mentioned in the section called "Creating a Lisp File" earlier in this chapter.

What we need is a way to get `update-writestamps` into `local-write-file-hooks` in buffers that need it, so that the first invocation of `local-write-file-hooks` can cause the autoloading of *timestamp*.

A good way to accomplish this is by using the *local variables list* that may appear near the end of any file. Whenever Emacs visits a new file, it scans near the end[*] for a block of text that looks like this:

```
Local variables:
var₁: value₁
var₂: value₂
...
End:
```

When Emacs finds such a block, it assigns each *value* to the corresponding *var*, which is automatically made buffer-local. Emacs can recognize this block even if each line begins with a prefix, as long as they all begin with the *same* prefix. This is necessary in a file of Lisp code, for example, to comment out the lines so they're not interpreted as Lisp:

```
; Local variables:
; var₁: value₁
; var₂: value₂
; ...
; End:
```

The *value*s are treated as if quoted; they are *not* evaluated before being assigned to their respective *var*s. So in a file that has

```
; Local variables:
; foo: (+ 3 5)
; End:
```

the buffer-local variable `foo` has the value `(+ 3 5)`, not 8.

Any file that needs `update-writestamps` in its `local-write-file-hooks` could therefore specify:

```
Local variables:
local-write-file-hooks: (update-writestamps)
End:
```

In fact, a file could set up all of the unique values it needs:

```
Local variables:
local-write-file-hooks: (update-writestamps)
writestamp-prefix: "Written:"
writestamp-suffix: "."
writestamp-format: "%D"
End:
```

One problem with setting `local-write-file-hooks` this way is that it's preferable to *add* `update-writestamps` to whatever value may already be in `local-write-file-hooks`, rather than replace `local-write-file-hooks`

---

[*] "Near the end" means: within the final 3000 bytes of the file—yes, it's arbitrary—and following the last line, if any, that begins with a CONTROL-L.

with a new list as in the example above. Doing so would require evaluating Lisp code, though. Specifically, you'd need to execute the expression

```
(add-hook 'local-write-file-hooks 'update-writestamps)
```

To allow this, Emacs recognizes a "pseudovariable" in the local variables list called `eval`. When

> eval: *value*

appears in a local variables list, *value* is evaluated. The result of evaluating it is discarded; it is *not* stored in a buffer-local variable named `eval`. So a complete solution is to include:

```
eval: (add-hook 'local-write-file-hooks 'update-writestamps)
```

among the local variables.

Actually, the right way to set up `local-write-file-hooks` for this purpose is to write a *minor mode*, which is the subject of Chapter 7.

Addendum: Security Consideration

The local variables list is a potential security hole, exposing the user to "Trojan horse" attacks. Imagine a variable setting that causes Emacs to behave in an unexpected way; or an `eval` that has unexpected side-effects, like deleting files or forging email in your name. All an attacker has to do is entice you to visit a file with such a setting in its local variables list. As soon as you visit the file, the code is executed.

The way to protect yourself is to put

```
(setq enable-local-variables 'query)
```

in your *.emacs*. This causes Emacs to present any local variables list to you for inspection before executing it. There's also `enable-local-eval`, specifically controlling the `eval` pseudovariable.

6

Lists

So far, we've seen lists in a few contexts, but we haven't really explored how they work and why they're useful. Since lists are central to Lisp, this chapter provides a thorough look at this data structure.

The Simple View of Lists

As we've already seen, a list in Lisp is a sequence of zero or more Lisp expressions enclosed in parentheses. Lists may be nested; that is, the enclosed subexpressions may include one or more lists. Here are a few examples:

```
(a b c)           ; list of three symbols
(7 "foo")         ; list of number and string
((4.12 31178))    ; list of one element: a sublist of two numbers
```

The empty list () is synonymous with the symbol `nil`.

The functions `car` and `cdr`[*] are used to access parts of a list: `car` yields the first element in a list, and `cdr` yields the remainder of the list (everything but the first element).

```
(car '(a b c))  ⇒ a
(cdr '(a b c))  ⇒ (b c)
(car (cdr '(a b c)))  ⇒ b
```

(Recall that quoting an expression—even a complete list—means to use that expression literally. So '(a b c) means the list containing a, b, and c, *not* the result of calling function a on arguments b and c.)

---

[*] Pronounced "could-er." These names are historical holdovers from the computer architecture on which Lisp was first designed.

The cdr of a one-element list is `nil`:

```
(cdr '(x)) ⇒ nil
```

The car and cdr of the empty list are both `nil`:

```
(car '()) ⇒ nil
(cdr '()) ⇒ nil
```

Note that this is also true of the list containing `nil`:

```
(car '(nil)) ⇒ nil
(cdr '(nil)) ⇒ nil
```

This does not mean that `()` is the same as `(nil)`.

You don't have to take my word for any of this. Just go into the `*scratch*` buffer and, as explained in the section on "Evaluating Lisp Expressions" in Chapter 1, try any of these examples for yourself.

Lists are constructed with the functions `list`, `cons`, and **append**. The function `list` makes a list out of any number of arguments:

```
(list 'a "b" 7) ⇒ (a "b" 7)
(list '(x y z) 3) ⇒ ((x y z) 3)
```

The function **cons** takes an arbitrary Lisp expression and an existing list. It makes a new list by prepending the arbitrary expression to the old list:

```
(cons 'a '(3 4 5)) ⇒ (a 3 4 5)
(cons "hello" '()) ⇒ ("hello")
(cons '(a b) '(c d)) ⇒ ((a b) c d)
```

Note that consing onto a list creates a new list without affecting the old list:

```
(setq x '(a b c))        ; assign (a b c) to variable x
(setq y (cons 17 x))     ; cons 17 onto it and put it in y
y ⇒ (17 a b c)           ; as expected
x ⇒ (a b c)              ; no change in x
```

The function **append** takes any number of lists and makes a new list by concatenating the top-level elements of all the lists. It effectively strips off the outer parentheses of each list, sticks all the resulting elements together, and surrounds them with a new pair of parentheses:

```
(append '(a b) '(c d)) ⇒ (a b c d)
(append '(a (b c) d) '(e (f))) ⇒ (a (b c) d e (f))
```

The function **reverse** takes a list and makes a new list by reversing its top-level elements.

```
(reverse '(a b c)) ⇒ (c b a)
(reverse '(1 2 (3 4) 5 6)) ⇒ (6 5 (3 4) 2 1)
```

Note that **reverse** does not reverse elements in sublists.

List Details

This section explains the inner workings of Lisp lists. Since most Lisp programs employ lists to some degree or other, it is beneficial to understand why they work the way they do. This will help you to understand what Lisp lists are and aren't good at.

Lists are composed of smaller data structures called *cons cells*. A cons cell is a structure that contains two Lisp expressions, referred to, you may not be surprised to learn, as the cell's *car* and *cdr*.

The function **cons** creates a new cons cell from its two arguments. Contrary to the implication in the preceding section, both arguments to **cons** may be arbitrary Lisp expressions. The second one need not be an existing list.

```
(cons 'a 'b) ⇒ a cons cell with car a and cdr b
(car (cons 'a 'b)) ⇒ a
(cdr (cons 'a 'b)) ⇒ b
```

The resulting cons cell is usually depicted as in Figure 6-1.

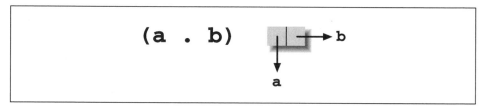

Figure 6-1. The result of (cons 'a 'b)

When you **cons** something onto a list, as in

```
(cons 'a '(b c))
```

the result is (a b c), which is merely a cons cell whose car is **a** and whose cdr is (b c). More about this below.

There's a special syntax for cons cells whose cdrs aren't lists. It's called *dotted pair notation,* and cons cells themselves are sometimes referred to as *dotted pairs*:

```
(cons 'a 'b) ⇒ (a . b)
(cons '(1 2) 3) ⇒ ((1 2) . 3)
```

When the cdr of a cons cell is `nil`, as in Figure 6-2, the dotted pair notation can be abbreviated to omit the dot and the `nil`.

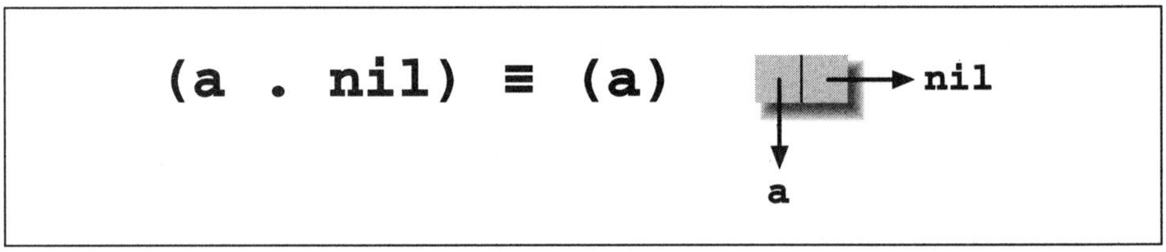

(a . nil) ≡ (a)
nil
a

Figure 6-2. A single-element list: (a)

Another abbreviation rule says that if the cdr of a cons cell is another cons cell, then the dot can be discarded along with the parentheses surrounding the cdr. See Figure 6-3.

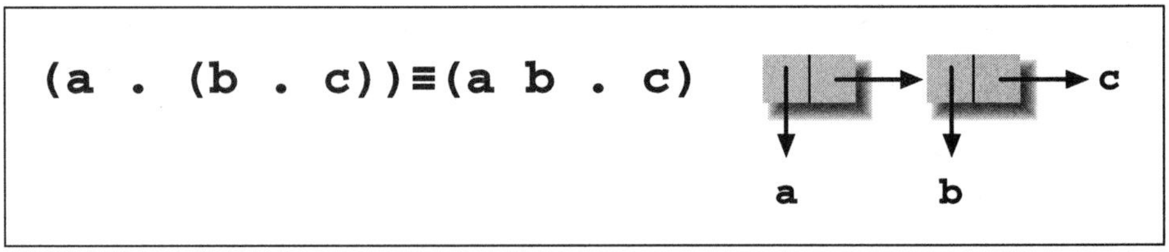

(a . (b . c))≡(a b . c)
c
a
b

Figure 6-3. One cons cell points to another

When combined with the abbreviation rule about `nil` cdrs, we recognize the lists with which we're already familiar:

```
(a . (b . nil)) ≡ (a b . nil) ≡ (a b)
```

Generally speaking, a Lisp list is a chain of cons cells where each cdr is another cons cell and the last cdr is `nil`. It doesn't matter what the cars of the cons cells are. Figure 6-4 shows a list as part of another list.

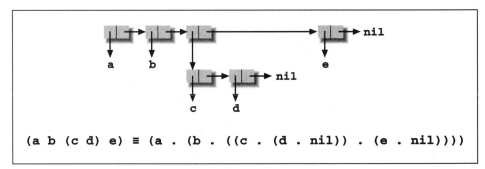

nil
a
b
e
nil
c
d
(a b (c d) e) ≡ (a . (b . ((c . (d . nil)) . (e . nil))))

Figure 6-4. A list containing a sublist

When you write

```
(setq x '(a b c))
```

you make **x** point to the first cons cell in a three-cons-cell chain. If you then write

```
(setq y (cdr x))        ; now y is (b c)
```

you make **y** point to the second cons cell in the *same chain*. A list is really only a pointer to a cons cell.

A list where the last cdr is not `nil` is sometimes called an *improper list*. Frequently, the entries in an *association list* (see below) are improper lists.

There are several functions for testing whether a Lisp object is a list or a list component.

* `consp` tests whether its argument is a cons cell. (`consp` *x*) is true when *x* is any list except the empty list, and false for all other objects.

* `atom` tests whether its argument is *atomic*. (`atom` *x*) is the opposite of (`consp` *x*)—everything that's not a cons cell, including `nil`, numbers, strings, and symbols, is an atom.

* `listp` tests whether its argument is a list. (`listp` *x*) is true for all cons cells and for `nil`, false for everything else.

* `null` tests whether its argument is `nil`.

Now that you know about cons cells, you might find it odd that (`car nil`) and (`cdr nil`) are both defined to be `nil`, when `nil` isn't even a cons cell and therefore has no car or cdr. Indeed, a few dialects of Lisp make it an error to call `car` and `cdr` on `nil`. Most Lisps behave like Emacs Lisp in this regard, however, mainly for convenience—but this special case does have the bizarre side effect (previously noted) of making () and (`nil`) behave the same way with respect to `car` and `cdr`.

Recursive List Functions

Traditional Lisp textbooks use a variety of short programming exercises to illustrate the behavior of lists and cons cells. Let's just take a moment now to look at two of the better-known examples, then move on.

Our goal in this exercise is to define a function called `flatten` that, given a list, undoes any nesting of sublists, causing all elements to be at the top level. For example:

```
(flatten '(a ((b) c) d)) ⇒ (a b c d)
```

The solution calls for recursion, flattening the car and the cdr separately, then recombining them in a way that preserves flatness. Suppose the input to `flatten` is the list

```
((a (b)) (c d))
```

The car is `(a (b))` which when flattened yields `(a b)`. The cdr is `((c d))` which when flattened becomes `(c d)`. The function `append` can be used to combine `(a b)` with `(c d)` and preserve flatness, yielding `(a b c d)`. So at the heart of `flatten` is this code:

```
(append (flatten (car lst))
        (flatten (cdr lst)))
```

(I've chosen `lst` as the name for `flatten`'s parameter. I prefer not to use `list`, which is the name of a Lisp function.) Now, `flatten` is only meant to work on lists, so `(flatten (car lst))` is an error if `(car lst)` is not a list. We must therefore elaborate as follows:

```
(if (listp (car lst))
    (append (flatten (car lst))
            (flatten (cdr lst))))
```

This `if` has no "else" clause. What if `(car lst)` is not a list? For example, suppose `lst` were

```
(a ((b) c))
```

The car, `a`, is not a list. In this case, we will simply need to flatten the cdr, `(((b) c))`, to get `(b c)`; then `cons` the car back onto it.

```
(if (listp (car lst))
    (append (flatten (car lst))
            (flatten (cdr lst)))
  (cons (car lst)
        (flatten (cdr lst))))
```

Finally, we need a way to terminate the recursion. In recursive functions that work on smaller and smaller pieces of lists, the smallest piece you can wind up with is `nil`, and `nil` is almost always used as the "basis case" for such functions. In this case, the result of flattening `nil` is simply `nil`, so our complete function is

```
(defun flatten (lst)
  (if (null lst)              ; Is lst nil?
      nil                     ; If so, return nil
    (if (listp (car lst))
        (append (flatten (car lst))
                (flatten (cdr lst)))
      (cons (car lst)
            (flatten (cdr lst)))))))
```

Try running this function on a few sample lists in the `*scratch*` buffer, and try following the logic of the function by hand on a few examples. Remember that the return value of a function in Lisp is the value of the last expression to execute.

Iterative List Functions

Recursion isn't always the right solution for a list-related programming problem. Sometimes plain old iteration is needed. In this example, we'll demonstrate the Emacs Lisp idiom for operating on a list of elements one at a time, sometimes called "cdr-ing down" a list (because in each iteration, the list is shortened by taking its cdr).

Suppose we need a function that counts the number of symbols in a list, skipping over other kinds of list elements like numbers, strings, and sublists. A recursive solution is wrong:

```
(defun count-syms (lst)
  (if (null lst)
      0
    (if (symbolp (car lst))
        (+ 1 (count-syms (cdr lst)))
      (count-syms (cdr lst)))))
```

Recursion—particularly deep recursion—introduces a fair amount of overhead in terms of keeping track of many nested function calls and return values, and should be avoided when possible. Furthermore, this problem naturally suggests an iterative solution, and code should usually reflect the natural approach to solving a problem, rather than obfuscating the solution by being too clever.

```
(defun count-syms (lst)
  (let ((result 0))
    (while lst
      (if (symbolp (car lst))
          (setq result (+ 1 result)))
      (setq lst (cdr lst)))
    result))
```

Other Useful List Functions

Here are some more list-related Lisp functions that Emacs defines.

- `length` returns the length of a list. It does not work on "improper" lists.

  ```
  (length nil) ⇒ 0
  (length '(x y z)) ⇒ 3
  (length '((x y z))) ⇒ 1
  (length '(a b . c)) ⇒ error
  ```

- `nthcdr` calls `cdr` on a list *n* times.

  ```
  (nthcdr 2 '(a b c)) ⇒ (c)
  ```

- nth returns the *n*th element of a list (where the first element is numbered zero). This is the same as the `car` of the `nthcdr`.

```
(nth 2 '(a b c)) ⇒ c
(nth 1 '((a b) (c d) (e f))) ⇒ (c d)
```

- mapcar takes a function and a list as arguments. It calls the function once for each element of the list, passing that element as an argument to the function. The result of `mapcar` is a list of the results of calling the function on each element. So if you have a list of strings and want to capitalize each one, you could write:

```
(mapcar '(lambda (x)
            (capitalize x))
        '("lisp" "is" "cool")) ⇒ ("Lisp" "Is" "Cool")
```

- equal tests whether its two arguments are equal. This is a different kind of equality test from `eq`, which we first encountered in the section called "Saving and Restoring Point," in Chapter 3. Whereas `eq` tests whether its arguments are the *same object*, `equal` tests whether two objects have the same structure and contents.

This distinction is important. In the following example:

```
(setq x (list 1 2 3))
(setq y (list 1 2 3))
```

x and y are two different objects. That is, the first call to `list` creates a chain of three cons cells, and the second call to `list` creates a chain of three more cons cells. So (`eq x y`) is `nil`, even though the two lists have the same structure and contents. But since they do have the same structure and contents, (`equal x y`) is true.

In Lisp programming, any time you wish to compare two objects for equality, you must be alert to whether `eq` or `equal` is appropriate. Another consideration is that `eq` is an instantaneous operation, whereas `equal` may have to recursively compare the structure of its two arguments.

Note that when you write

```
(setq x (list 1 2 3))
(setq y x)
```

(eq x y) becomes true.

- assoc is a function that helps you use lists as lookup tables. When a list has the form

```
((key₁ . value₁)
 (key₂ . value₂)
 ...
 (keyₙ . valueₙ))
```

it is called an *association list,* or *assoc list* for short.[*] The function `assoc` finds the first sublist of an assoc list whose car (the *key$_i$* "field") matches the argument you give. So:

```
(assoc 'green
       '((red . "ff0000")
         (green . "00ff00")
         (blue . "0000ff"))) ⇒ (green . "00ff00")
```

If no matching sublist is found, `assoc` returns `nil`.

This function uses `equal` to test whether each *key$_i$* matches the argument you give. Another function, `assq`, is like `assoc` but uses `eq` instead.

Some programmers do not like dotted pairs, so instead of setting up a lookup table in this form:

```
((red . "ff0000")
 (green . "00ff00")
 (blue . "0000ff"))
```

they'll do this instead:

```
((red "ff0000")
 (green "00ff00")
 (blue "0000ff"))
```

This is fine, because as far as `assoc` is concerned, each element of the list is still a dotted pair:

```
((red . ("ff0000"))
 (green . ("00ff00"))
 (blue . ("0000ff")))
```

The only difference is that in the earlier example, each entry in the assoc list can be stored in a single cons cell, but now each entry requires two cons cells. And retrieving the value associated with a key could previously be done like this:

```
(cdr (assoc 'green ...)) ⇒ "00ff00"
```

but now must be done like this:

```
(car (cdr (assoc 'green ...))) ⇒ "00ff00"
```

Destructive List Operations

So far, all the list operations we've looked at have been non-destructive. For instance, when you `cons` an object onto an existing list, the result is a brand new cons cell whose cdr points to the unaltered old list. Any other objects or variables that refer to the old list are unaffected. Similarly, `append` works by making a

---

[*] I've never found consensus on whether this should be pronounced a-SOAK, a-SOASH, or a-SOCK list. I've heard all three. Some avoid the problem by calling it an "a-list."

brand new list, creating as many new cons cells as necessary to hold the elements of the lists in its arguments. It cannot make the last cdr of **x** point directly to **y**, or the last cdr of **y** point directly to **z**, because the **nil** pointer at the end would be changed. **x** and **y** could no longer be used in their original forms. Instead **append** makes an unnamed copy of those lists as shown in Figure 6-5. Note that the value of **z** need not be copied; **append** always uses its last argument directly.[*]

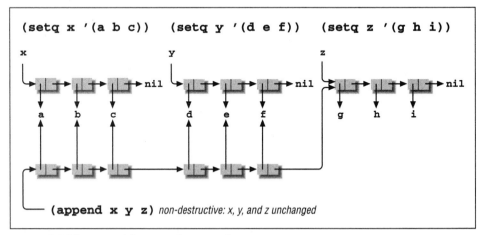

Figure 6-5: The append function does not alter its arguments.

Here's what the non-destructiveness of **append** means in Lisp code:

```
(setq x '(a b c))
(setq y '(d e f))
(setq z '(g h i))
(append x y z) ⇒ (a b c d e f g h i)
```

Because **append** does not destructively modify its arguments, these three variables continue to have their old values:

```
x ⇒ (a b c)
y ⇒ (d e f)
z ⇒ (g h i)
```

But if destructive modification were used, then each variable would refer to some part of a single, long cons chain made when the three shorter cons chains are strung together as shown in Figure 6-6. The function that performs a destructive append is called **nconc**.

```
(nconc x y z) ⇒ (a b c d e f g h i)
x ⇒ (a b c d e f g h i)
y ⇒ (d e f g h i)
z ⇒ (g h i)
```

---

* Because it's pointed to directly, the last argument to **append** doesn't even have to be a list! Try it and see.

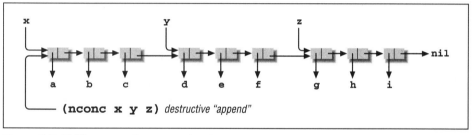

Figure 6-6. Unlike append, nconc *alters its arguments*

Usually it's unwise to destructively modify lists. Many other variables and data structures may be using the same copies of the lists you modify, so it's best not to change them in ways that would have unpredictable effects.

On the other hand, sometimes you *do* want to destructively modify a list. Perhaps you need the efficiency of nconc and you know that no other code depends on the data structure remaining unchanged.

One of the most common uses of destructive list operations is when changing values in an assoc list. For example, suppose you have an assoc list that maps people's names to their email addresses:

```
(setq e-addrs
      '(("robin" . "rl@sherwood.uk")
        ("marian" . "mf@sherwood.uk")
        ...))
```

Now suppose someone's email address changes. You could update the list like this:

```
(setq e-addrs
      (alist-replace e-addrs "john" "johnl@exile.fr"))
```

where alist-replace is some hideously expensive recursive operation that basically recopies the whole list:

```
(defun alist-replace (alist key new-value)
  (if (null alist)
      nil
    (if (and (listp (car alist))
             (equal (car (car alist))
                    key))
        (cons (cons key new-value)
              (cdr alist))
      (cons (car alist)
            (alist-replace (cdr alist) key new-value)))))
```

Not only is this slow (especially if the input is large), but this is a case where you probably *do* want to affect any other objects or variables referring to this data structure. Unfortunately, alist-replace doesn't actually change the data struc-

ture. It makes a brand-new copy, and anything referring to the old copy does not
see the update. In code, this means:

```
(setq alist '((a . b) (c . d)))            ;alist is an assoc list.
(setq alist-2 alist)                       ;alist-2 refers to the same list.

(setq alist (alist-replace alist 'c 'q))   ;alist is a new list.

alist ⇒ ((a . b) (c . q))                  ;alist reflects the change.
alist-2 ⇒ ((a . b) (c . d))                ;alist-2 still refers to the old list.
```

Enter **setcar** and **setcdr**.[*] Given a cons cell and a new value, these functions
replace the cell's car or cdr with the new value. Examples:

```
(setq x (cons 'a 'b)) ⇒ (a . b)
(setcar x 'c)
x ⇒ (c . b)
(setcdr x 'd)
x ⇒ (c . d)
```

We can now easily write a destructive version of **alist-replace** like so:

```
(defun alist-replace (alist key new-value)
  (let ((sublist (assoc key alist)))
    (if sublist
        (setcdr sublist new-value))))
```

This finds the sublist of **alist** whose car is the sought-for *key*—e.g., the sublist
(`"john"` . `"jl@nottingham.co.uk"`)—and replaces the cdr with **new-
value**. Since this changes the data structure in place—that is, since it doesn't
work by making a new copy of anything—all variables and other objects that
refer to the cons cell, particularly the assoc list containing it, reflect the change.

There is one other important destructive list operation: **nreverse**, a non-copying
version of **reverse**.

```
(setq x '(a b c))
(nreverse x) ⇒ (c b a)
x ⇒ (a)
```

Why does **x** equal (a) after the last example? It's because **x** continues to refer to
the same cons cell, which has gotten shuffled around. Consider: the list (a b
c) consists of three cons cells, one whose car is a, one whose car is b, and one
whose car is c. At first, **x** refers to the list by referring to the first cons cell—the
one whose car is a and whose cdr refers to the next cons cell in the chain (which
is the one containing b). But after **nreverse**, the cdrs of all the cons cells are
changed. Now the cons cell whose car is c is the first in the chain, and its cdr is

---

[*] Also called rplaca and rplacd, for the same historical reasons that gave us car and cdr.

the cons cell containing **b**. Meanwhile, **x**'s value hasn't changed: it still refers to the original cons cell, whose car is **a**. But now that cell's cdr is `nil` because it's at the end of the chain, so **x** is `(a)`.

If you need **x** to reflect the change in the list, you'd have to write

```
(setq x (nreverse x)) ⇒ (c b a)
```

Circular Lists?!

Because we can destructively modify lists after they're created, we're not limited to building lists only out of pre-existing parts. A list can be made to refer to part of itself! Consider:

```
(setq x '(a b c))
(nthcdr 2 x) ⇒ (c)
(setcdr (nthcdr 2 x) x)          ; don't try this yet!
```

What's happening in this example? First we create a three-element list and place it in **x**. Next, we find the last cons cell with `nthcdr`. Finally, we replace that cell's cdr with **x**—which is the first cons cell in the list. The list is now circular: the former end of the list now points back to the beginning.

What does this list look like? Well, it starts out like this:

```
(a b c a b c a b c a b c a b c a b c a b c ...
```

and it never stops. The reason I wrote *don't try this yet!* above is that if you executed the `setcdr` in the `*scratch*` buffer, Emacs would try to display the result—and would never finish. It would get caught in an infinite loop, albeit one that you can interrupt with **C-g**. Go ahead and try it now, but press **C-g** as soon as Emacs locks up. The longer you wait, the more it fills up the `*scratch*` buffer with repetitions of **a b c**.

Obviously, printing isn't the only thing you can do to a circular data structure that can make Emacs loop forever. Any operation that iterates over all the elements in a list will never terminate. Here's an important illustration:

```
(eq x (nthcdr 3 x)) ⇒ t        ; 3rd cdr is same object as x
(equal x (nthcdr 3 x)) ⇒ never terminates!
```

If circular lists throw Emacs for a loop (pun intended), what good are they? One doesn't normally think of lists as being circular, but if you stop thinking of them as lists and start thinking of them as connected cons cells, you can build any kind of linked data structure, from trees to lattices. Some data structures are self-referential, i.e., circular. If you ever find yourself needing to build such a data structure, you should not be daunted by the fact that Emacs loops forever trying to display it. Simply don't evaluate it in a context where the result needs to be displayed. For instance, if we changed the **setcdr** above to

```
(setq x '(a b c))
(progn
  (setcdr (nthcdr 2 x) x)
  nil)
```

then Emacs would not try to display the result of the **setcdr**, and now **x** is a circular data structure that we can manipulate without trying to display the whole thing.

```
(nth 0 x)   ⇒ a
(nth 1 x)   ⇒ b
(nth 412 x) ⇒ b
```

7

Minor Mode

In this chapter we'll ratchet our Emacs programming dexterity up a notch by considering times when we don't want extensions to apply to all buffers, but just to a particular type of buffer. For instance, when you're in Lisp mode it's nice to press **C-M-a** and have Emacs jump backwards to the beginning of the nearest function definition, but you don't want or need that ability when you're editing a textual document. The Emacs "mode" mechanism arranges things so that **C-M-a** does its magic only when you're in Lisp mode.

The subject of modes in Emacs is a complex one. We'll ease into it by first studying so-called *minor modes*. A minor mode coexists with a major mode in a buffer, adding a typically small amount of new editing behavior. Every Emacs user is familiar with major modes like Lisp and C and Text, but they may not be aware of little strings that appear on the "mode line" saying things like Fill when you're *also* in Auto Fill minor mode.

We'll create a minor mode that builds on Emacs's idea of filling paragraphs. Our minor mode, Refill, dynamically fills paragraphs as you edit them.

Paragraph Filling

Filling a paragraph is the process of making all the lines in the paragraph the right length. Every line should be more or less equally long without extending past the right margin. Long lines should be split up at the spaces between words. Short lines should be lengthened with text from subsequent lines. Filling optionally includes *justification,* which is the process of adding whitespace throughout each line to make both margins come out even.

Most modern word processors keep paragraphs filled at all times. After every change, the text in the paragraph "flows" to keep the layout correct. Some detractors of Emacs point out that Emacs isn't as good as these other applications when it comes to filling paragraphs. Emacs does provide `auto-fill-mode`, but that only wraps the current line, and only when you insert whitespace beyond the "right margin." It doesn't keep paragraphs filled after deletions; it doesn't fill any lines besides the current one; and it does nothing when insertions that occur near the left margin push other text past the right margin.

As an Emacs enthusiast, you can give one of three responses to the detractor who holds up some other program as the *ne plus ultra* of text editing:

1. Glitzy features like on-the-fly filling of paragraphs are needed only to hide the program's many inadequacies compared to Emacs (which you may feel free to list).

2. You value content over form so don't need to see a paragraph continually refilled, but when you do feel the need, it's a simple matter of pressing **M-q** to invoke `fill-paragraph`.

3. Given a little Lisp hacking, Emacs can do on-the-fly paragraph filling just like the other program (and you may ask whether the other program can likewise be made to emulate Emacs).

This chapter is about option 3.

In order to make sure that the current paragraph is correctly filled at all times, we'll need to recheck it after each insertion and each deletion. This may be computationally expensive, so we'll want to be able to turn it on or off at will; and when we turn it on, we'll want the behavior only in the current buffer, since it may not be suitable behavior for all buffers.

Modes

Emacs uses the concept of a *mode* to encapsulate a set of editing behaviors. In other words, Emacs behaves differently in buffers with different modes. To take a small example, while the **TAB** key inserts an ASCII tab character in Text mode, in Emacs Lisp mode it inserts or deletes enough whitespace to indent a line of code to the correct column. As another example, when you invoke the command `indent-for-comment` in an Emacs Lisp mode buffer, you get an empty comment beginning with the Lisp comment character, `;`. When you invoke it in a C mode buffer, you get an empty comment using C comment syntax: `/* */`.

Every buffer in Emacs is always in exactly one *major mode*. A major mode specializes a buffer for a particular kind of editing such as Text, Lisp, or C. A major mode called Fundamental isn't specialized for anything in particular and can be thought of as sort of a null mode. Usually the major mode for a buffer is chosen automatically by the name of the file you visit, or by some cues in the buffer itself. You can change major modes by invoking a mode's command, such as `text-mode`, `emacs-lisp-mode`, or `c-mode`.[*] When you do so, the buffer is in the new major mode and is no longer in the old major mode.

A *minor mode,* by contrast, adds to a buffer a package of functionality that doesn't fundamentally change the way editing in the buffer is performed. Minor modes can be turned on and off independently of the major mode and of each other. A buffer can be in zero, one, two, three, or more minor modes in addition to the major mode. Examples of minor modes are: `auto-save-mode`, which causes a buffer to be periodically saved to a specially-named file during editing (which can prevent losses in case of a system crash); `font-lock-mode`, which (on capable displays) colors the text in a buffer according to its syntactic meaning; and `line-number-mode`, which shows the current line number in the buffer's *mode line* (see below).

Generally speaking, a package should be implemented as a minor mode if one should be able to turn it off and on separately in individual buffers, regardless of the major mode. This is exactly how we defined the requirements for our paragraph filling mechanism in the last section, so we now know that our paragraph filling project calls for a minor mode. We'll take the plunge into implementing major modes in Chapter 9, *A Major Mode.*

Defining a Minor Mode

These are the steps involved in defining a minor mode.

1. Choose a *name*. The name for our mode is `refill`.

2. Define a variable named *name*-mode. Make it buffer-local. The minor mode is "on" in a buffer if that buffer's value of *name*-mode is non-`nil`, "off" otherwise.

   ```
   (defvar refill-mode nil
     "Mode variable for refill minor mode.")
   (make-variable-buffer-local 'refill-mode)
   ```

3. Define a command called *name*-mode.[†] The command should take one optional argument. With no arguments, it should toggle the mode on or off. With an argument, it should turn the mode on if the `prefix-numeric-value` of the argument is greater than zero, off otherwise. Thus, **C-u M-x** *name*-mode **RET** always turns it on, and **C-u — M-x** *name*-mode **RET** always

---

[*] There are many other major modes than the few I'm using as examples here. There are modes for editing HTML files, LATEX files, ASCII art files, troff files, files of binary data, directories, and on and on. Also, major modes are used to implement many non-editing features such as newsreading and Web browsing. Try **M-x finder-by-keyword RET** to browse Emacs's many modes and other extensions.

[†] You can use the same name for a function and a variable; they won't conflict.

turns it off (refer to the section entitled "Addendum: Raw Prefix Argument" in Chapter 2). Here's the command for toggling Refill mode:

```
(defun refill-mode (&optional arg)
  "Refill minor mode."
  (interactive "P")
  (setq refill-mode
        (if (null arg)
            (not refill-mode)
          (> (prefix-numeric-value arg) 0)))
  (if refill-mode
      code for turning on refill-mode
    code for turning off refill-mode))
```

That `setq` is a little hairy, but it's a common idiom in minor mode definitions. If `arg` is `nil` (because no prefix argument was given), it sets `refill-mode` to (not `refill-mode`)—i.e., the opposite of `refill-mode`'s previous value, `t` or `nil`. Otherwise, it sets `refill-mode` to the truth value of

```
(> (prefix-numeric-value arg) 0)
```

which is `t` if `arg` has a numeric value greater than 0, `nil` otherwise.

4. Add an entry to `minor-mode-alist`, a variable whose value is an assoc list (refer to the section entitled "Other Useful List Functions" in Chapter 6) of the form:

```
((mode₁ string₁)
 (mode₂ string₂)
 ...)
```

The new entry maps *name*-`mode` to a short string to use in the buffer's *mode line*. The mode line is the informative banner that appears at the bottom of every Emacs window and that includes, among other things, the names of the buffer's major mode and all active minor modes. The short string describing this minor mode should begin with a space, since it is appended to the other strings that appear in the mode portion of the mode line. Here's how to do this for Refill mode:

```
(if (not (assq 'refill-mode minor-mode-alist))
    (setq minor-mode-alist
          (cons '(refill-mode " Refill")
                minor-mode-alist)))
```

(The surrounding `if` prevents (`refill-mode " Refill"`) being added a second time if it's already in `minor-mode-alist`, such as if *refill.el* is loaded twice.) This makes the mode line of buffers that use `refill-mode` look something like this:

```
--**-Emacs: foo.txt (Text Refill) --L1--Top---
```

There are other steps involved in defining some minor modes that don't apply in this example. For instance, the minor mode may have a *keymap*, a *syntax table*, or an *abbrev table* associated with it, but since `refill-mode` won't, let's skip them for now.

Mode Meat

With the basic structure in place, let's start defining the guts of Refill mode.

We've already identified the basic feature of `refill-mode`: each insertion and deletion must ensure that the current paragraph is correctly filled. The correct way to execute code when the buffer is changed, as you may recall from Chapter 4, is by adding a function to the hook variable `after-change-functions` when `refill-mode` is turned on (and removing it when it is turned off). We'll add a function called `refill` (which does not yet exist) that will do all the work of making sure the current paragraph remains correctly filled.

```
(defun refill-mode (&optional arg)
  "Refill minor mode."
  (interactive "P")
  (setq refill-mode
        (if (null arg)
            (not refill-mode)
          (> (prefix-numeric-value arg) 0)))
  (make-local-hook 'after-change-functions)
  (if refill-mode
      (add-hook 'after-change-functions 'refill nil t)
    (remove-hook 'after-change-functions 'refill t)))
```

The extra arguments to **add-hook** and **remove-hook** ensure that only the buffer-local copies of `after-change-functions` are altered. Whether `refill-mode` is being turned on or off when this function is called, we call `make-local-hook` on `after-change-functions` to make it buffer-local. This is because in both cases—turning `refill-mode` on or turning it off—we need to manipulate `after-change-functions` separately in each buffer. Unconditionally calling `make-local-hook` first is the simplest way to do this, especially since `make-local-hook` has no effect if the named hook variable is already buffer-local in the current buffer.

Now all that remains is to define the function `refill`.

Naïve First Try

As mentioned in Chapter 4, the hook variable `after-change-functions` is special because the functions in it take three arguments (whereas normal hook functions take no arguments). The three arguments refer to the change that took place in the buffer before `after-change-functions` was executed.

- The position where the change began, which we'll call *start*

- The position where the change ended, which we'll call *end*

- The length of the affected text, which we'll call *len*

The numbers *start* and *end* refer to positions in the buffer *after* the change. The length *len* refers to the text *before* the change. After an insertion, *len* is zero (because no previously existing text in the buffer was affected), and the newly inserted text lies between *start* and *end*. After a deletion, *len* is the length of the deleted text, now gone, and *start* and *end* are the same number, since deleting the text closed the gap, so to speak, between the two ends of the deletion.

Now that we know what the parameters to `refill` have to be, we can make an artless first attempt at defining it:

```
(defun refill (start end len)
  "After a text change, refill the current paragraph."
  (fill-paragraph nil))
```

This is a totally inadequate solution because `fill-paragraph` is far too expensive a function to invoke on every keystroke! It also has the problem that each time you try to add a space to the end of a line, `fill-paragraph` immediately deletes it—it cleans up trailing whitespace when it fills a paragraph—and since, while you're typing, the cursor spends most of its time at the end of a line, the only way to get a space between words is to type the two words together, likethis, then go back and put a space between them. But this first try does prove the concept, and gives us a starting point for refinement.[*]

Constraining refill

To optimize `refill`, let's analyze the problem a bit. First of all, does the *entire* paragraph have to be filled every time?

No. When text is inserted or deleted, only the affected line and subsequent lines in the paragraph need to be refilled. Prior lines needn't be. If text is inserted, the line may become too long, which may cause some text to spill over onto the next line (which may become too long in turn, at which point the process is repeated). If text is deleted, the line may become too short, which may call for some text being slurped up from the following line (which may become too short in turn, and the process is repeated). So changes can't affect any lines prior to the one in which they occur.

---

[*] Sharp-eyed readers might object that the call to `fill-paragraph` could alter the buffer, causing `after-change-functions` to execute again, invoking `refill` recursively and perhaps leading to an infinite loop, or rather an infinite recursion. Good call, but to avoid this very problem Emacs unsets `after-change-functions` while the functions in it are executing.

Actually, there's one case where changes *can* affect at most one prior line. Consider the following paragraph:

```
Glitzy features like on-the-fly filling of paragraphs are
needed only to hide the program's many inadequacies
compared to Emacs
```

Suppose we delete the word "compared" from the beginning of the third line:

```
Glitzy features like on-the-fly filling of paragraphs are
needed only to hide the program's many inadequacies
to Emacs
```

The word "to" can now be filled onto the end of the prior line, like so:

```
Glitzy features like on-the-fly filling of paragraphs are
needed only to hide the program's many inadequacies to
Emacs
```

A moment's reflection should convince you that at most one prior line needs to be refilled—and then only when the first word on the current line is shortened or removed.

So we can constrain the paragraph-filling operation to the affected line, perhaps the line before it, and the subsequent lines in the current paragraph. Instead of using `fill-paragraph`, which determines the paragraph boundaries itself, we'll choose our own "paragraph boundaries" and use `fill-region`.

The boundaries we choose for `fill-region` should enclose the entire affected portion of the paragraph. For an insertion, the "left" boundary is simply *start*, the point of insertion, and the "right" boundary is the end of the current paragraph. For a deletion, the left boundary is the beginning of the previous line (that is, the line prior to the one containing *start*), and the right boundary is again the end of the paragraph. So here's the outline of the new `refill`:

```
(defun refill (start end len)
  "After a text change, refill the current paragraph."
  (let ((left (if this is an insertion
                  start
                  beginning of previous line))
        (right end of paragraph))
    (fill-region left right ...)))
```

Filling in *this is an insertion* is easy. Recall that when `refill` is called, a zero value for *len* means insertion and a non-zero *len* means deletion.

```
(defun refill (start end len)
  "After a text change, refill the current paragraph."
  (let ((left (if (zerop len)        ; is len zero?
                  start
                  beginning of previous line))
        (right end of paragraph))
    (fill-region left right ...)))
```

To compute *beginning of previous line*, we first move the cursor to *start*, then move the cursor to the end of the previous line (oddly, this can be done with (beginning-of-line 0)), then take the value of (point), all inside a save-excursion:

```
(defun refill (start end len)
  "After a text change, refill the current paragraph."
  (let ((left (if (zerop len)
                  start
                (save-excursion
                 (goto-char start)
                 (beginning-of-line 0)
                 (point))))
        (right end of paragraph))
    (fill-region left right ...)))
```

We could do something similar for *end of paragraph*, but instead we'll use a convenient feature of fill-region: it'll find the end of the paragraph for us. The fifth argument to fill-region (there are two mandatory arguments and three optional ones), if non-nil, tells fill-region to keep filling through the end of the region until the next paragraph boundary. So there's no need to compute right.

Our new version of refill is not complete. We must first solve the problem of fill-region positioning the cursor at the end of the affected region. Naturally, it is unacceptable for the cursor to jump to the end of the paragraph on every keystroke! Wrapping the call to fill-region in a call to save-excursion solves the problem.

```
(defun refill (start end len)
  "After a text change, refill the current paragraph."
  (let ((left (if (zerop len)
                  start
                (save-excursion
                 (goto-char start)
                 (beginning-of-line 0)
                 (point))))
    (save-excursion
      (fill-region left end nil nil t)))))
```

(The second argument to fill-region is ignored because we're using the feature that finds the end of the paragraph. We pass in end just because it's handy and not entirely meaningless to a human reader.)

Minor Adjustments

Well, that's the basic idea, but there's still plenty to do. For one thing, when computing left, we shouldn't back up to the previous line if the previous line is not in the same paragraph. So we should locate the beginning of the paragraph *and* the beginning of the previous line, then use whichever position is greater.

```
(defun refill (start end len)
  "After a text change, refill the current paragraph."
  (let ((left (if (zerop len)
                  start
                (max (save-excursion
                       (goto-char start)
                       (beginning-of-line 0)
                       (point))
                     (save-excursion
                       (goto-char start)
                       (backward-paragraph 1)
                       (point))))))
    (save-excursion
      (fill-region left end nil nil t))))
```

(The function **max** returns the larger of its arguments.)

We now have three calls to **save-excursion**, which is a moderately expensive function. It might be better to combine two of them into one and compute both values inside it.

```
(defun refill (start end len)
  "After a text change, refill the current paragraph."
  (let ((left (if (zerop len)
                  start
                (save-excursion
                  (max (progn
                         (goto-char start)
                         (beginning-of-line 0)
                         (point))
                       (progn
                         (goto-char start)
                         (backward-paragraph 1)
                         (point)))))))
    (save-excursion
      (fill-region left end nil nil t))))
```

Next, recall our earlier observation about filling the prior line: "at most one prior line needs to be refilled—and then only when the first word on the current line is shortened or removed." But in the code we've written, we're backing up to the previous line on every deletion. Let's see if we can avoid that in the case where the deletion occurred in or beyond the second word of a line.

We'll do this by changing this

```
(if (zerop len)
    start
  find previous line)
```

to

```
(if (or (zerop len)
        (not (before-2nd-word-p start)))
```

```
    start
    find previous line)
```

where `before-2nd-word-p` is a function that tells whether its argument, a buffer position, lies before the second word on a line.

Now we must write `before-2nd-word-p`. It should locate the second word on the line, then compare its position with its argument.

How shall we locate the second word on a line?

We could go to the beginning of the line, then call `forward-word` to skip over the first word. The problem with that solution is that it puts us at the end of the first word, not at the beginning of the second word, which may follow after much whitespace.

We could go to the beginning of the line, then call `forward-word` twice (actually, we'd call `forward-word` once, with an argument of 2), then call `backward-word`, which *will* put us at the beginning of the second word. That's fine, but now we realize that the way `forward-word` and `backward-word` define a "word" isn't the same as the definition we need. According to those functions, punctuation (such as a hyphen) separates words, so that (for example) "forward-word" is actually two words. That's bad for us, because our function needs to count words as separate only when they're separated by whitespace.

We could go to the beginning of the line, then skip over all non-whitespace characters (the first word), then skip over all whitespace characters (the whitespace after the first word), which will leave us positioned at the second word. That sounds promising; let's give it a try.

```
(defun before-2nd-word-p (pos)
  "Does POS lie before the second word on the line?"
  (save-excursion
    (goto-char pos)
    (beginning-of-line)
    (skip-chars-forward "^ ")
    (skip-chars-forward " ")
    (< pos (point))))
```

The function **skip-chars-forward** is very useful. It moves the cursor forward until encountering a character either in or not in a set of characters you specify. The set of characters works exactly like the inside of a square-bracketed regular expression (see regular expression rule 3 in the section "Regular Expressions" in Chapter 4). So

```
(skip-chars-forward "^ ")
```

means "skip over characters that aren't a space," while

```
(skip-chars-forward " ")
```

means "skip over spaces."

One problem with this approach is that if the line has no spaces,

```
(skip-chars-forward "^ ")
```

will skip right on to the next line! We don't want that. So let's make sure we don't skip too far by adding a newline (written `"\n"` in strings) to the first `skip-chars-forward`:

```
(skip-chars-forward "^ \n")        ; skip to first space or newline
```

The next problem is that a tab character (`"\t"` in strings) may be used to separate words just like spaces. So we must modify our two `skip-chars-forward` calls like so:

```
(skip-chars-forward "^ \t\n")
(skip-chars-forward " \t")
```

Are there other characters like space and tab that are considered whitespace? Possibly. The formfeed character (ASCII 12) is usually considered to be whitespace. And if the buffer is using some character set other than ASCII, there may be other characters that are word-separating whitespace. For example, in the 8-bit character set known as Latin-1, character numbers 32 and 160 are both spaces—though 160 is a "non-breaking space" which means lines should not be broken there.

Rather than worry about these details, why not let Emacs worry about them? This is where *syntax tables* come in handy. A syntax table is a mode-specific mapping from characters to "syntax classes." Classes include "word constituent" (usually letters and apostrophes and sometimes digits), "balanced brackets" (usually pairs like (), [], {}, and sometimes <>), "comment delimiters" (which are ; and newline for Lisp mode, /* and */ for C mode), "punctuation," and of course, "whitespace."

The syntax table is used by commands like `forward-word` and `backward-word` to figure out just what a word is. Because different buffers can have different syntax tables, the definition of a word can vary from one buffer to another. We're going to use the syntax table to figure out which characters are to be considered whitespace in the current buffer.

All we need to do is replace our two calls to `skip-chars-forward` with two calls to `skip-syntax-forward` like so:

```
(skip-syntax-forward "^ ")
(skip-syntax-forward " ")
```

For each syntax class, there's a code letter.* Space is the code letter meaning "whitespace," so the two lines above mean "skip all non-whitespace" and "skip all whitespace."

Unfortunately, we again have the problem that our first call to `skip-syntax-forward` might traverse to the next line. Worse, this time we can't simply add \n to `skip-syntax-forward`'s argument, because \n isn't the code letter for the syntax of newline characters. In fact, the code letter for the syntax of newline characters will be different in different buffers.

What we *can* do is ask Emacs to tell us the code letter for the syntax of newline characters, then use that result to construct the argument to `skip-syntax-forward`:

```
(skip-syntax-forward (concat "^ "
                             (char-to-string
                              (char-syntax ?\n))))
```

The function `char-syntax` returns a character's syntax code as another character. That's then converted to a string with `char-to-string` and appended to "^ ".

Here's the final form of `before-2nd-word-p`:

```
(defun before-2nd-word-p (pos)
  "Does POS lie before the second word on the line?"
  (save-excursion
    (goto-char pos)
    (beginning-of-line)
    (skip-syntax-forward (concat "^ "
                                 (char-to-string
                                  (char-syntax ?\n))))
    (skip-syntax-forward " ")
    (< pos (point))))
```

Bear in mind that the cost of computing `before-2nd-word-p` might outweigh the benefit it's meant to provide (i.e., avoiding the calls to `end-of-line` and `backward-paragraph` in `refill`). If you're interested, you can try using the *profiler* (see Appendix B, *Debugging and Profiling*) to see which version of `refill` is faster, the one with a call to `before-2nd-word-p` or the one without.

Eliminating Unwanted Filling

We needn't refill the paragraph every time an insertion occurs. A small insertion that doesn't push any text beyond the right margin doesn't affect any line but its

---

* For more details about syntax tables, run `describe-function` on `modify-syntax-entry`.

own, so if the current change is an insertion, and *start* and *end* are on the same line, and the end of the line isn't beyond the right margin, let's not call `fill-region` at all.

This means we must surround our call to `fill-region` with an `if` that looks something like this:

```
(if (and (zerop len)                    ; if it's an insertion...
         (same-line-p start end)        ; ...that doesn't span lines...
         (short-line-p end))            ; ...and the line's still short
    nil                                 ; then do nothing
  (save-excursion
    (fill-region ...)))                 ; otherwise, refill
```

We must now define `same-line-p` and `short-line-p`.

Writing `same-line-p` should be easy by now. We simply test whether *end* falls between *start* and the end of the line.

```
(defun same-line-p (start end)
  "Are START and END on the same line?"
  (save-excursion
    (goto-char start)
    (end-of-line)
    (<= end (point))))
```

Writing `short-line-p` is similarly straightforward. The variable controlling the "right margin" is called `fill-column`, and `current-column` returns the horizontal position of point.

```
(defun short-line-p (pos)
  "Does line containing POS stay within 'fill-column'?"
  (save-excursion
    (goto-char pos)
    (end-of-line)
    (<= (current-column) fill-column)))
```

Here's the new definition of `refill`:

```
(defun refill (start end len)
  "After a text change, refill the current paragraph."
  (let ((left (if (or (zerop len)
                      (not (before-2nd-word-p start)))
                  start
                (save-excursion
                  (max (progn
                         (goto-char start)
                         (beginning-of-line 0)
                         (point))
                       (progn
                         (goto-char start)
                         (backward-paragraph 1)
                         (point)))))))
    (if (and (zerop len)
```

```
                        (same-line-p start end)
                        (short-line-p end))
                  nil
                (save-excursion
                  (fill-region left end nil nil t)))))
```

Trailing Whitespace

We still haven't dealt with the problem that `fill-region` deletes trailing whitespace from each line, particularly the one you're editing, requiring you to type words likethis, then back up and insert a space!

Our strategy will be to avoid refilling altogether whenever the cursor follows whitespace at the end of a line, or if the cursor is *in* whitespace at the end of a line. This condition can be expressed by

```
(and (eq (char-syntax (preceding-char))
         ?\ )
     (looking-at "\\s *$"))
```

which is true when the character preceding the cursor is whitespace and when nothing but whitespace follows the cursor on the line. Let's take a closer look at this.

First we compute `(char-syntax (preceding-char))`, which gives the syntax class of the character preceding the cursor, and compare it with '`?\ `'. That strange construct—question mark, backslash, space—is the Emacs Lisp way of writing a space character. Recall that the space character is the code letter for the "whitespace" syntax class, so this test tells whether the preceding character is whitespace.

Next we call `looking-at`, a function that tells whether the text following the cursor matches a given regular expression. The regexp in this case is `\s *$` (remember, backslashes get doubled in Lisp strings). In Emacs Lisp regexps, `\s` introduces a syntax class based on the current buffer's syntax table. The character following `\s` tells which syntax class to use. In this case, it's space, meaning "whitespace." So `'\s '` is a regexp meaning "match a character of whitespace," and `\s *$` means "match zero or more whitespace characters, followed by end of line."

Our final version of `refill` includes this new test.

```
(defun refill (start end len)
  "After a text change, refill the current paragraph."
  (let ((left (if (or (zerop len)
                      (not (before-2nd-word-p start)))
                  start
                (save-excursion
                  (max (progn
```

```
                        (goto-char start)
                        (beginning-of-line 0)
                        (point))
                      (progn
                        (goto-char start)
                        (backward-paragraph 1)
                        (point)))))))
    (if (or (and (zerop len)
                 (same-line-p start end)
                 (short-line-p end))
            (and (eq (char-syntax (preceding-char))
                     ?\ )
                 (looking-at "\\s *$")))
        nil
      (save-excursion
        (fill-region left end nil nil t)))))
```

For performance reasons, it's normally a good idea to avoid putting functions, especially complicated ones like **refill**, in **after-change-hooks**. If your computer is fast enough, you may not notice the cost of executing this function on every keypress; otherwise, you might find it makes Emacs unusably sluggish. In the next chapter, we'll examine a way to speed it up.

8

Evaluation and Error Recovery

In the previous chapter, we noted that **save-excursion** is a moderately expensive function, and we tried to reduce the number of times it is called in **refill** (which, since it's invoked on every buffer change, needs to be as fast as possible). Nevertheless, the code for **refill** contains five calls to **save-excursion**.

We could try to coalesce the uses of **save-excursion**—for example, by surrounding the entire body of **refill** with a call to **save-excursion**, discarding all the **save-excursion**s within, and rewriting everything else to make sure the cursor is properly positioned at all times. But this would harm the clear layout of the code. Of course, clarity does sometimes have to be sacrificed in the name of optimization, but before we consider coalescing the calls to **save-excursion**, let's see if we can do without them. It turns out we can replace them with a different function with less overhead.

In this chapter we will explore ways to write a faster, limited form of **save-excursion**. We'll encounter many interesting features of Emacs that have a common purpose: to control when things are evaluated and what effect they have on the surrounding code. We will be considering such issues as return values and cleaning up in case of error. We'll see how you can make the Lisp interpreter refrain from evaluating expressions until you are ready for them. We'll even find ways to change the order in which functions are evaluated.

limited-save-excursion

The purpose of **save-excursion** is to restore the original value of "point" after executing some Lisp expressions; but that's not all. It also restores the value of the "mark," and it restores Emacs's idea of which buffer is current. That's more overhead than we need for `refill`; after all, we're only changing the value of point. We're not switching buffers or moving the mark.

We can write a limited form of `save-excursion` that does only what we need and no more. Specifically, we need to write a function that, given any number of Lisp expressions as arguments, does the following:

1. Records the position of point

2. Evaluates the subexpressions in order

3. Restores point to its original location

The first problem we run into is that when a Lisp function is called, its arguments are all evaluated *before* the function gets control. In other words, if we write a function named `limited-save-excursion` and call it like this:

```
(limited-save-excursion
  (beginning-of-line)
  (point))
```

then the sequence of events is:

1. `(beginning-of-line)` is evaluated, moving point to the beginning of the current line and returning `nil`.

2. `(point)` is evaluated, returning the position to which the cursor has just moved.

3. `limited-save-excursion` is invoked with the *values* of the arguments it was passed—namely, `nil` and some number.

In this scenario, there is no way for `limited-save-excursion` to record the position of point prior to evaluation of the subexpressions; and it certainly can't do anything useful with the arguments `nil` and a cursor position.

eval

We could get around this problem by requiring the caller to quote every argument to `limited-save-excursion`:

```
(limited-save-excursion
  '(beginning-of-line)
  '(point))
```

This time `limited-save-excursion` is called with the two arguments `(beginning-of-line)` and `(point)`. It could record the value of point, explicitly evaluate each subexpression in turn, then restore point and return. It would look like the following example.

```
(defun limited-save-excursion (&rest exprs)
  "Like save-excursion, but only restores point."
  (let ((saved-point (point)))        ; memorize point
    (while exprs
      (eval (car exprs))              ; evaluate the next argument
      (setq exprs (cdr exprs)))
    (goto-char saved-point)))         ; restore point
```

This function contains something new: a call to **eval**, which takes a Lisp expression as an argument and evaluates it. At first that may not seem like much since, after all, the Lisp interpreter is already evaluating Lisp expressions automatically, with no calls to **eval** needed. But sometimes the result of evaluation is another Lisp expression which you'd like to evaluate, and Lisp won't do the second one automatically. If we were to execute only **(car exprs)**, we'd be extracting the first subexpression, then discarding it! We need **eval** to make that subexpression do something useful once we have it.

Here's an simple example to illustrate the difference between the evaluation that Emacs does normally and the need for **eval**:

```
(setq x '(+ 3 5))
x ⇒ (+ 3 5)              ; evaluating x
(eval x) ⇒ 8             ; evaluating the value of x
```

Macro Functions

Although **limited-save-excursion** works when we require its arguments to be quoted, it's cumbersome for the caller, and it doesn't really qualify as a substitute for **save-excursion** (since **save-excursion** doesn't have that restriction).

It is possible to write a special kind of function, called a *macro function,*[*] that behaves as though its arguments are quoted. That is, when a macro function is invoked, its arguments are *not* evaluated before the function gets control. Instead, the macro function produces some value, typically a rearrangement of its arguments, and then *that* is evaluated.

Here's a simple example. Suppose we wanted a function called **incr** that could increment the value of a numeric variable. We'd like to be able to write:

```
(setq x 17)
(incr x)
x ⇒ 18
```

---

[*] Don't confuse macro functions with keyboard macros, from which Emacs ("editor macros") gets its name.

But if `incr` were an ordinary function, then it would be invoked with the argument 17, not `x`, and could not therefore affect `x`. So `incr` must be a macro function. Its output must be an expression that, when evaluated, adds one to the value of the variable named in its argument.

Macro functions are defined with `defmacro` (whose syntax resembles `defun`). The way to write `incr` is:

```
(defmacro incr (var)
  "Add one to the named variable."
  (list 'setq var (list '+ var 1)))
```

The body of a macro function produces an *expansion* of its input. The expansion then gets evaluated. The expansion of `(incr x)` is:

```
(setq x (+ x 1))
```

When that expression is evaluated, `x` is incremented.

You can debug macro functions using the function `macroexpand`. This is an ordinary function that takes a Lisp expression and returns it after macro-expanding it. If the expression is not a macro call, it's returned unchanged. So:

```
(macroexpand '(incr x)) ⇒ (setq x (+ x 1))
```

Backquote and Unquote

Knowing that `limited-save-excursion` must be a macro function, all we have to do is imagine how a call to `limited-save-excursion` should expand. Here's a start:

```
(limited-save-excursion
  subexpr₁
  subexpr₂
  ...)
```

expands to

```
(let ((orig-point (point)))
  subexpr₁
  subexpr₂
  ...
  (goto-char orig-point))
```

Here's how to write that as a Lisp macro function:

```
(defmacro limited-save-excursion (&rest subexprs)
  "Like save-excursion, but only restores point."
  (append '(let ((orig-point (point))))
          subexprs
          '((goto-char orig-point))))
```

Remember that **append** works by effectively stripping off the outer parentheses of each list, gluing the results together, and putting a new pair of parentheses around the result. So this call to **append** takes three lists:

```
(let ((orig-point (point)))))
(subexpr₁ subexpr₂ ...)
((goto-char orig-point))
```

strips off their outer parentheses:

```
let ((orig-point (point)))
subexpr₁ subexpr₂ ...
(goto-char orig-point)
```

and surrounds the result with new parentheses:

```
(let ((orig-point (point)))
  subexpr₁
  subexpr₂
  ...
  (goto-char orig-point))
```

That's the expansion of the macro, which then gets evaluated.

That would do the trick, but it's hard to read the macro definition and understand what's going on. Fortunately, there's a better way. It turns out that nearly all macros recombine their arguments with calls to such functions as **list** and **append**, with some expressions quoted and others not. In fact, that's so common that Emacs Lisp has a special syntax making it possible to write *templates* for how macro expansions should appear.

Remember ´*expr*, which expands to (**quote** *expr*)? Well, there's also `*expr*, which expands to (**backquote** *expr*).[*] Backquote is just like quote, meaning that the result of evaluating a backquoted expression is the expression itself:

```
`(a  b  c) ⇒ (a  b  c)
```

There is one important difference, however. A backquoted list's subexpressions may be individually *unquoted* using yet more special syntax. This means that when the backquoted expression is evaluated, the unquoted subexpressions actually do get evaluated—but the rest of the list remains quoted!

```
`(a ,b  c) ⇒ (a value-of- b  c)
```

To understand why this is useful, let's return to the **incr** example. We could rewrite **incr** this way:

```
(defmacro incr (var)
  "Add one to the named variable."
  `(setq ,var (+ ,var 1)))
```

---

[*] This syntax is new as of Emacs 19.29. In prior versions, before backquote and company were well-integrated into the language, they had to be invoked as functions, like this: (` *expr*).

Each comma introduces a subexpression to be unquoted, so in this example, a literal list is built up containing:

```
(setq ... (+ ... 1))
```

and the *value* of `var` (i.e., some variable name) is plugged in twice. The result is exactly the same as our first version of `incr`, but this time it's much more clearly expressed.

Applying backquoting and unquoting to `limited-save-excursion` gives us the not-yet-correct:

```
(defmacro limited-save-excursion (&rest subexprs)
  "Like save-excursion, but only restores point."
  '(let ((orig-point (point)))
     ,subexprs        ; wrong!
     (goto-char orig-point)))
```

There's one more detail to learn about backquoting. Since `subexprs` is a `&rest` parameter, it is a list containing all the arguments passed to `limited-save-excursion`. When its value is substituted into the template above, the result is necessarily also a list. In other words,

```
(limited-save-excursion
  (beginning-of-line)
  (point))
```

expands to:

```
(let ((orig-point (point)))
  ((beginning-of-line)
   (point))
  (goto-char orig-point))
```

which is a syntax error, because of too many parentheses. What we need instead is a way to *splice* the value of `subexprs` into the surrounding list, removing the outer parentheses. For this purpose, Emacs Lisp has one more special bit of syntax (last one, I promise): the splicing unquote operator, `,@`. This version:

```
(defmacro limited-save-excursion (&rest subexprs)
  "Like save-excursion, but only restores point."
  '(let ((orig-point (point)))
     ,@subexprs
     (goto-char orig-point)))
```

yields the correct result:

```
(let ((orig-point (point)))
  (beginning-of-line)
  (point)
  (goto-char orig-point))
```

Return Value

There's still a long way to go in developing `limited-save-excursion`. For one thing, it doesn't return the value of the last expression in `subexprs`, whereas `save-excursion` does. Instead, `limited-save-excursion` unhelpfully returns the value of `(goto-char orig-point)`, which is the same as `orig-point` since `goto-char` returns its argument. This is particularly useless if you were expecting to do something like:

```
(setq line-start (limited-save-excursion
                    (beginning-of-line)
                    (point)))
```

To fix this problem, we must be sure to memorize the value of the last subexpression, then restore point, then return the memorized value. We might try this:

```
(defmacro limited-save-excursion (&rest subexprs)
  "Like save-excursion, but only restores point."
  `(let ((orig-point (point))
         (result (progn ,@subexprs)))
     (goto-char orig-point)
     result))
```

Note the use of `progn`, which simply executes everything passed to it and returns the value of its last argument—exactly what we need the result of the overall macro to be. However, this version is wrong for two reasons. The first reason has to do with the way `let` works. When this expression runs:

```
(let ((var₁ val₁)
      (var₂ val₂)
      ...
      (varₙ valₙ))
  body ...)
```

all the *vals* are evaluated before any of the *vars* are assigned, so no *val* may refer to any of the *vars*. Furthermore, *the order in which they are evaluated is undefined*. So, if we use the above version of `limited-save-excursion` to expand

```
(limited-save-excursion
  (beginning-of-line)
  (point))
```

into

```
(let ((orig-point (point))
      (result (progn (beginning-of-line)
                     (point))))
  (goto-char orig-point)
  result)
```

it's quite possible that, when this expansion is evaluated, the call to `beginning-of-line` may occur before the "first" call to `point`, causing `orig-point` to have the wrong value.

The solution to this problem is to use `let*` instead of `let`. With `let*`, there is no ambiguity: the order in which the *vals* are evaluated is the same as the order in which they're written.* Furthermore, each *var* is assigned as soon as the corresponding *val* is computed, so val_i may contain references to var_1 through var_{i-1}.

```
(defmacro limited-save-excursion (&rest subexprs)
  "Like save-excursion, but only restores point."
  `(let* ((orig-point (point))
          (result (progn ,@subexprs)))
     (goto-char orig-point)
     result))
```

The next problem isn't so easily fixed. Suppose one of the `subexprs` refers to a global variable named `orig-point`. As we just noted, each *val* can refer to preceding *vars*, so if `subexprs` contains a reference to a global `orig-point`, it will instead refer to `limited-save-excursion`'s internal copy—almost certainly not what the writer of the subexpressions had in mind. The variable reference is said to be *captured* by the macro expansion. This will wreak havoc with the subexpressions, which expect to manipulate an entirely different variable. And if those subexpressions happen to *modify* `orig-point`, it will wreak havoc with `limited-save-excursion` itself.

By embedding the execution of `subexprs` within a `let*` that defines a local `orig-point`, we've effectively hidden the "real" `orig-point` from the code that hopes to use it.

You might think that a good way to work around this problem is simply to choose a different name for `orig-point`, one that is very unlikely to appear in any of the `subexprs`. This is an unsatisfactory approach because (a) no matter how uniquely you name your variables, there's always the possibility of a collision, and (b) it can be done right. The right way is to generate a brand-new symbol that's *guaranteed* not to conflict with any other symbols in use. How can we do that?

To answer this question, we must first understand what it means for two symbols to conflict. Two symbols conflict when they are the *same object*, not merely when they have the same name. When you type a symbol name into a Lisp program, the Lisp interpreter internally converts that name into a symbol object. A symbol

---

* If `let` is ambiguous and `let*` isn't, why not always use `let*`? The answer: `let` may be more efficient in some cases. Also, you may want all the *vals* to evaluate in a context where none of the *vars* yet exist. In general, you should use `let` unless you need `let*`—but as you can probably imagine, using the wrong one is a common source of program errors.

object contains much more information than just its name. It includes the symbol's local and global variable bindings; it includes any function definition bound to the symbol (as with `defun`); and it includes the symbol's property list (see the section on "Symbol Properties" in Chapter 3).

The process of converting written Lisp code into internal data structures like symbol objects (or cons cells, etc.) is called *reading*. When the Lisp "reader" sees the same symbol name twice, it doesn't create two internal symbol objects—it reuses the same one.

It does this by storing symbols in a *symbol table*, also called an *obarray* (short for "object array"). Each time the reader sees a symbol name, it uses the corresponding symbol object from this table. If no corresponding symbol object exists, one is created and used for subsequent lookups of that name. Creating a new symbol and putting it in an obarray is called *interning* the symbol. Because of interning, symbols with identical names are really the same object.

Perhaps you can see where this is headed: if you can obtain a distinct symbol object, bypassing Lisp's tendency to intern symbols and reuse them, then Lisp won't consider it to be the same object as any other symbol, even one that has the same name. The way to create such a symbol is with the function `make-symbol`, which takes the symbol's name (as a string) and creates a brand-new, uninterned object guaranteed not to be equal, in the sense of `eq`, to any other Lisp object.

In other words, the result of

```
(make-symbol "orig-point")
```

cannot conflict with any occurrence of `orig-point` that appears anywhere else. The newly created `orig-point` is a different object from any that may have been previously created.

It's safe, then, to use a new, uninterned symbol in a situation where you want to avoid capturing variable references. Here's a revised version of our function:

```
(defmacro limited-save-excursion (&rest subexprs)
  "Like save-excursion, but only restores point."
  (let ((orig-point-symbol (make-symbol "orig-point")))
    `(let* ((,orig-point-symbol (point))
            (result (progn ,@subexprs)))
       (goto-char ,orig-point-symbol)
       result)))
```

The first `let` creates a new symbol object whose name is `orig-point`, but which isn't the same object as any other symbol, including any that happen to be named `orig-point`. This new symbol object is assigned to the variable orig-

`point-symbol`, then used twice (via unquoting) in the backquote template that follows.

At first glance, it might seem that we've simply traded the danger of capturing `orig-point` for the danger of capturing `orig-point-symbol`. But `orig-point-symbol` doesn't appear in the expansion of the macro, which looks like this (where `orig-point´` denotes the uninterned symbol created with `make-symbol`):

```
(let* ((orig-point´ (point))
       (result (progn subexprs)))
  (goto-char orig-point´)
  result)
```

so at the point where the *subexprs* are evaluated—after macro expansion—the only temporary variable is `orig-point´`, which is known to be unique. The temporary variable `result` does not yet exist at that point. So the problem of variable capture has definitely gone away.

Failing Gracefully

When an error occurs in Emacs, the current computation is aborted and Emacs returns to the top of its main loop, where it waits for keyboard or other input. When an error occurs while executing a `limited-save-excursion` subexpression, the whole `limited-save-excursion` is aborted before reaching the call to `goto-char`, leaving point who knows where. But the real `save-excursion` manages to correctly restore point (and the mark and the current buffer) even when an error occurs. How is this possible?

Information about pending function calls is kept in an internal data structure called a *stack*. Getting back to the top of the main loop after an error involves *unwinding* the stack, one function call at a time, in reverse order—so if *a* called *b*, and *b* called *c*, and then an error occurred, *c* will be unwound, followed by *b*, then *a*, until Emacs is back at "top level."

It is possible to write Lisp code that gets executed while the stack is being unwound! This is the key to writing code that fails "gracefully," cleaning up after itself if it doesn't get the chance to finish due to some error (or due to the user interrupting the operation with **C-g**). The function to use is called `unwind-protect`, which takes one expression to evaluate normally, followed by any number of expressions to execute afterward—even if an error interrupted the first expression. It looks like this:

```
(unwind-protect
    normal
  cleanup₁
```

cleanup₂
  ...)

Clearly, we'd like to restore the value of point in the "cleanup" portion of an
`unwind-protect`:

```
(defmacro limited-save-excursion (&rest subexprs)
  "Like save-excursion, but only restores point."
  (let ((orig-point-symbol (make-symbol "orig-point")))
    `(let ((,orig-point-symbol (point)))
       (unwind-protect
           (progn ,@subexprs)
         (goto-char ,orig-point-symbol)))))
```

One side benefit of `unwind-protect` is that in the non-error case, its return
value is the value of the "normal" subexpression. (When there is an error, the
return value doesn't matter.) In this case, that's `(progn ,@subexprs)`, which is
exactly the return value we want `limited-save-excursion` to have, so we're
able to do away with our earlier `result` variable, and we've turned the `let*`
back into a `let`.

Point Marker

As a final enhancement to `limited-save-excursion`, rather than recording
point as a number, we should record it as a marker, for the same reason we used
markers in the definition of `unscroll` (see the "Markers" section in Chapter 3):
namely, that executing the *subexprs* may render the saved buffer position inaccurate, because text may be inserted or deleted earlier in the buffer.

This is trivial to change. All that's necessary is to replace the call to `point`, which
returns a number, with a call to `point-marker`, which returns point's current
position as a marker.

```
(defmacro limited-save-excursion (&rest subexprs)
  "Like save-excursion, but only restores point."
  (let ((orig-point-symbol (make-symbol "orig-point")))
    `(let ((,orig-point-symbol (point-marker)))
       (unwind-protect
           (progn ,@subexprs)
         (goto-char ,orig-point-symbol)))))
```

Now all that remains is to put this definition, followed by

```
(provide 'limited)
```

into a file named *limited.el* in a directory on your `load-path` and byte-compile
the file (see Chapter 5, *Lisp Files*). Then in *refill.el* we can replace the calls to
`save-excursion` with calls to `limited-save-excursion`; add:

```
(require 'limited)
```

to the beginning of *refill.el*, and byte-compile it. Now *limited* won't be loaded until *refill* is loaded, and if you also put

```
(autoload 'refill-mode "refill" "Refill minor mode." t)
```

in your *.emacs*, then *refill* won't be loaded until you invoke `refill-mode`.

9

A Major Mode

Writing a simple major mode is very much like writing a minor mode, which we covered in Chapter 7, *Minor Mode*. We'll just touch on the basic ideas of major modes in this chapter, preparing us for the creation of a substantial major mode—indeed, a whole new application—in the next chapter.

My Quips File

For several years I have been collecting witty quotations from various sources on the Internet, storing them in a file called *Quips* whose format is the same one used by the old UNIX *fortune* program. Each quotation is introduced by a line containing the string `%%`. Here's an example:

```
%%
I like a man who grins when he fights.
   - Winston Churchill
%%
The human race has one really effective weapon, and that is laughter.
   - Mark Twain
```

Apart from the `%%` lines, the file is completely free-form.

After my *Quips* file had been growing for a while, I found that I edited it a bit differently from the way I edit ordinary text files. For one thing, I frequently needed to confine my editing to a single quip in order to avoid accidentally straying into a neighboring quip. For another, whenever I needed to fill a paragraph at the beginning of a quip, I first had to separate it from the leading `%%`

with a blank line. Otherwise, the %% would become filled as if it were part of the paragraph:

%%
I like a man who grins when he fights.
  - Winston Churchill
%% The human race has one really effective weapon, and that is laughter.
  - Mark Twain

Inserting a blank line told Emacs that the %% wasn't part of the paragraph. After filling the paragraph, I'd rejoin the text to the leading %% by deleting the blank line.

A new editing mode was clearly called for, one in which these workarounds were not necessary. The question was, should it be a major mode or a minor mode? Recall that a major mode excludes all other major modes, while a minor mode can be turned on and off independently of the major mode and other active minor modes. In this case, the need for an editing mode arose from the format of the data itself, which suggested that the mode should be major, not minor. Files using this data format would always want this major mode and no other. You wouldn't, for example, use a Lisp-editing major mode in combination with a quip-editing minor mode.[*]

Major Mode Skeleton

These are the steps involved in defining a major mode.

1. Choose a *name*. The name for our mode is `quip`.

2. Create a file called name.*el* to contain the code for the mode.

3. Define a variable called *name*-`mode-hook`. This will contain the user's hook functions to execute when entering the mode.

   ```
   (defvar quip-mode-hook nil
     "*List of functions to call when entering Quip mode.")
   ```

4. If appropriate, define a mode-specific keymap (see "Keymaps" later in this chapter). Put it in a variable called *name*-`mode-map`. Create a mode's keymap like this:

   ```
   (defvar name-mode-map nil
     "Keymap for name major mode.")

   (if name-mode-map
       nil
     (setq name-mode-map (make-keymap))
   ```

---

[*] The choice of major mode or minor mode can be considerably less clear-cut in other cases.

```
(define-key name-mode-map keysequence command)
...)
```

Instead of `make-keymap`, you could use `make-sparse-keymap`, which is better suited to keymaps that contain only a few keybindings.

5. If appropriate, define a mode-specific syntax table (see the section called "Minor Adjustments" in Chapter 7). Put it in a variable named *name*-`mode-syntax-table`.

6. If appropriate, define a mode-specific abbrev table. Put it in a variable named *name*-`mode-abbrev-table`.

7. Define a command named *name*-`mode`. This is the major mode command, and it takes no arguments (unlike a minor mode command, which takes one optional argument). When executed, it should cause the current buffer to enter *name*-`mode` by performing the following steps:

   (a) It must call `kill-all-local-variables`, which removes the definitions for all buffer-local variables. This effectively turns off whatever modes, major and minor, were previously active.

   ```
   (kill-all-local-variables)
   ```

   (b) It must set the variable `major-mode` to *name*-`mode`.

   ```
   (setq major-mode 'quip-mode)
   ```

   (c) It must set the variable `mode-name` to a short string describing the mode, to be used in the buffer's mode line.

   ```
   (setq mode-name "Quip")
   ```

   (d) It must install the mode-specific keymap, if any, by calling `use-local-map` on *name*-`mode-map`.

   (e) It must run the user's hook functions by calling `run-hooks` on *name*-`mode-hook`.

   ```
   (run-hooks 'quip-mode-hook)
   ```

8. It must "provide" the feature implemented by this mode (see the section on "Programmatic Loading" in Chapter 5) by calling `provide` on *name*.

   ```
   (provide 'quip)          ; allows users to (require 'quip)
   ```

Our first version of Quip mode will not include a keymap, syntax table, or abbrev table, so at first *quip.el* looks like this:

```
(defvar quip-mode-hook nil
  "*List of functions to call when entering Quip mode.")

(defun quip-mode ()
  "Major mode for editing Quip files."
  (interactive)
  (kill-all-local-variables)
```

```
(setq major-mode 'quip-mode)
(setq mode-name "Quip")
(run-hooks 'quip-mode-hook))

(provide 'quip)
```

Those are the basics, shared among all major modes. Now let's start fleshing out the specifics of Quip mode.

Changing the Definition of a Paragraph

First, we must arrange for a line consisting of `%%` not to be considered part of a paragraph. This means we must change the variable `paragraph-separate`, whose value is a regexp that describes lines that separate paragraphs. We'll also have to change `paragraph-start`, a regexp that describes lines that serve as *either* the first line of a paragraph *or* (despite the name) as a line that separates paragraphs.[*]

Emacs uses the regexps in `paragraph-start` and `paragraph-separate` to match at the beginnings of lines, even though the regexps do not explicitly begin with the magic ∧ ("match at the beginning of a line") character.

In Text mode, the value of `paragraph-start` is `"[ \t\n\^L]"`, which means that if a line starts with a space, tab, newline,[†] or Control-L (the ASCII "formfeed" character), it's either the first line of a paragraph or a line that separates paragraphs.

Text mode's value for `paragraph-separate` is `"[ \t\^L]*$"`, which means that a line containing zero or more spaces, tabs, or formfeeds, or some combination thereof, *and nothing else*, is not part of any paragraph.

What we'd like to do is augment these patterns to say "a line containing `%%` is a paragraph separator, too."

The first step is to make these variables have separate values for the current buffer when in Quip mode. (That is, setting these variables, which are global, should not affect other buffers that may not be in Quip mode.) Therefore, in addition to the basic skeleton described in the last section, the function `quip-mode` should do this:

```
(make-local-variable 'paragraph-start)
(make-local-variable 'paragraph-separate)
```

---

[*] No regexp variable exists to match just the start of a paragraph. Instead, the start of a paragraph is a line that matches `paragraph-start` but not `paragraph-separate`.

[†] A line that "starts" with a newline is, of course, a blank line.

Next, `quip-mode` must set the buffer-local values for both `paragraph-start` and `paragraph-separate`.

```
(setq paragraph-start "%%\\|[ \t\n\^L]")
(setq paragraph-separate "%%$\\|[ \t\^L]*$")
```

The value for `paragraph-start` means "%% *or* a space, tab, newline, or control-L." The value for `paragraph-separate` means "%% and nothing else *or* zero or more spaces, tabs, or formfeeds and nothing else." See the section on "Regular Expressions" in Chapter 4.

Quip Commands

What else should Quip mode be able to do?

- It should allow the user to move forward and backward a quip at a time.

- It should allow the user to restrict editing operations to a single quip.

- It should be able to report the number of quips in the file, and the number of the quip that point is on.

- Apart from that, it should work by and large the same way Text mode works. After all, the contents are mostly plain text.

Let's pause a moment to consider the different kinds of cursor motion commands in Emacs. There's `forward-char` and `backward-char` for moving one character at a time. There's `forward-word` and `backward-word`. There's `forward-line` and `previous-line`. There are also commands for moving forward and backward in units of sentences, paragraphs, sexps, and pages.

What's a page? Conventionally, a new page begins at a formfeed character (control-L), because in the ancient days of teletypes and line printers, the way to begin a new page was to send a control-L to the device. In true Emacs style, however, we can redefine what constitutes a "page" by changing the regexp in `page-delimiter`.

```
(make-local-variable 'page-delimiter)
(setq page-delimiter "^%%$")
```

This single insight—making a "page" equal a "quip"—solves most of the requirements we've stipulated for Quip mode! Now Emacs's many built-in page commands will operate on quips:

- `backward-page` and `forward-page`, normally bound to **C-x [** and **C-x]**, allow moving back and forth a quip at a time

- `narrow-to-page`, bound to **C-x n p**, confines editing to a single quip by "narrowing" the buffer (see the section on "Narrowing" later in this chapter).

- `what-page` reports the number of the current quip

We've essentially co-opted Emacs's page commands, but that's okay: in Quip mode, those commands would otherwise be unused, since a Quip file is not divided into pages.

Keymaps

Unfortunately, the names of the commands—`backward-page` and `what-page` and so on—obscure their function in Quip mode, which is to operate on quips, not pages. Therefore it might be wise to do this:

```
(defalias 'backward-quip 'backward-page)
(defalias 'forward-quip 'forward-page)
(defalias 'narrow-to-quip 'narrow-to-page)
(defalias 'what-quip 'what-page)
```

But that's not quite enough. Even with these aliases defined, the existing keybindings—C-x [, C-x], and C-x n p—are still bound to the "page" commands, so that if users list the keybindings in Quip mode using `describe-bindings`, they'll see:

C-x [	backward-page
C-x]	forward-page
C-x n p	narrow-to-page

(among many others) but nothing relating to quips. It would be better if these keysequences referred to the quip variant of the command names—in Quip mode only, of course. While we're at it, we should also change **C-x n p** (so chosen because it means narrow to page) to **C-x n q** (narrow to quip). We could also give a keybinding to `what-quip`, which doesn't have one by default. At this point we need a *keymap* specific to Quip mode.

A keymap is a Lisp data structure that maps keystrokes to the commands they should invoke. When you press C-f, for instance, Emacs consults the "global" keymap and finds the binding for C-f, namely `forward-char`. Each entry in a keymap represents a single keystroke.

Key *sequences*, such as **C-x C-w** (`write-file`), are implemented by *nesting* keymaps. In the global keymap, the entry for **C-x** contains a nested keymap instead of a command. The nested keymap contains an entry for **C-w**, which maps to `write-file`. The nested keymap for **C-x** also contains an entry for **n**, which maps to yet another nested keymap. That doubly-nested keymap contains an entry for **p**, which maps to `narrow-to-page`.

Any key whose binding is a nested keymap is called a *prefix key*; thus **C-x** is a prefix for many other commands, and **C-x n** is a prefix for a handful more. (As of

Emacs 19.16, you can press a prefix key followed by **C-h** to see all the keybindings for which that key is a prefix.)

At any time, there may be several keymaps *active*. The *global keymap*, mentioned
above, is always active. It can be superseded by entries in a buffer's *local keymap*,
which contains special keybindings for the current major mode. That, in turn, can
be superseded by the entries in the *minor mode keymap* corresponding to any
minor modes that are active.[*]

Let's create a local map for Quip mode as described earlier in this chapter. First
we create the variable to contain the keymap. Its initial value should be `nil`.

```
(defvar quip-mode-map nil
  "Keymap for quip major mode.")
```

Next we'll write a block of code at the top level of *quip.el* that sets up `quip-
mode-map` as soon as *quip.el* is loaded, if the keymap hasn't already been set up.
The way this block is structured, if `quip-mode-map` already exists—for instance,
because *quip.el* has been previously loaded—it is left alone. Otherwise, it's
created and populated with the desired keybindings.

```
(if quip-mode-map
    nil          ; do nothing if quip-mode-map exists
  (setq quip-mode-map (make-sparse-keymap))
  (define-key quip-mode-map "\C-x[" 'backward-quip)
  (define-key quip-mode-map "\C-x]" 'forward-quip)
  (define-key quip-mode-map "\C-xnq" 'narrow-to-quip)
  (define-key quip-mode-map "\C-cw" 'what-quip))
```

We use `make-sparse-keymap` because Quip mode has only a few special
keybindings beyond the ones found in the global keymap. Only when a keymap
has more than a couple dozen keybindings should a full keymap be created with
`make-keymap`.

Each call to `define-key` adds a new entry to `quip-mode-map`. When the
keysequence contains more than one key (as all the examples in this chapter do),
`define-key` automatically creates nested keymaps as necessary.[†]

We've chosen to bind `what-quip` to **C-c w**. By convention, mode-specific
commands are often bound to sequences beginning with **C-c**. The other Quip
mode commands correspond to existing keybindings elsewhere, so there's no
point moving them to new prefixes.

---

[*] It's possible to subvert this ordering of keymap precedence slightly with a variable called `overriding-
local-map`, but that's useful only in very unusual cases.

[†] The function `current-global-map` returns the current global keymap. (It's possible to change global
keymaps with `use-global-keymap`, though that's very rare.) Thus, `(global-set-key ...)` is equivalent to `(define-key (current-global-map) ...)`.

Finally, we make sure to install the new keymap when Quip mode is entered.

```
(defun quip-mode ()
  "Major mode for editing Quip files."
  (interactive)
  (kill-all-local-variables)
  (setq major-mode 'quip-mode)
  (setq mode-name "Quip")
  (make-local-variable 'paragraph-separate)
  (make-local-variable 'paragraph-start)
  (make-local-variable 'page-delimiter)
  (setq paragraph-start "%%\\|[ \t\n\^L]")
  (setq paragraph-separate "%%$\\|[ \t\^L]*$")
  (setq page-delimiter "^%%$")
  (use-local-map quip-mode-map)      ; this installs the keymap
  (run-hooks 'quip-mode-hook))
```

If users wish to alter Quip mode's keybindings, they can do so using a mode hook and `local-set-key` (which, within Quip mode, alters `quip-mode-map`):

```
(add-hook 'quip-mode-hook
          '(lambda ()
             (local-set-key "\M-p" 'backward-quip)
             (local-set-key "\M-n" 'forward-quip)
             (local-unset-key "\C-x[")    ; removes a keybinding
             (local-unset-key "\C-x]")))
```

It is customary to include a mode's local keybindings in the docstring that describes the mode. However, it's a bad idea to "hardwire" the default keybindings into the docstring like this:

```
(defun quip-mode ()
  "Major mode for editing Quip files.

Keybindings include `C-x [' and `C-x ]' for backward-quip
and forward-quip, `C-x n p' for narrow-to-quip, and `C-c w'
for what-quip."
  ...)
```

since as we've seen, the user may redefine which keys do what, rendering the docstring inaccurate. Instead, we can write:

```
(defun quip-mode ()
  "Major mode for editing Quip files.
Special commands:
\\{quip-mode-map}"
  ...)
```

This special syntax causes Emacs to substitute a description of the keybindings currently in `quip-mode-map` whenever the user requests the docstring with `describe-function`, or with `describe-mode` (which uses the docstrings of all relevant mode commands to describe the current major and minor modes).

Narrowing

You may already be familiar with the Emacs concept of *narrowing*. It is possible to define a region of a buffer and narrow the buffer to that region. Emacs then makes it appear that that region *is* the entire buffer, hiding any text that comes before or after it. All editing operations, and most Lisp functions, are confined to the narrowed region (although when the file is saved, all of it is saved regardless of any narrowing) until the user undoes the narrowing with `widen`, normally bound to C-x n w.* So `narrow-to-quip` satisfies the requirement, "It should allow the user to restrict editing operations to a single quip."

Emacs Lisp code must be written to be aware of the possibility that a buffer is narrowed. Most of the time, Lisp functions won't care. They can behave as if the narrowed portion *is* the whole buffer. Some functions that normally deal with buffer boundaries actually deal with narrowed-region boundaries when narrowing is in effect. For instance, `eobp` ("end-of-buffer-p"), which normally tests whether point is at the end of the buffer, returns true if point is at the end of a narrowed region. Similarly, `point-min` and `point-max` return the boundaries of the narrowed region if there is one, not of the whole buffer. In a sense, these functions are preserving a fiction for the benefit of Lisp programmers, who might otherwise have to go to extreme lengths to keep all their code aware of the possibility of narrowing.

There is a price to pay, however. On some occasions, functions do need to care about the buffer outside any narrowed region. In those cases, it is necessary to call `widen`, so that the function can have access to the entire buffer. If this is placed inside a call to `save-restriction`, then narrowing is restored after the code is executed. (We used this approach in Chapter 4, *Searching and Modifying Buffers*.)

As an example, let's define `count-quips`, which we must write ourselves since Emacs doesn't have any page-counting commands for us to co-opt. Clearly `count-quips` needs access to the entire buffer, regardless of any narrowing in effect. Therefore, a good way to define it is as follows:

```
(defun count-quips ()
  "Count the quips in the buffer."
  (interactive)
  (save-excursion
    (save-restriction
      (widen)
      (goto-char (point-min))
      (count-matches "^%%$"))))
```

---

* Narrowing does not nest. If you narrow a buffer to a region, then narrow that region to a smaller region, C-x n w will still restore a view of the entire buffer (i.e., it won't revert to the previous narrowing).

The function `count-matches` returns a string such as `"374 matches"` that tells how many matches for the given regexp were found following point.

Derived Modes

We've now satisfied all the requirements for Quip mode save one: "It should work by and large the same way Text mode works." One way to achieve this is actually to call `text-mode` as part of initializing Quip mode; then perform whatever specialization is required by Quip mode. In conjunction with calling `text-mode`, we'd create `quip-mode-map` not from scratch with `make-sparse-keymap`, but as a *copy* of `text-mode-map` using `copy-keymap`:

```
(defvar quip-mode-map nil
  "Keymap for Quip major mode.")

(if quip-mode-map
    nil
  (setq quip-mode-map (copy-keymap text-mode-map))
  (define-key quip-mode-map "\C-x[" 'backward-quip)
  (define-key quip-mode-map "\C-x]" 'forward-quip)
  (define-key quip-mode-map "\C-xnq" 'narrow-to-quip)
  (define-key quip-mode-map "\C-cw" 'what-quip))

(defun quip-mode ()
  "Major mode for editing Quip files.
Special commands:
\\{quip-mode-map}"
  (interactive)
  (kill-all-local-variables)
  (text-mode)                              ; first, set things up for Text mode
  (setq major-mode 'quip-mode)             ; now, specialize for Quip mode
  (setq mode-name "Quip")
  (use-local-map quip-mode-map)
  (make-local-variable 'paragraph-separate)
  (make-local-variable 'paragraph-start)
  (make-local-variable 'page-delimiter)
  (setq paragraph-start "%%\\|[ \t\n\^L]")
  (setq paragraph-separate "%%$\\|[ \t\^L]*\$")
  (setq page-delimiter "^%%$")
  (run-hooks 'quip-mode-hook))

(provide 'quip)
```

For closer conformance with Text mode, we should clone `text-mode-syntax-table` too (using `copy-syntax-table`), not just `text-mode-map`. And there's also `text-mode-abbrev-table` (but there's no corresponding `copy-abbrev-table` function, perhaps because abbrev tables are not used quite so often and no one ever lamented its absence).

Actually, a lot of bookkeeping can be required when you clone another mode and specialize it for a new purpose. It's easy to miss something. Fortunately, it's so common to *derive* new modes by varying existing ones—just as we've varied Text mode to get Quip mode—that there's an Emacs Lisp package to simplify this task. The package is called *derived* and the central function it provides is called `define-derived-mode`. (Actually, `define-derived-mode` is a macro.) Here's how we can use it to derive Quip mode from Text mode:

```
(require 'derived)

(define-derived-mode quip-mode text-mode "Quip"
  "Major mode for editing Quip files.
Special commands:
\\{quip-mode-map}"
  (make-local-variable 'paragraph-separate)
  (make-local-variable 'paragraph-start)
  (make-local-variable 'page-delimiter)
  (setq paragraph-start "%%\\|[ \t\n\^L]")
  (setq paragraph-separate "%%$\\|[ \t\^L]*$")
  (setq page-delimiter "^%%$"))

(define-key quip-mode-map "\C-x[" 'backward-quip)
(define-key quip-mode-map "\C-x]" 'forward-quip)
(define-key quip-mode-map "\C-xnq" 'narrow-to-quip)
(define-key quip-mode-map "\C-cw" 'what-quip)

(provide 'quip)
```

The syntax of `define-derived-mode` is

```
(define-derived-mode new-mode old-mode mode-line-string
  docstring
  body1
  body2
  ...)
```

This creates the command *new-mode* and all the associated data structures. By the time the *body* expressions execute, *new-mode*-`map`, *new-mode*-`syntax-table`, and *new-mode*-`abbrev-table` exist. The last thing that the constructed *new-mode* command does is to run *new-mode*-`hook`.

This chapter has shown us what it's like to change Emacs's behavior slightly for editing a particular kind of data. Quip mode isn't much different from Text mode, because quips aren't much different from text. But in the next chapter, we'll create a major mode that's very different from anything else in Emacs, for editing data that's very much unlike text.

10

A Comprehensive Example

This chapter is the culmination of our programming examples. It is a substantial major mode implementing a crossword puzzle editor—clearly a use which the designers of Emacs didn't foresee, but implementable nonetheless. The straightforwardness of designing and implementing Crossword mode demonstrates Emacs's true potential as an application-building toolkit.

After devising a data model for a crossword puzzle editing application, we'll construct a user interface for it, creating functions for displaying a representation of our data model and restricting input to the set of operations we allow on it. We'll write commands that go on the Emacs menu and commands that communicate with external processes. In doing so, we'll exploit the Lisp techniques we've learned for performing complex logic and string manipulation.

New York Times Rules

I'm a big fan of crossword puzzles. I used to do the *New York Times* crossword puzzle daily. I frequently found myself amazed at the skill that must go into constructing a crossword puzzle, and wanted to try my hand at it. My initial attempts were on graph paper, but I quickly found that crossword puzzle creation involves so much trial and error (at least for me) that by the time I was halfway through, my eraser would be tearing holes in the paper! I hit on the idea of writing a computer program to help me create crossword puzzles.

A crossword diagram, or grid, contains "blanks" and "blocks." A blank is an empty square where a letter may be placed. A block is a blackened square where no letter goes, used to separate words. Skillful crossword puzzle creators try to use as few blocks as possible.

Crossword mode should enforce what I call the "*New York Times* rules" of crossword puzzles (of course, they're similar to, or the same as, rules used by countless other crossword puzzle writers):

1. The crossword grid is an $n \times n$ square, where n is odd. The daily *New York Times* crossword puzzle is 15×15. The Saturday puzzle is 21×21.

2. The grid has "180° symmetry," meaning that if you rotate the grid 180 degrees, the pattern of blocks and non-blocks is the same.[*] Mathematically, this means that if grid square (x,y) is blank, then so must grid square $(n-x+1, n-y+1)$ be (where n is the width of the grid and x and y count from 0); and if (x,y) contains a block, then so must $(n-x+1, n-y+1)$. See Figure 10-1 for an example of 180° symmetry.

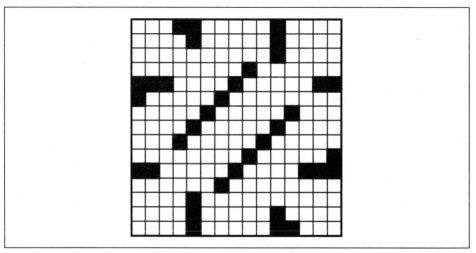

Figure 10-1. An example of 180° symmetry

3. All words in the puzzle must be at least two letters long. (Actually, I'm informed that *The New York Times* never uses words shorter than *three* letters, but for simplicity in this programming example, we'll leave it at two.)

Data Representation

Let's start by choosing a data representation. An obvious approach is to store the cells of the crossword grid in a two-dimensional array, or matrix. Emacs Lisp doesn't have such a data type, but we can create one using *vectors*.

---

[*] 180° symmetry is also known as "two-way symmetry." There's also "four-way symmetry," meaning that the pattern is the same every time you rotate the grid 90 degrees.

Vectors

A Lisp *vector* resembles a list, in that it is a sequence of zero or more arbitrary subexpressions (including nested vectors or lists). However, vectors permit random access to their elements, whereas one must traverse a list from its beginning to find a particular element. (That doesn't necessarily make vectors superior to lists. Unlike lists, vectors can't be lengthened or shortened except by copying. As always, use the right tool for the job.)

Vectors are written with square brackets instead of parentheses:

```
[a   b   c ...]
```

Vectors are self-evaluating; that is, the result of evaluating a vector is the vector itself. Its subexpressions are not evaluated. So if you write:

```
[a b c]
```

you'll get a vector containing the three symbols, a, b, and c. If you want a vector containing the *values* of variables a, b, and c, you must construct the vector using the `vector` function:

```
(vector a b c) ⇒ [17 37 42]        ; or whatever the values happen to be
```

Matrix Package

It is straightforward to design a matrix package using vectors. We'll choose to represent a matrix as a vector of rows, with each row being a nested vector of columns. Here's how to create one of these:

```
(defun make-matrix (rows columns &optional initial)
  "Create a ROWS by COLUMNS matrix."
  (let ((result (make-vector rows nil))
        (y 0))
    (while (< y rows)
      (aset result y (make-vector columns initial))
      (setq y (+ y 1)))
    result))
```

The argument `initial` specifies a Lisp expression to use as the initial value for every element in the matrix. The first call to `make-vector` creates a vector of nils, `rows` elements long. One by one, we replace each `nil` with a new vector of length `columns`. The function `aset` is used for setting vector elements; `aref` retrieves them.[*] Vectors are indexed starting at 0. Calling (`aset` *vector index*

---

[*] The "a" in these function names stands for "array." Why not `vset` and `vref`, with "v" for "vector"? The answer is that in Emacs Lisp, vectors are just one kind of *array*. Strings are another kind of array. So `aset` and `aref` can be used on strings as well as on vectors—but that doesn't mean that strings are vectors.

value) changes the element at position *index* in *vector* to be *value*. Calling (`aref` *vector index)* retrieves the element at position *index*.

The call to `make-vector` inside the `while` loop sets each element of the nested vectors to `initial`, so at the end of `make-matrix`, `result` is a vector of `rows` nested vectors, where each nested vector is a vector of `columns` copies of `initial`.

Why couldn't we have written this function more simply, like this?

```
(defun make-matrix (rows columns &optional initial)
  "Create a ROWS by COLUMNS matrix."
  (make-vector rows (make-vector columns initial)))      ; wrong!
```

The reason is that the inner call to `make-vector` yields a single new vector. The outer call would use that *single vector* as the initial value for every element in the outer vector. In other words, every element in the outer vector would share the same inner vector, when what we want is for every element in the outer vector to be a *separate* nested vector.

Given the structure of a matrix, it's a simple matter to define the basic operations on one:

```
(defun matrix-set (matrix row column elt)
  "Given a MATRIX, ROW, and COLUMN, put element ELT there."
  (let ((nested-vector (aref matrix row)))
    (aset nested-vector column elt)))

(defun matrix-ref (matrix row column)
  "Get the element of MATRIX at ROW and COLUMN."
  (let ((nested-vector (aref matrix row)))
    (aref nested-vector column)))
```

It might also be useful to have functions that report the width and height of the matrix:

```
(defun matrix-columns (matrix)
  "Number of columns in MATRIX."
  (length (aref matrix 0)))          ; length of one of the subvectors

(defun matrix-rows (matrix)
  "Number of rows in MATRIX."
  (length matrix))                   ; length of the outer vector
```

When function definitions are very short, like these last four, it's usually a good idea to turn them into *inline functions* using `defsubst` instead of `defun`. Inline functions defined with `defsubst` work the same way ordinary `defun` functions do, except that when you compile a function that *calls* an inline function, the call is replaced with a copy of the inline function itself. This has one major benefit: at run time, the current function doesn't have to set up a call to another function. This is marginally faster, but the savings can add up in loops that run thousands or millions of times. Unfortunately, there are also two drawbacks to inline functions. One is that the inline function is duplicated everywhere it's used, which can increase memory requirements. The other drawback is, if the inline function definition changes, the old definition will still be "frozen" into compiled files that use it. (In all these respects, `defsubst` functions are equivalent to `inline` functions in C++, or macro functions in C .)

We can put the above code into *matrix.el*, stick a `(provide 'matrix)` at the end of it, and use it in subsequent programs with `(require 'matrix)`.

Crossword Variant of Matrix

Now let's consider a crossword grid, which is a specialized kind of matrix. Each cell in the grid can be in only one of four states:

1. Empty, meaning we may place a letter or a block in it.

2. Semi-empty, meaning we may only place a letter in it, not a block (because of the requirement of 180° symmetry).

3. Filled with a block.

4. Filled with a letter.

Let's use `nil` to stand for a cell that is empty, the symbol `letter` to stand for a semi-empty cell that must be filled with a letter, the symbol `block` to stand for a cell containing a block, and the letter itself (which is represented in Emacs by a number, its ASCII value) for cells containing a letter.

Given all that, let's define a new data type for crossword grids, implemented in terms of matrices.

```
(require 'matrix)

(defun make-crossword (size)
  "Make a crossword grid with SIZE rows and columns."
  (if (zerop (% size 2))            ; Is size even? (% is the remainder function)
      (error "make-crossword: size must be odd"))
  (if (< size 3)                    ; Is size too small?
      (error "make-crossword: size must be 3 or greater"))
  (make-matrix size size nil))

(defsubst crossword-size (crossword)
  "Number of rows and columns in CROSSWORD."
  (matrix-rows crossword))          ; or matrix-columns, it doesn't matter

(defsubst crossword-ref (crossword row column)
  "Get the element of CROSSWORD at ROW and COLUMN."
  (matrix-ref crossword row column))

(defsubst crossword--set (crossword row column elt)
```

```
"Internal function for setting a crossword grid square."
(matrix-set crossword row column elt))
```

The function `crossword--set` has a double hyphen in its name. This is the conventional way to denote a "private" function that isn't part of a package's advertised programming interface. In this case, `crossword--set` is private because it doesn't implement the *New York Times* rules we want to preserve in the crossword grid. Users of the Crossword package won't use `crossword--set`; instead they'll use `crossword-store-letter`, `crossword-store-block`, and `crossword-clear-cell`, defined below. Only the Crossword package itself will use `crossword--set`, plus some logic for preserving 180° symmetry and word lengths greater than 2.

Using Cons Cells

Let's coin the term "cousin" to mean the grid square symmetrically opposite a given square.

```
(defun crossword-cousin-position (crossword row column)
  "Give the cousin position for CROSSWORD ROW and COLUMN."
  (let ((size (crossword-size crossword)))
    (cons (- size row 1) (- size column 1))))
```

This function returns the position of the cousin of `row` and `column` as a dotted pair (see the section entitled "List Details" in Chapter 6): (*cousin-row . cousin-column*). Here are two functions for referencing and setting cousins directly:

```
(defun crossword-cousin-ref (crossword row column)
  "Get the cousin of CROSSWORD's ROW,COLUMN position."
  (let ((cousin-position (crossword-cousin-position crossword
                                                     row
                                                     column)))
    (crossword-ref crossword
                   (car cousin-position)
                   (cdr cousin-position))))

(defun crossword--cousin-set (crossword row column elt)
  "Internal function for setting the cousin of a cell."
  (let ((cousin-position (crossword-cousin-position crossword
                                                     row
                                                     column)))
    (crossword--set crossword
                    (car cousin-position)
                    (cdr cousin-position)
                    elt)))
```

Note that `crossword--cousin-set` is another "private" function with a double hyphen in its name.

Now let's create functions for storing blocks and letters, preserving *New York Times* rules. First, letters. When storing a letter in a cell, we must make sure that the cell's cousin already contains a letter (which we can test with **numberp**). If it doesn't, we must store the symbol **letter** there:

```
(defun crossword-store-letter (crossword row column letter)
  "Given CROSSWORD, ROW, and COLUMN, put LETTER there."
  (crossword--set crossword row column letter)
  (if (numberp (crossword-cousin-ref crossword row column))
      nil
    (crossword--cousin-set crossword row column 'letter)))
```

Inserting blocks is a little bit simpler:

```
(defun crossword-store-block (crossword row column)
  "Given CROSSWORD, ROW, and COLUMN, put a block there."
  (crossword--set crossword row column 'block)
  (crossword--cousin-set crossword row column 'block))
```

Now let's write a function to erase a cell. When erasing a cell, the following situations are possible:

- The cell and its cousin both contain letters. If so, the cell becomes "semi-empty" and the cousin is unaffected.

- The cell and its cousin both contain blocks. If so, the cell and its cousin both become empty.

- The cell is already semi-empty (because its cousin contains a letter). If so, nothing changes.

- The cell contains a letter but the cousin is semi-empty. If so, both cells become empty.

- The cell and its cousin are both empty. If so, nothing changes.

We can handle all those cases with this simple logic: If the cell's cousin contains a letter, then the cell becomes semi-empty and the cousin is unaffected; otherwise the cell and its cousin both become empty. Here's how that looks in code.

```
(defun crossword-clear-cell (crossword row column)
  "Erase the CROSSWORD cell at ROW,COLUMN."
  (if (numberp (crossword-cousin-ref crossword row column))
      (crossword--set crossword row column 'letter)
    (crossword--set crossword row column nil)
    (crossword--cousin-set crossword row column nil)))
```

Now observe that the center square of an *n*×*n* grid is its own cousin, if *n* is odd. This means that a slight correction is needed in **crossword-clear-cell**. It must never set the center square to **letter**. (Luckily, **crossword-store-block** and **crossword-store-letter** happen to work correctly already.)

```
(defun crossword-clear-cell (crossword row column)
  "Erase the CROSSWORD cell at ROW,COLUMN."
  (let ((cousin-position (crossword-cousin-position crossword
                                                     row
```

```
                                                      column)))
      (if (and (not (equal cousin-position
                            (cons row column)))
               (numberp (crossword-ref crossword
                                        (car cousin-position)
                                        (cdr cousin-position))))
          (crossword--set crossword row column ´letter)
        (crossword--set crossword row column nil)
        (crossword--set crossword
                        (car cousin-position)
                        (cdr cousin-position)
                        nil))))
```

In this version, the cell is set to `letter` only if `cousin-position` is not equal to *(row . column)*—i.e., if the cell is not its own cousin. If the cell is its own cousin, or if its cousin does not contain a letter, then (as in the original version) it's set to `nil`, and so is its cousin. That last call to `crossword--set` is redundant in the case of the center square, but harmlessly so. Note that since we compute the cousin's position at the beginning of the function, we've replaced a call to `crossword-cousin-ref` with a call to `crossword-ref`, and replaced a call to `crossword--cousin-set` with a call to `crossword--set`, to avoid computing the cousin's position a second and third time.

One-Letter Words

A one-letter word is created any time three cells in a row contain block, non-block, block; or when a non-block cell is between the border and a block. Here's a function to test whether a given square is a one-letter word.

```
(defun crossword-one-letter-p (crossword row column)
  "Is CROSSWORD cell at ROW,COLUMN a one-letter word?"
  (and (not (eq (crossword-ref crossword row column)
                'block))
       (or (and (crossword-block-p crossword (- row 1) column)
                (crossword-block-p crossword (+ row 1) column))
           (and (crossword-block-p crossword row (- column 1))
                (crossword-block-p crossword row (+ column 1))))))
```

This is a complicated bit of logic, but recall our technique from Chapter 3, *Cooperating Commands*, for making sense of such expressions: move inward one subexpression level at a time.

```
(and ...)
```

The result of `crossword-one-letter-p` will be true if all of some subexpressions are true, false otherwise.

```
(and (not ...)
     (or ...))
```

"True if something's not true *and* one or more other things are true."

```
(and (not (eq ...))
     (or (and ...)
         (and ...)))
```

"True if something's not equal to something else *and* if one set of things are all true *or* another set of things are all true."

```
(and (not (eq (crossword-ref crossword row column)
              'block))
     (or (and (crossword-block-p crossword (- row 1) column)
              (crossword-block-p crossword (+ row 1) column))
         (and (crossword-block-p crossword row (- column 1))
              (crossword-block-p crossword row (+ column 1)))))
```

"True if the current cell is not a block *and* if the cells above and below are blocks *or* the cells to the left and right are blocks." This relies on a minor convenience hack: `crossword-block-p` must allow referring to squares outside the boundaries of the grid, and must report that they contain blocks.

Here's how we define `crossword-block-p`:

```
(defun crossword-block-p (crossword row column)
  "Does CROSSWORD's ROW,COLUMN cell contain a block?"
  (or (< row 0)
      (>= row (crossword-size crossword))
      (< column 0)
      (>= column (crossword-size crossword))
      (eq (crossword-ref crossword row column) 'block)))
```

User Interface

We now have a complete suite of functions for manipulating a crossword data structure, obeying the rules we've chosen; but there's not yet any way for a user to interact with a crossword grid. We must write the user interface, which includes commands to invoke the various crossword operations and a means of displaying the crossword grid and keeping the display up to date.

Display

Let's choose a visual representation for a crossword grid, to be used in an Emacs buffer.

Each row of the crossword grid should be represented by one line of the buffer. Each column of the grid, however, should take up *two* screen columns—because, on most displays, this helps the grid look squarer. (In most display fonts, the space for a single character is much higher than it is wide, making an $n{\times}n$ block of characters look ludicrously narrow.)

Empty grid squares will be represented by a dot (.). Blocks will be represented by a hash mark (#). Semi-empty cells will be represented by a question mark (?). And of course, cells containing letters will display that letter.

Here is a function that inserts a representation of a crossword grid into the current buffer. It doesn't erase the buffer first, or position the cursor; that's up to the caller of this function, which we'll define later.

```
(defun crossword-insert-grid (crossword)
  "Insert CROSSWORD into the current buffer."
  (mapcar 'crossword-insert-row crossword))
```

Recall from "Other Useful List Functions" in Chapter 6 that `mapcar` applies a function to each element of a list. It works on vectors, too; so, since `crossword` is a vector of rows, `crossword-insert-grid` calls `crossword-insert-row` on each row of the grid.

Here's the definition of `crossword-insert-row`, used above:

```
(defun crossword-insert-row (row)
  "Insert ROW into the current buffer."
  (mapcar 'crossword-insert-cell row)
  (insert "\n"))
```

This works the same way, calling `crossword-insert-cell` on each cell in row. At the end of the row, we begin a new line.

Finally, here's `crossword-insert-cell`, needed by `crossword-insert-row`:

```
(defun crossword-insert-cell (cell)
  "Insert CELL into the current buffer."
  (insert (cond ((null cell) ".")
                ((eq cell 'letter) "?")
                ((eq cell 'block) "#")
                ((numberp cell) cell))
          " "))
```

This inserts two characters: a dot, a question mark, a hash mark, or a letter; followed by a blank space (to make the cell take up two screen columns). The choice of which first character to insert is made with `cond`, which is a variation of `if`. Each argument to `cond` is called a *clause*, and each clause is a list. The first element of each clause, called its *condition*, is evaluated in turn. When a clause is found whose condition evaluates true, then that clause's remaining elements (if any) are evaluated, and the value of the last one is returned from `cond`. Clauses that follow a successful *condition* are skipped.

```
(cond ((condition₁  body ...)
       (condition₂  body ...)
       ...))
```

If you want an "else" clause in the `cond`—a clause that executes if no other condition is true—add a final clause whose condition is `t`:

```
(cond ((condition₁ body ...)
       (condition₂ body ...)
       ...
       (t body ...)))
```

The function `insert` takes any number of strings or characters to insert into the current buffer; that's why we can pass the value of `cell`, a number, as well as `" "`, a string, to `insert`.

Cursor Positioning

Let's continue building the components that our complete mode will ultimately need.

Now that we can display a crossword grid, it will be useful to have a way to position the cursor on an arbitrary cell. The position of the cursor indicates to the user which cell will be affected by the next operation he or she invokes.

This function assumes that a crossword grid has been drawn in the current buffer, and that it begins at `(point-min)`.*

```
(defun crossword-place-cursor (row column)
  "Move point to ROW,COLUMN."
  (goto-char (point-min))
  (forward-line row)
  (forward-char (* column 2)))
```

Next, when the user does invoke some operation, it will be necessary to deduce the current crossword coordinates from the cursor's position.

```
(defun crossword-cursor-coords ()
  "Compute (ROW . COLUMN) from cursor position."
  (cons (- (current-line) 1)
        (/ (current-column) 2)))
```

The function `/`, which performs division in Emacs Lisp, performs *integer division* when its arguments are all integers. The result is rounded toward zero. Thanks to this,

```
(/ (current-column) 2)
```

returns the correct grid column whether the cursor is in the proper *screen* column or in the blank space that follows it.

---

* Although we won't use this fact in this chapter, remember that `(point-min)` isn't necessarily the beginning of the buffer; it could be somewhere in the middle, if narrowing is in effect.

Unfortunately, while `current-column` is built into Emacs, there is no `current-line` function.* Here is one way to write it:

```
(defun current-line ()
  "Return line number containing point."
  (let ((result 1))                        ; Emacs counts lines starting from 1.
    (save-excursion
      (beginning-of-line)                  ; so bobp will work
      (while (not (bobp))
        (forward-line -1)
        (setq result (+ result 1)))))
    result))
```

The function `bobp` tests whether the cursor is at the beginning of the buffer.

Updating the Display

As the user edits the crossword grid, changes to the underlying data structure have to be reflected in the buffer. It would be wastefully inefficient to erase the whole buffer and call `crossword-insert-grid` every time the user makes a change. Instead, we'd like to redraw just the affected grid cells.

We already have the tools for doing this: `crossword-place-cursor` and `crossword-insert-cell`. Here's a function that uses those components. It presumes that the cursor is on the affected cell, and redraws it and its cousin.

```
(defun crossword-update-display (crossword)
  "Called after a change, keeps the display up to date."
  (let* ((coords (crossword-cursor-coords))
         (cousin-coords (crossword-cousin-position crossword
                                                   (car coords)
                                                   (cdr coords))))
    (save-excursion
      (crossword-place-cursor (car coords)
                              (cdr coords))
      (delete-char 2)
      (crossword-insert-cell (crossword-ref crossword
                                            (car coords)
                                            (cdr coords)))
      (crossword-place-cursor (car cousin-coords)
                              (cdr cousin-coords))
      (delete-char 2)
      (crossword-insert-cell (crossword-ref crossword
                                            (car cousin-coords)
                                            (cdr cousin-coords))))))
```

---

* There is `what-line`, but that function is meant to be used interactively, not in a program. It displays a message about the current line number, and doesn't return a useful value. We need a function with the opposite behavior: no message should be displayed, and the current line number should be returned.

You might think that the first call to `crossword-place-cursor` in this function is redundant, since it's placing the cursor at the same position that it just read with `crossword-cursor-coords`. But remember that the depiction of a grid cell is two screen columns wide, and the cursor may have somehow gotten into the righthand column. In order for `crossword-insert-cell` to work, the cursor must be in the lefthand column. Calling `crossword-place-cursor` ensures that it is. The surrounding call to `save-excursion` makes sure that the cursor returns to where it started after the display is updated.

User Commands

Now we need to define the interactive commands that will allow users to operate Crossword mode.

Grid-changing commands

Let's start by assuming that a buffer in Crossword mode has a buffer-local variable named `crossword-grid` that holds the crossword grid. (We'll address how and when to create `crossword-grid` when we define the `crossword-mode` command in the next section.) The user command to erase a cell can therefore be written as in the following example.

```
(defun crossword-erase-command ()
  "Erase current crossword cell."
  (interactive)
  (let ((coords (crossword-cursor-coords)))
    (crossword-clear-cell crossword-grid
                          (car coords)
                          (cdr coords)))
  (crossword-update-display crossword-grid))
```

Likewise, here's a command to insert a block:

```
(defun crossword-block-command ()
  "Insert a block in current cell and cousin."
  (interactive)
  (let ((coords (crossword-cursor-coords)))
    (crossword-store-block crossword-grid
                           (car coords)
                           (cdr coords)))
  (crossword-update-display crossword-grid))
```

The command for inserting a letter is trickier. There are twenty-six possible letters, but we don't wish to write twenty-six different commands with names like `crossword-insert-a` and `crossword-insert-b` and so on. We want one single function bound to all twenty-six letter keys that, when invoked, inserts whatever letter was used to invoke it. One such function for ordinary modes is `self-insert-command`. We'll define `crossword-self-insert`, which inserts the letter that the user pressed.

```
(defun crossword-self-insert ()
  "Self-insert letter in current cell."
  (interactive)
  (let ((coords (crossword-cursor-coords)))
    (crossword-store-letter crossword-grid
                            (car coords)
                            (cdr coords)
                            (aref (this-command-keys) 0)))
  (crossword-update-display crossword-grid))
```

This function uses `this-command-keys` to determine what key the user pressed. The return value of `this-command-keys` is a string of characters or a vector of symbolic events (more about those in the section on "Mouse Commands" later in this chapter); but `crossword-store-letter` expects a character, not a string, symbol, or vector. By using `aref` to select the first element and passing it to `crossword-store-letter`, we're trusting that it is indeed a string, and that we don't care about anything other than the first letter. This should be okay, because when we set up the keybindings in the section on "Keybindings" later in this chapter, we'll bind `crossword-self-insert` only to single keys (namely, the letters of the alphabet), and later on we'll make it impossible, or at least somewhat hard, for the user to enter invalid characters.

Navigation

The user must have some way of navigating from cell to cell other than Emacs's ordinary cursor-motion commands, which don't translate well to crossword-grid navigation. For one thing, each grid is two columns wide, so it would take two presses of **C-f** just to move one cell to the right. For another thing, trying to move rightward at the right boundary of the grid should not wrap around to the beginning of the next line, like **C-f** would. It should just stop.

Defining navigation commands is very straightforward. It's just a matter of figuring out in what directions the user may want to move, and in what size jumps. We'll define commands for moving one grid square left, right, up, and down; for moving to the beginning and end of each grid row; for moving to the top and bottom of each grid column; and for moving to the beginning (upper left corner) and end (bottom right corner) of the grid.

First, the horizontal cellwise motion commands:

```
(defun crossword-cursor-right (arg)
  "Move ARG cells to the right."
  (interactive "p")        ; prefix arg as number
  (let* ((coords (crossword-cursor-coords))
         (new-column (+ arg (cdr coords))))
    (if (or (< new-column 0)
            (>= new-column (crossword-size crossword-grid)))
        (error "Out of bounds"))
    (crossword-place-cursor (car coords)
```

```
                              new-column)))

(defun crossword-cursor-left (arg)
  "Move ARG cells to the left."
  (interactive "p")
  (crossword-cursor-right (- arg)))
```

Likewise for the vertical cellwise motion commands:

```
(defun crossword-cursor-down (arg)
  "Move ARG cells down."
  (interactive "p")
  (let* ((coords (crossword-cursor-coords))
         (new-row (+ arg (car coords))))
    (if (or (< new-row 0)
            (>= new-row (crossword-size crossword-grid)))
        (error "Out of bounds"))
    (crossword-place-cursor new-row
                            (cdr coords))))

(defun crossword-cursor-up (arg)
  "Move ARG cells up."
  (interactive "p")
  (crossword-cursor-down (- arg)))
```

Now the commands for moving to the beginning or end or a row or column.

```
(defun crossword-beginning-of-row ()
  "Move to beginning of current row."
  (interactive)
  (let ((coords (crossword-cursor-coords)))
    (crossword-place-cursor (car coords) 0)))

(defun crossword-end-of-row ()
  "Move to end of current row."
  (interactive)
  (let ((coords (crossword-cursor-coords)))
    (crossword-place-cursor (car coords)
                            (- (crossword-size crossword-grid)
                               1))))

(defun crossword-top-of-column ()
  "Move to top of current column."
  (interactive)
  (let ((coords (crossword-cursor-coords)))
    (crossword-place-cursor 0 (cdr coords))))

(defun crossword-bottom-of-column ()
  "Move to bottom of current row."
  (interactive)
  (let ((coords (crossword-cursor-coords)))
    (crossword-place-cursor (- (crossword-size crossword-grid)
                               1)
                            (cdr coords))))
```

Finally, the beginning- and end-of-grid commands.

```
(defun crossword-beginning-of-grid ()
  "Move to beginning of grid."
  (interactive)
  (crossword-place-cursor 0 0))

(defun crossword-end-of-grid ()
  "Move to end of grid."
  (interactive)
  (let ((size (crossword-size crossword-grid)))
    (crossword-place-cursor size size)))
```

As an afterthought, here's something that might be useful: a command to jump to the current cell's cousin.

```
(defun crossword-jump-to-cousin ()
  "Move to cousin of current cell."
  (interactive)
  (let* ((coords (crossword-cursor-coords))
         (cousin (crossword-cousin-position crossword-grid
                                            (car coords)
                                            (cdr coords))))
    (crossword-place-cursor (car cousin)
                            (cdr cousin))))
```

Setting Up the Mode

There are two circumstances under which a user expects to enter Crossword mode. One is when visiting a file that contains a crossword grid from an earlier session. Another is when creating a brand-new crossword grid.

Creating a brand-new crossword grid requires creating an empty buffer and filling it in using `crossword-insert-grid`. The act of entering a major mode shouldn't change buffers or alter a buffer's contents, so `crossword-mode` will only be for entering Crossword mode in a buffer already containing a crossword grid. We'll devise a separate command, `crossword`, for creating a grid from scratch.

Here's a start at defining `crossword`:

```
(defun crossword (size)
  "Create a new buffer with an empty crossword grid."
  (interactive "nGrid size: ")
  (let* ((grid (make-crossword size))
         (buffer (generate-new-buffer "*Crossword*")))
    (switch-to-buffer buffer)
    (crossword-insert-grid grid)
    (crossword-place-cursor 0 0)          ; start in upper-left corner
    ...))
```

We'll leave this function unfinished for now, but before we move on, let's note some interesting things about this function:

1. (`interactive` "`nGrid size: `"). The letter `n` is one of a few code letters for `interactive` that instruct Emacs to prompt the user for a value. These letters allow you to specify a prompt string, as we've done here. This `interactive` declaration means, "Prompt the user with the string "Grid size: ", and read a number in response."

   What if this command took two arguments, a number and, say, a string? What would the `interactive` declaration look like?

   Emacs considers everything after the `n` to be part of the prompt string, *up to the first newline*. So just embed a newline in the string to introduce the next code letter, like this:

   ```
   (interactive "nFirst prompt: \nsSecond prompt: ")
   ```

2. We use `let*` instead of `let` to make sure `grid` gets created before `buffer`. This isn't strictly necessary, because the creation of `buffer` doesn't depend on `grid`. But it is a good idea, because we don't want to create `buffer` if there's an error creating `grid` (such as, `size` is an illegal value). The reason is that buffer creation is fairly expensive in Emacs, and because buffers don't go away by themselves (they don't get garbage-collected) the way other Lisp values do. Once a buffer is created, it stays around until killed with `kill-buffer`.

3. The name of the new buffer is `*Crossword*`. By convention, buffers that are not associated with files have names beginning and ending with an asterisk—witness `*scratch*` and `*Help*`. Once the user begins editing the buffer, he or she can save it to a file (e.g., with **C-x C-w**), at which time Emacs will rename the buffer to correlate with the chosen filename.

Let's turn our attention momentarily to the **crossword-mode** command. As we've already decided, it should be used only on buffers that already contain a crossword grid. It should somehow *parse* the buffer. This means constructing a new crossword grid object based on the text in the buffer. The parsed grid must be assigned to **crossword-grid**. Here's a first attempt, following the major mode guidelines laid out in Chapter 9, *A Major Mode*:

```
(defun crossword-mode ()
  "Major mode for editing crossword puzzles.
Special commands:
\\{crossword-mode-map}"
  (interactive)
  (kill-all-local-variables)
  (setq major-mode 'crossword-mode)
  (setq mode-name "Crossword")
  (use-local-map crossword-mode-map)
```

```
(make-local-variable 'crossword-grid)
(setq crossword-grid (crossword-parse-buffer))
(crossword-place-cursor 0 0)                    ; start in upper-left corner
(run-hooks 'crossword-mode-hook))
```

We'll define `crossword-mode-map` and `crossword-parse-buffer` later.

Now let's return to the `crossword` command. After placing a grid representation in an empty buffer, it must cause the buffer to enter Crossword mode. How? The obvious answer is for it to call `crossword-mode`:

```
(defun crossword (size)
  "Create a new buffer with an empty crossword grid."
  (interactive "nGrid size: ")
  (let* ((grid (make-crossword size))
         (buffer (generate-new-buffer "*Crossword*")))
    (switch-to-buffer buffer)
    (crossword-insert-grid grid)
    (crossword-place-cursor 0 0)        ; start in upper-left corner
    (crossword-mode)))
```

This is fine, but a little inefficient. Note that `crossword-mode` calls `crossword-parse-buffer` to create a crossword data structure, *even though* `crossword` *has already set one up*. If we can preserve `crossword`'s copy of that data structure, we can skip the parsing step.

The best way to do this is to create a third function, used by both `crossword` and `crossword-mode`, that performs the steps common to both ways of entering Crossword mode.

```
(defun crossword--mode-setup (grid)
  "Auxiliary function to set up crossword mode."
  (kill-all-local-variables)
  (setq major-mode 'crossword-mode)
  (setq mode-name "Crossword")
  (use-local-map crossword-mode-map)
  (make-local-variable 'crossword-grid)
  (setq crossword-grid grid)
  (crossword-place-cursor 0 0)
  (run-hooks 'crossword-mode-hook))
```

We've make `crossword--mode-setup` take the crossword grid as an argument. So `crossword` should call it with the grid it constructs:

```
(defun crossword (size)
  "Create a new buffer with an empty crossword grid."
  (interactive "nGrid size: ")
  (let* ((grid (make-crossword size))
         (buffer (generate-new-buffer "*Crossword*")))
    (switch-to-buffer buffer)
    (crossword-insert-grid grid)
    (crossword--mode-setup grid)))
```

and by `crossword-mode` should call it with the result of parsing the buffer:

```
(defun crossword-mode ()
  "Major mode for editing crossword puzzles.
Special commands:
\\{crossword-mode-map}"
  (interactive)
  (crossword--mode-setup (crossword-parse-buffer)))
```

Keybindings

Earlier, we defined several user commands, such as `crossword-erase-command` and `crossword-block-command`. Now let's define `crossword-mode-map` and choose keybindings for these commands.

```
(defvar crossword-mode-map nil
  "Keymap for Crossword mode.")

(if crossword-mode-map
    nil
  (setq crossword-mode-map (make-keymap))
  ...)
```

Most of these commands are natural analogues for ordinary Emacs commands. For instance, `crossword-beginning-of-row` and `crossword-end-of-row` correspond pretty well with `beginning-of-line` and `end-of-line`, which are normally bound to **C-a** and **C-e**. Does that mean we should bind those commands like this?

```
(define-key crossword-mode-map "\C-a"
            'crossword-beginning-of-row)
(define-key crossword-mode-map "\C-e"
            'crossword-end-of-row)
```

Maybe. But suppose the user doesn't use **C-a** for `beginning-of-line`? In that case, **C-a** is the wrong choice. Because of their similarity, the user will expect to use the same key for `crossword-beginning-of-row` as for `beginning-of-line`. It would be best if we could find the user's keybinding for `beginning-of-line` and bind `crossword-beginning-of-row` accordingly. This is exactly what `substitute-key-definition` does.

```
(substitute-key-definition 'beginning-of-line
                           'crossword-beginning-of-row
                           crossword-mode-map
                           (current-global-map))
```

This means, "Wherever `beginning-of-line` is now bound in the current global keymap, create a binding for `crossword-beginning-of-row` in `crossword-mode-map`."

We can set up `crossword-mode-map` using a series of calls to `substitute-key-definition`; or, more concisely, one call inside a loop.

```
(let ((equivs
       ´((forward-char . crossword-cursor-right)
         (backward-char . crossword-cursor-left)
         (previous-line . crossword-cursor-up)
         (next-line . crossword-cursor-down)
         (beginning-of-line . crossword-beginning-of-row)
         (end-of-line . crossword-end-of-row)
         (beginning-of-buffer . crossword-beginning-of-grid)
         (end-of-buffer . crossword-end-of-grid))))
  (while equivs
    (substitute-key-definition (car (car equivs))
                               (cdr (car equivs))
                               crossword-mode-map
                               (current-global-map))
    (setq equivs (cdr equivs)))))
```

We create a list of "equivalence pairs" in equivs. Each time through this loop,
(car equivs) is one of the equivalence pairs, such as (next-line .
crossword-cursor-down). Thus, (car (car equivs)) is the command to
find in the global keymap (e.g., next-line) and (cdr (car equivs)) is the
corresponding command to place in crossword-mode-map (e.g., crossword-
cursor-down).

Now we must bind the letter keys to crossword-self-insert.

```
(let ((letters
       ´(?A ?B ?C ?D ?E ?F ?G ?H ?I ?J ?K ?L ?M
         ?N ?O ?P ?Q ?R ?S ?T ?U ?V ?W ?X ?Y ?Z
         ?a ?b ?c ?d ?e ?f ?g ?h ?i ?j ?k ?l ?m
         ?n ?o ?p ?q ?r ?s ?t ?u ?v ?w ?x ?y ?z)))
  (while letters
    (define-key crossword-mode-map
                (char-to-string (car letters))
                ´crossword-self-insert)
    (setq letters (cdr letters)))))
```

This only leaves crossword-erase-command, crossword-block-
command, crossword-top-of-column, crossword-bottom-of-column,
and crossword-jump-to-cousin without keybindings (because they have
no obvious equivalents in other ordinary editing modes). Let's bind the first two
as:

```
(define-key crossword-mode-map " " ´crossword-erase-command)
(define-key crossword-mode-map "#" ´crossword-block-command)
```

because those seem natural for clearing a cell and inserting a block, respectively.
For the remaining three, let's use two-keystroke keybindings beginning with **C-c**.
Recall that by convention, **C-c** is the prefix for mode-specific keybindings.

```
(define-key crossword-mode-map "\C-ct"
            ´crossword-top-of-column)
(define-key crossword-mode-map "\C-cb"
```

```
                            ´crossword-bottom-of-column)
      (define-key crossword-mode-map "\C-c\C-c"
                  ´crossword-jump-to-cousin)        ; by analogy with C-x C-x
```

Those are all the keybindings we need for the moment; but unfortunately, like all local keymaps, this one will inherit keybindings from the current global keymap for any keys that aren't locally bound. That means, for example, that there remain several keystrokes that could wreak havoc on our carefully formatted crossword grid. Digits and typographical characters remain bound to **self-insert-command**; **C-w**, **C-k**, and **C-d** can still eradicate part of the buffer; **C-y** can still insert who-knows-what at any given point; and so on.

This situation is partially alleviated with **suppress-keymap**, which causes all self-inserting keys to become undefined. We should call **suppress-keymap** immediately after creating the keymap, before starting to define keys in it.

```
(if crossword-mode-map
    nil
  (setq crossword-mode-map (make-keymap))
  (suppress-keymap crossword-mode-map)
  ...)
```

This only gets rid of self-inserting keys, leaving other dangerous keys like **C-w** and **C-y** lurking about. A more complete (and more drastic) solution is to place a catch-all binding in **crossword-mode-map**:

```
(define-key crossword-mode-map [t] ´undefined)
```

In this call to **define-key**, the "key" argument isn't a string of characters, as we've seen before; it's a vector containing the symbol **t**. Recall that vectors and strings are related; each is a kind of *array*. In fact, a vector of characters means the same thing as a string of characters in a call to **define-key**; and a vector of *symbols* is a useful extension at which we'll look more closely in the next section. But the vector [t] stands for an entry that catches all keystrokes not otherwise bound by this keymap. Normally, if the current local keymap doesn't bind a key, the key's definition is sought in the current global keymap. A binding for [t] means "stop here." So this is a way to disable any keystrokes that we haven't explicitly *en*abled.

Mouse Commands

When running Emacs under a windowing system such as X, the mouse can be used to invoke actions just like keystrokes. In fact, mouse actions are under the control of the same keymaps that contain the bindings for ordinary keys. The main difference is in how Emacs looks up the binding.

The keymap data structure can be a vector, an assoc list, or a combination of the two. When you press a key, you generate a numeric code that can be used to index the vector, or it can be used as the search key in an assoc search. When you press a mouse button, you generate a *symbol* that can only be used in an assoc search. The symbol `down-mouse-1`, for instance, represents a press of mouse button 1 (usually the left mouse button), while the symbol `mouse-1` represents button 1 being released. (It is customary for a button press to initiate an action by noting the position of the mouse pointer, and for a button *release* to complete an action by noting whether the mouse has moved since the corresponding button press.) Other mouse-event symbols include `C-down-mouse-2` (pressing the middle mouse button while holding the control key), `S-drag-mouse-3` (shift key plus mouse motion with button 3 depressed), and `double-mouse-1` (after releasing mouse button 1 for the second time in a double-click).

Another difference between mouse input and keyboard input is that when you press a mouse button, there is additional data associated with the button press: for instance, there's the location in the window where you pressed it. Keyboard input always happens at "point," but mouse input happens wherever the mouse is. For this reason, mouse input is represented by a data structure called an *input event*. A command bound to a mouse action can access the current event by calling `last-input-event`, or by using the `e` code letter in its `interactive` declaration.

To demonstrate this, let's define three simple mouse commands for Crossword mode. Mouse button 1 will place the cursor on a grid cell, mouse button 2 will place a block, and mouse button 3 will clear a cell.

In each case, the initial `down-` event will place the cursor and memorize the location in a variable, `crossword-mouse-location`. When the button is released, the new location is compared with the saved location. If they differ, no action is taken.

Let's start with `crossword-mouse-set-point`, the function that responds to the mouse-down event.

```
(defvar crossword-mouse-location nil
  "Location of last mouse-down event, as crossword coords.")

(defun crossword-mouse-set-point (event)
  "Set point with the mouse."
  (interactive "@e")
  (mouse-set-point event)
  (let ((coords (crossword-cursor-coords)))
    (setq crossword-mouse-location coords)
    (crossword-place-cursor (car coords)
                            (cdr coords)))))
```

The `@` in the `interactive` declaration means, "Before doing anything else, find the mouse click (if any) that invoked this command, and select the window in which the mouse was clicked." The code letter `e` tells `interactive` to bundle up the mouse event that invoked this command as a list and assign it to `event`. We don't need any information from the event structure, but we do need to pass it to `mouse-set-point`, which uses the window location data inside `event` to compute a new position for point. Once point is placed, we can call `crossword-cursor-coords` to compute and memorize the resulting grid coordinates. Finally we call `crossword-place-cursor`, because each grid cell is two screen columns wide and `mouse-set-point` may have placed the cursor in the wrong column of the selected cell.

Here's how to set up the bindings for all three mouse-down events:

```
(define-key crossword-mode-map [down-mouse-1]
        'crossword-mouse-set-point)
(define-key crossword-mode-map [down-mouse-2]
        'crossword-mouse-set-point)
(define-key crossword-mode-map [down-mouse-3]
        'crossword-mouse-set-point)
```

Now for the individual mouse-up actions. Releasing button 1 is supposed to do the same thing as pressing button 1, so simply bind `mouse-1` to the same command as `down-mouse-1`:

```
(define-key crossword-mode-map [mouse-1]
        'crossword-mouse-set-point)
```

Here are mouse commands for placing a block and erasing a cell:

```
(defun crossword-mouse-block (event)
  "Place a block with the mouse."
  (interactive "@e")
  (mouse-set-point event)
  (let ((coords (crossword-cursor-coords)))
    (if (equal coords crossword-mouse-location)
        (crossword-block-command))))

(defun crossword-mouse-erase (event)
  "Erase a cell with the mouse."
  (interactive "@e")
  (mouse-set-point event)
  (let ((coords (crossword-cursor-coords)))
    (if (equal coords crossword-mouse-location)
        (crossword-erase-command))))
```

and here are the bindings for those commands:

```
(define-key crossword-mode-map [mouse-2]
        'crossword-mouse-block)
(define-key crossword-mode-map [mouse-3]
        'crossword-mouse-erase)
```

Menu Commands

We still have no user command for checking the crossword grid for one-letter words; but we do have `crossword-one-letter-p`, defined back in the section on "One-Letter Words" earlier in this chapter. Let's use that to define a command, `crossword-find-singleton`, that finds a one-letter word in the grid (if one exists) and moves the cursor there.

```
(defun crossword-find-singleton ()
  "Jump to a one-letter word, if one exists."
  (interactive)
  (let ((row 0)
        (size (crossword-size crossword-grid))
        (result nil))
    (while (and (< row size)
                (null result))
      (let ((column 0))
        (while (and (< column size)
                    (null result))
          (if (crossword-one-letter-p crossword-grid
                                      row column)
              (setq result (cons row column)))
          (setq column (+ column 1)))))
      (setq row (+ row 1)))
    (if result
        (crossword-place-cursor (car result)
                                (cdr result))
      (message "No one-letter words."))))
```

This function iterates over every cell in the grid, testing whether it's a one-letter word, stopping when it finds the first one or displaying the message, "No one-letter words."

We can now bind this function to a key. **C-c 1** suggests itself.

```
(define-key crossword-mode-map "\C-c1"
            'crossword-find-singleton)
```

But checking for one-letter words isn't likely to be a very common operation, like cursor motion and other commands. The user may not wish to memorize a keybinding for it. Since it will be infrequently used, it's a good candidate for placement in a menu.

Defining menu items is easy, and involves yet another aspect of keymaps. First we must define a new keymap to contain the items that belong on a single menu "card." Later we'll arrange for this menu card to have a top-level menubar entry called "Crossword."

```
(defvar crossword-menu-map nil
  "Menu for Crossword mode.")

(if crossword-menu-map
```

```
                nil
        (setq crossword-menu-map (make-sparse-keymap "Crossword"))
        (define-key crossword-menu-map [find-singleton]
                    '("Find singleton" . crossword-find-singleton)))
```

Menu keymaps must have an "overall prompt string." That's the meaning of the optional argument `"Crossword"` in this call to `make-sparse-keymap`.

Our menu card has only one entry at the moment. It is bound to the made-up event symbol, `find-singleton`. The binding for that "event" is a cons cell containing the string, `"Find singleton"`, and the symbol `crossword-find-singleton`. The string is used on the menu as the menu item description. The symbol is the name of the function to invoke when the menu item is selected. The made-up event symbol `find-singleton` is meaningless, other than that it must be different from all other such symbols on the same menu card.

In order to place this menu card under a heading in the overall menu bar, we must choose another symbol to stand for the menu card as a whole; we'll use `crossword`. Now, installing the menu card is a simple matter of binding the menu keymap to the made-up event sequence `[menu-bar crossword]`.

```
        (define-key crossword-mode-map [menu-bar crossword]
                (cons "Crossword" crossword-menu-map))
```

This time, the binding is placed in `crossword-mode-map`, which is the way to make the entries in `crossword-menu-map` "reachable" from the set of keymaps in use. The event symbol `menu-bar` represents the menubar as a whole. The event sequence `[menu-bar crossword]` selects the Crossword menu keymap, and the event sequence `[menu-bar crossword find-singleton]` means the user navigated the menus to select the "Find singleton" item.

Tracking Unauthorized Changes

Suppose that, in spite of our precautions against unwanted buffer-modifying commands, the user manages to invoke one anyway. The state of the crossword grid on the screen won't match the data structure in `crossword-grid`. How can we recover?

One way is to attach a function to `after-change-functions` (see the section called "Clever Approach" in Chapter 4) that is invoked every time the buffer changes. If the change was "unauthorized," we must somehow resynchronize the buffer and the `crossword-grid` data structure.

What's "unauthorized"? Trivially, it's the opposite of "authorized," so let's add a mechanism to "authorize" changes to the buffer.

```
        (defvar crossword-changes-authorized nil
          "Are changes currently authorized?")
```

```
(make-variable-buffer-local 'crossword-changes-authorized)

(defmacro crossword-authorize (&rest subexprs)
  "Execute subexpressions, authorizing changes."
  '(let ((crossword-changes-authorized t))
     ,@subexprs))
```

This is a macro that can be wrapped around function bodies where buffer
changes happen. It temporarily sets `crossword-changes-authorized` to `t`,
executes the function body, then reverts `crossword-changes-authorized` to
its previous value. By default, changes are not authorized. So to prevent the user
from corrupting the buffer, we must rewrite `crossword-insert-grid` and
`crossword-update-display` to authorize the changes they make:

```
(defun crossword-insert-grid (crossword)
  "Insert CROSSWORD into the current buffer."
  (crossword-authorize
    (mapcar 'crossword-insert-row crossword)))

(defun crossword-update-display (crossword)
  "Called after a change, keeps the display up to date."
  (crossword-authorize
    (let* ((coords (crossword-cursor-coords))
           (cousin-coords (crossword-cousin-position crossword
                                                     (car coords)
                                                     (cdr coords))))
      (save-excursion
        (crossword-place-cursor (car coords)
                                (cdr coords))
        (delete-char 2)
        (crossword-insert-cell (crossword-ref crossword
                                              (car coords)
                                              (cdr coords)))
        (crossword-place-cursor (car cousin-coords)
                                (cdr cousin-coords))
        (delete-char 2)
        (crossword-insert-cell (crossword-ref crossword
                                              (car cousin-coords)
                                              (cdr cousin-coords)))))))
```

and we must attach a function to `after-change-functions` that detects
changes made when `crossword-changes-authorized` is not true:

```
(defun crossword-after-change-function (start end len)
  "Recover if this change is not authorized."
  (if crossword-changes-authorized
      nil        ; do nothing if this change is authorized
    recover somehow))

(make-local-hook 'after-change-functions)
(add-hook 'after-change-functions
          'crossword-after-change-function)
```

Recognizing that many individual changes can occur during the course of executing a single user command, we should not try to "recover somehow" more than once per command. This means that *after* the current command completes (and after possibly many changes), we should check to see whether any unauthorized changes occurred, and resynchronize *then*. Therefore we also need to install a function in `post-command-hook` (which executes once after each complete user command).

We'll create another new variable, `crossword-unauthorized-change`, which tells whether an unauthorized change occurred during the current command. We'll revise `crossword-after-change-function` to set it, and a new function, `crossword-post-command-function`, will test it:

```
(defvar crossword-unauthorized-change nil
  "Did an unauthorized change occur?")
(make-variable-buffer-local 'crossword-unauthorized-change)

(defun crossword-after-change-function (start end len)
  "Recover if this change is not authorized."
  (if crossword-changes-authorized
      nil
    (setq crossword-unauthorized-change t)))

(defun crossword-post-command-function ()
  "After each command, recover from unauthorized changes."
  (if crossword-unauthorized-change
      resynchronize)
  (setq crossword-unauthorized-change nil))
```

These calls should be added to **crossword--mode-setup**:

```
(make-local-hook 'after-change-functions)
(add-hook 'after-change-functions
          'crossword-after-change-function)

(make-local-hook 'post-command-hook)
(add-hook 'post-command-hook
          'crossword-post-command-function)
```

When resynchronizing, we have two choices: trust the contents of the buffer and update the data structure in `crossword-grid`; or trust `crossword-grid`, erasing the buffer and reinserting the grid with `crossword-insert-grid`.

On the surface, there doesn't seem to be any reason to trust the visible buffer more than our internal data structure, because the buffer is more likely than the data structure to become corrupted. However, there is one big reason to at least *try* to trust the buffer: the undo command. If the user invokes undo, it will revert the buffer to its state before the last command executed. That's useful. But it won't revert the state of `crossword-grid`. For that, we should use our unauthorized-change detector and attempt to re-parse the grid in the buffer (which we know we can do, since we've already stipulated the existence of **crossword-parse-buffer**). If that fails, presumably because the buffer is incorrectly formatted, we should erase the buffer and insert a corrected grid.

Here's how we can fill in the rest of **crossword-post-command-function** to do this:

```
(defun crossword-post-command-function ()
  "After each command, recover from unauthorized changes."
  (if crossword-unauthorized-change
      (let ((coords (crossword-cursor-coords)))
        (condition-case nil
            (setq crossword-grid (crossword-parse-buffer))
          (error (erase-buffer)
                 (crossword-insert-grid crossword-grid)))
        (crossword-place-cursor (car coords)
                                (cdr coords)))))
  (setq crossword-unauthorized-change nil))
```

This function uses **condition-case**, a special form that is related to **unwind-protect** (which we first encountered in the section entitled "Failing Gracefully" in Chapter 8). Recall that **unwind-protect** looks like this:

```
(unwind-protect
    body
  unwind ...)
```

It executes the *body*, which may or may not complete depending on whether an error is signaled while it's running. Whether or not *body* completes successfully, *unwind* is executed afterward.

The difference between **condition-case** and **unwind-protect** is that **condition-case** contains expressions to execute *only* in the case of an error. It's used like this:

```
(condition-case var
    body
  (symbol₁ handler ...)
  (symbol₂ handler ...)
  ...)
```

If *body* aborts because of a "signaled condition," one of the subsequent handler clauses is executed to "catch" the error. The clause that executes is the one whose *symbol* matches the signaled condition. For now, we're only interested in the signaled condition called **error** (which is signaled when the **error** function is called), so our use of **condition-case** looks like this:

```
(condition-case var
    body
  (error handler ...))
```

If *var* is non-`nil`, then it's the name of a variable into which Emacs will put information about the current error—namely, the arguments to the `error` call that signaled this condition—when one of the handlers runs. But in our example, *var* is `nil` because we don't need access to that information.

We attempt to set `crossword-grid` to the result of calling `crossword-parse-buffer`. If parsing fails, `crossword-parse-buffer` signals an error, which causes the body of the `condition-case` to abort before replacing the value of `crossword-grid`. If that happens, the error handler runs, erasing the buffer and inserting the known-to-be-correct copy of `crossword-grid`.

In either case, we finish by placing the cursor at the grid coordinates we memorized at the beginning of the function; but suppose the buffer is so badly mangled that even trying to memorize the current coordinates fails? We should then have two separate calls to `condition-case`:

```
(defun crossword-post-command-function ()
  "After each command, recover from unauthorized changes."
  (if crossword-unauthorized-change
      (condition-case nil
          (let ((coords (crossword-cursor-coords)))
            (condition-case nil
                (setq crossword-grid (crossword-parse-buffer))
              (error (erase-buffer)
                     (crossword-insert-grid crossword-grid)))
            (crossword-place-cursor (car coords)
                                    (cdr coords)))
        (error (erase-buffer)
               (crossword-insert-grid crossword-grid)
               (crossword-place-cursor 0 0)))
    (setq crossword-unauthorized-change nil)))
```

The outer `condition-case` handles errors in `crossword-cursor-coords`. It erases the buffer, re-inserts the grid, and places the cursor in the upper left corner. The inner `condition-case` handles errors in `crossword-parse-buffer`, erasing and re-inserting the grid, and restoring the memorized cursor position.

Now that we can track and recover from unauthorized changes in the buffer, I recommend removing the catch-all keybinding,

```
(define-key crossword-mode-map [t] 'undefined)
```

from `crossword-mode-map`, which after all is a little *too* restrictive, making many harmless and useful commands as inaccessible as **C-k** and **C-y**.

Since crosswords are stored in plain text files, it's still possible for users to corrupt them by editing them with another editor, or with Emacs when not in Crossword mode. But most such changes would cause Crossword mode to fail on startup when it tries to parse the corrupted file.

Parsing the Buffer

Here is a definition for `crossword-parse-buffer`:

```
(defun crossword-parse-buffer ()
  "Parse the crossword grid in the current buffer."
  (save-excursion
    (goto-char (point-min))
    (let* ((line (crossword-parse-line))
           (size (length line))
           (result (make-crossword size))
           (row 1))
      (crossword--handle-parsed-line line 0 result)
      (while (< row size)
        (forward-line 1)
        (setq line (crossword-parse-line))
        (if (not (= (length line) size))
            (error "Rows vary in length"))
        (crossword--handle-parsed-line line row result)
        (setq row (+ row 1)))
      result)))
```

It calls `crossword-parse-line`, which parses a line of text and returns it in
list form. The length of that list gives us the horizontal and vertical size of the
crossword grid (remember, our crossword grids are always square). We then call
`crossword-parse-line` on the `size` − 1 remaining lines. Each time we parse
a line, we fill in a row of the crossword data structure held in `result` by calling
`crossword--handle-parsed-line`, which we can define like this:

```
(defun crossword--handle-parsed-line (line row grid)
  "Take LINE and put it in ROW of GRID."
  (let ((column 0))
    (while line
      (cond ((eq (car line) 'block)
             (crossword-store-block grid row column))
            ((eq (car line) nil)
             (crossword-clear-cell grid row column))
            ((numberp (car line))
             (crossword-store-letter grid row column (car line))))
      (setq line (cdr line))
      (setq column (+ column 1)))))
```

Here's `crossword-parse-line`, which does the real work of `crossword-parse-buffer`:

```
(defun crossword-parse-line ()
  "Parse a line of a Crossword buffer."
  (beginning-of-line)
  (let ((result nil))
    (while (not (eolp))
      (cond ((eq (char-after (point)) ?#)
             (setq result (cons 'block result)))
            ((eq (char-after (point)) ?.)
```

```
                    (setq result (cons nil result)))
                   ((eq (char-after (point)) ??)
                    (setq result (cons nil result)))
                   ((looking-at "[A-Za-z]")
                    (setq result (cons (char-after (point))
                                       result)))
                   (t (error "Unrecognized character"))))
            (forward-char 1)
            (if (eq (char-after (point)) ?\ )
                (forward-char 1)
              (error "Non-blank between columns")))
          (reverse result)))
```

This moves along a line two characters at a time. The first one is expected to be pound sign (#), period (.), question mark (?, which is treated the same way as .), or a letter. The cond expression tells us what to do in each case. If it's none of those, an error is signaled—"Unrecognized character." Otherwise, the next character is expected to be the blank space separating columns of the grid. Again, if it isn't, an error is signaled.

The resulting data is accumulated in result using cons, which means that the first item on the line appears at the end of the list, the second appears next-to-last, and so on. So the last thing the function does is call reverse to produce a correctly ordered list.

One more thing: when an Emacs mode is appropriate only for editing specially prepared text, the mode symbol should be given the special property like this:

```
(put 'crossword-mode 'mode-class 'special)
```

This tells Emacs not to use Crossword mode as the default mode for any buffers, since it only works on buffers that already contain parseable crossword grids.

Word Finder

So far, Crossword mode isn't much more than very fancy graph paper. Apart from keeping track of what letters you want to put where, it offers little help to the aspiring crossword puzzle creator. The really hard part of designing a crossword puzzle isn't keeping track of what belongs in each grid square; it's trying to find words that will fit with other words you've already chosen, such as when you need a five-letter word whose last three letters have to be "fas".

It's possible to use standard UNIX utilities to find suitable words. The UNIX program *grep*, given a suitable regular expression, can find matching words from a word file. Most UNIXes have a word file in */usr/dict/words* or */usr/lib/dict/words* or, on modern GNU systems, */usr/local/share/dict/words*.

If the word file contains one word per line, it is possible to find a five-letter word ending in "fas" with this UNIX command:

```
grep -i '^..fas$'  word-file
```

(The `-i` tells *grep* to match case-insensitively.) Running this command gives us the answer, "sofas".

Wouldn't it be nice if we could just hit a key and have Emacs construct the correct regular expression and run *grep* for us?

Here's how it would work. With the cursor on a grid cell, you press **C-c h** to find a word that fits horizontally through the current cell, **C-c v** to find a word that fits vertically. In each case, the function searches left and right, or up and down, for the nearest enclosing blocks. The intervening cells are used to construct a regular expression. Empty or "letter" cells become dots (`.`); letters become themselves. The regular expression is bracketed with `^` at the beginning and `$` at the end. This regular expression is handed to *grep*, whose output appears in a temporary buffer.

First Try

For simplicity, let's start by designing just the horizontal version of this command. Let's call it **crossword-hwords**. The first thing we do is get the cursor position and test the type of the current cell.

```
(defun crossword-hwords ()
  "Pop up a buffer listing horizontal words for current cell."
  (interactive)
  (let ((coords (crossword-cursor-coords)))
    (if (eq (crossword-ref crossword-grid
                           (car coords)
                           (cdr coords))
            'block)
        (error "Cannot use this command on a block"))
```

We abort if the current cell is a block. No words can cross a block (horizontally or vertically). Otherwise:

```
(let ((start (- (cdr coords) 1))
      (end (+ (cdr coords) 1)))
```

We'll use **start** and **end** to record the column number of the first block to the left and the first block to the right of the current cell.

```
(while (not (crossword-block-p crossword-grid
                               (car coords)
                               start))
  (setq start (- start 1)))
```

This moves `start` to the left until we hit a block. Remember that `crossword-block-p` maintains the fiction that the border of the grid is surrounded by "blocks," so this loop is guaranteed to terminate when we reach the edge of the grid at the latest.

```
(while (not (crossword-block-p crossword-grid
                               (car coords)
                               end))
       (setq end (+ end 1)))
```

This does the same thing with `end`, but to the right instead of to the left.

```
(let ((regexp "^")
      (column (+ start 1)))
  (while (< column end)
```

This prepares to build up the regular expression, starting one cell after `start` and ending one cell before `end`.

```
(let ((cell (crossword-ref crossword-grid
                           (car coords)
                           column)))
  (if (numberp cell)
      (setq regexp (concat regexp
                           (char-to-string cell)))
    (setq regexp (concat regexp "."))))
```

This tests whether the present cell in the `while` loop is a letter. If it is, we add that letter to the regular expression; otherwise we add a dot (`.`).

(We use `char-to-string` to turn a character such as `?a` into a string such as `"a"`, since only strings may be passed to `concat`.)

Now we advance `column` for the next iteration of the loop:

```
(setq column (+ column 1)))
```

After the loop exits, we end the regular expression with `$`:

```
(setq regexp (concat regexp "$"))
```

Next, we create a buffer to hold the *grep* output:

```
(let ((buffer (get-buffer-create "*Crossword words*")))
```

The function `get-buffer-create` returns a *buffer object* with the specified name. If a buffer of that name already exists, that buffer is returned, otherwise a suitable buffer is created. (When you don't want to reuse an old buffer, you can use `generate-new-buffer` to unconditionally create a new one.)

```
(set-buffer buffer)
```

We temporarily select the `*Crossword words*` buffer, making it "current." The effect of `set-buffer` lasts only for the duration of the current command, and doesn't change the user's idea of the current buffer. (For that, we would use `switch-to-buffer`.)

```
(erase-buffer)
```

This makes sure the buffer is empty, in case we're reusing a buffer that's lingering from a previous run of **crossword-hwords**.

Now for the call to **call-process**, the function that invokes the *grep* program:

```
(call-process "grep"
              nil t nil
              "-i" regexp
              "/usr/local/share/dict/words")
```

Instead of invoking *grep* by name, it would be better to create a variable—say, **crossword-grep-program**—and use it in the above call instead of **"grep"**. If another *grep* program is desired, the user can change the variable. We can do the same thing for the *words* file, declaring and using a variable called **crossword-words-file** instead of explicitly naming */usr/local/share/dict/words*.

The arguments **nil**, **t**, and **nil** in the middle of the **call-process** call mean:

1. "The program does not need 'standard input'." Its input will come from the file named in its command-line arguments. If a string is used instead of **nil**, that string names a file to use as input to the program. If **t** is given, the current buffer is used as input to the program.

2. "Send output to the current buffer" (i.e., the ***Crossword words*** buffer). An argument of **nil** means "discard the output." An argument of **0** means "discard the output and return immediately (don't wait for the program to finish)." An argument that is a buffer object means to send output to that buffer.

   The argument may also be a two-element list, where each element is one of the arguments just described. The first element of the list tells Emacs where to put the program's "standard output." The second element tells Emacs where to put the program's "standard error."

3. "Do not incrementally redisplay the buffer as data arrives" (which would slow things down). Emacs waits for the program to finish before showing any of the output in the ***Crossword words*** buffer.

The remaining arguments to **call-process** are passed as command-line arguments to *grep*: **-i** to turn off case-sensitivity; **regexp**, which contains the regular expression we've computed; and **/usr/local/share/dict/words**, the file that *grep* will search for matches.

The last thing `crossword-hwords` must do is to show the `*Crossword words*` buffer containing the output of *grep*. This is done with `display-buffer`:

```
(display-buffer buffer))))))
```

This completes our first version of `crossword-hwords`.

This version of `crossword-hwords` is fine if you always want to find words that completely fill the space between two existing blocks; but sometimes you'd settle for shorter words and insert more blocks as necessary. For instance, if you have a crossword row that looks like this:

```
. . . . . . . a d a c . . . .
```

and you press **C-c h**, you'll get back one suggestion: "asclepiadaceous". But you might be satisfied with turning this line into:

```
. . . . # h e a d a c h e # #
```

The problem is, `crossword-hwords` computes the regular expression `^.......adac....$`, but "headache" doesn't match that regexp.

We could try removing the `^` and the `$` from the regexp, along with the leading and trailing dots, leaving us with `adac`. If that regexp is handed to *grep*, it *will* find "headache". But it will also find "tetracadactyly", which is one letter too long (and which has the `adac` in the wrong place at any rate).

Second Try

A good way to solve this problem is to construct regexps that look like this: `^.?.?.?.?.?.?.?adac.?.?.?.?$`. Each `.?` matches zero characters or one; so the overall regexp matches from zero to seven characters, followed by "adac", followed by zero to four more characters. This pattern includes "headache" and excludes "tetracadactyly".

Let's give `crossword-hwords` another try:

```
(defun crossword-hwords ()
  "Pop up a buffer listing horizontal words for current cell."
  (interactive)
  (let ((coords (crossword-cursor-coords)))
    (if (eq (crossword-ref crossword-grid
                           (car coords)
                           (cdr coords))
            'block)
        (error "Cannot use this command on a block"))
    (let ((start (- (cdr coords) 1))
          (end (+ (cdr coords) 1)))
      (while (not (crossword-block-p crossword-grid
                                     (car coords)
                                     start))
```

```
                (setq start (- start 1)))
         (while (not (crossword-block-p crossword-grid
                                        (car coords)
                                        end))
                (setq end (+ end 1)))
```

So far, this is the same as before: `start` and `end` point to the enclosing blocks.

Now let's introduce a new concept into this function: that of the regexp's *core*. We'll use this term to refer to the part of the regexp that must match character-for-character.

Leading and trailing blanks don't have to be matched; they're optional. But everything starting from the first letter and ending at the last letter *must* be matched, even intervening blanks. So when we construct the regexp to match this line:

```
    . . . b a r . f o o . . . . .
```

the "core" is `bar.foo`, and the overall regexp has three optional characters at the beginning and five at the end: `^.?.?.?bar.foo.?.?.?.?.?$` is the final result.

This means that we must find the core in the crossword grid. Any blanks outside the core must be turned into `.?` in the regexp. Any blanks inside the core must be turned into `.` (a dot).

We'll start at `start` and `end` and work our way inward:

```
         (let ((corestart (+ start 1))
               (coreend (- end 1)))
           (while (null (crossword-ref crossword-grid
                                       (car coords)
                                       corestart))
             (setq corestart (+ corestart 1)))
           (while (null (crossword-ref crossword-grid
                                       (car coords)
                                       coreend))
             (setq coreend (- coreend 1)))
```

This advances `corestart` rightward and `coreend` leftward to skip over blank cells. Note that there may be no "core" between `start` and `end`. In this case, `corestart` advances all the way to `end` and `coreend` backs up all the way to `start`. That's okay, because the way we use `corestart` and `coreend` in this next bit of code is insensitive to that peculiarity:

```
         (let ((regexp "^")
               (column (+ start 1)))
           (while (< column end)
             (if (or (< column corestart)
                     (> column coreend))
                 (setq regexp
                       (concat regexp ".?"))
```

Here, if we haven't yet reached the core, or if we've already passed it, we append
`.?` to `regexp`. Note that if there was no core, we *always* append `.?`.[*]

If we're in the core, we proceed exactly as before—except that we now invoke
egrep instead of *grep*, because *grep* doesn't understand the ? syntax in regular
expressions and *egrep* does:

```
              (let ((cell (crossword-ref crossword-grid
                                         (car coords)
                                         column)))
                (if (numberp cell)
                    (setq regexp (concat regexp
                                         (char-to-string cell)))
                  (setq regexp (concat regexp "."))))))
            (setq column (+ column 1)))
          (setq regexp (concat regexp "$"))
          (let ((buffer (get-buffer-create "*Crossword words*")))
            (set-buffer buffer)
            (erase-buffer)
            (call-process "egrep"
                          nil t nil
                          "-i" regexp
                          "/usr/local/share/dict/words")
            (display-buffer buffer)))))))
```

Again, you may wish to use variables called `crossword-egrep-program` and
`crossword-words-file` instead of referring to *egrep* and */usr/local/share/dict/
words* by name. In fact, the remainder of this chapter will take that approach.

The command `crossword-vwords`—the vertical counterpart of `crossword-`
`hwords`—is substantially identical to `crossword-hwords`. Defining it, along
with factoring out common code into a separate function for both commands to
use, is left as an exercise for the reader.

Asynchronous egrep

The way `crossword-hwords` is presently written, it runs *egrep*, waits for it to
finish, then displays its output. But suppose you're using some program other
than *egrep*; or suppose your setting for `crossword-words-file` is a file on the
far side of a slow network. It could take `crossword-hwords` quite a while to
run, and Emacs will be unavailable the whole time.

It would be better if `crossword-hwords` could start the *egrep* program running,
and let it run "in the background" while you continue to interact with Emacs. For
this, we can use Emacs's *asynchronous process* objects.

---

[*] Invoking `crossword-hwords` where there is no "core" isn't exactly an error, but it might be worth
alerting the user in such a case, since the resulting regexp would match *all* words in the dictionary that
are the right length or shorter—probably not what the user wishes to see!

An asynchronous process object is a Lisp data structure that represents another running program on your computer. New processes are created with `start-process`, which resembles `call-process` (which we saw in the previous section). Unlike `call-process`, however, `start-process` does not wait for the executed program to complete. Instead, it returns a process object.

There are many things one can do with a process object. You can send input to a running process; you can send signals; you can kill the process. You can query the process's state (e.g., to find out whether it's running or has exited). You can associate the process with an Emacs buffer.

Let's rewrite `crossword-hwords` to use `start-process`. To save space, we'll concentrate on just the end of `crossword-hwords`. Here's the original version:

```
(let ((buffer (get-buffer-create "*Crossword words*")))
  (set-buffer buffer)
  (erase-buffer)
  (call-process crossword-egrep-program
                nil t nil
                "-i" regexp
                crossword-words-file)
  (display-buffer buffer))))))
```

Here's a version using `start-process`.

```
(let ((buffer (get-buffer-create "*Crossword words*")))
  (set-buffer buffer)
  (erase-buffer)
  (start-process "egrep"
                buffer
                crossword-egrep-program
                "-i" regexp
                crossword-words-file)
  (display-buffer buffer))))))
```

The *only* change here was to replace `call-process` with `start-process` and shuffle the arguments around appropriately. The first argument to `start-process` (`"egrep"` in this example) is a name that Emacs uses internally to refer to the process. (It is not necessarily the name of the program to run.) Next comes the buffer, if any, that will receive the process's output; then the program to run, and its arguments.

As soon as the process is started, `start-process` returns, which means `display-buffer` is called immediately. But we may not wish for the *Crossword words* buffer to appear right away. It would be better if it only appeared after *egrep* has run. So we would like a way to find out when the process exits. When that happens, that's when we want to call `display-buffer`.

To do this, we need to install a *sentinel* on the process object. A sentinel is a Lisp function that gets called when the process changes state. We're interested in the state change that happens when the program exits; but state changes can also happen when the process receives a signal.

Here's a version that calls `start-process`, then installs a sentinel to display the buffer when the process exits. In order to install the sentinel, we must save the process object that is returned from `start-process` so we can pass it to `set-process-sentinel`:

```
(let ((buffer (get-buffer-create "*Crossword words*")))
  (set-buffer buffer)
  (erase-buffer)
  (let ((process
          (start-process "egrep"
                         buffer
                         crossword-egrep-program
                         "-i" regexp crossword-words-file)))
     (set-process-sentinel process
                           'crossword--egrep-sentinel)))))))
```

We can define `crossword--egrep-sentinel` as:

```
(defun crossword--egrep-sentinel (process string)
  "When PROCESS exits, display its buffer."
  (if (eq (process-status process)
          'exit)
      (display-buffer (process-buffer process))))
```

Process sentinels are called with two arguments: the process object, and a string describing the state change. We ignore the string. Instead, we test the process's status to see whether it has exited. If it has, we display the process's buffer, which we find with `process-buffer`. This is the buffer originally associated with the process in the `start-process` call.

Suppose we don't want to wait for *egrep* to exit before we display the buffer, but we don't want to display the buffer immediately either. Instead, we want to display the buffer as soon as the first input arrives in it. For this, we need to install a *filter* on the process object.

A filter is a function that gets called whenever output from the process arrives. When a process has no filter, output goes into the associated buffer. But when there is a filter, the filter function is responsible for putting the output wherever it belongs. So let's modify our example a little more, to use a filter function that (a) puts output in the buffer and (b) displays the buffer:

```
(let ((buffer (get-buffer-create "*Crossword words*")))
  (set-buffer buffer)
  (erase-buffer)
  (let ((process
          (start-process "egrep"
                         buffer
                         crossword-egrep-program
```

```
                              "-i" regexp
                              crossword-words-file)))
         (set-process-filter process
                              'crossword--egrep-filter)
         (set-process-sentinel process
                              'crossword--egrep-sentinel)))))))))
```

We're keeping the sentinel in addition to the filter so that the buffer is sure to be displayed when *egrep* exits, even if there was no output.

Here's how we can define **crossword--egrep-filter**:

```
(defun crossword--egrep-filter (process string)
  "Handle output from PROCESS."
  (let ((buffer (process-buffer process)))
    (save-excursion
      (set-buffer buffer)
      (goto-char (point-max))
      (insert string))
    (display-buffer buffer)))
```

Filters are called with two arguments: the process object, and the chunk of output that has just arrived, as a string. We find the process's buffer and insert the output at the end. Then we make sure the buffer is displayed by calling **display-buffer**.

Because filters (and sentinels) can be called at unpredictable times (which is the nature of asynchronous programming), they must take care not to have any unexpected side effects. This means there are some things they must do that synchronous functions needn't worry about. For example, every time a command finishes, Emacs restores the selected buffer; so during the command, functions may call **set-buffer** to change buffers without affecting what the user sees. But resetting the selected buffer only happens when a command ends—around the same time that **post-command-hook** is invoked. Since an asynchronous function may be invoked when there is no command in progress, any calls to **set-buffer** may not be reset, and so may have unwanted effects. That's why **crossword--egrep-filter** uses **save-excursion**.

One more thing about **start-process**. When Emacs creates the process, it maintains a connection to it (through which input and output flow) using either UNIX *pipes* or UNIX *pseudo-ttys*. Pipes are more appropriate for non-interactive processes like *egrep*, while pseudo-ttys, or *ptys*, are more appropriate for interactive programs—e.g., command interpreters like the UNIX shell. The kind of connection that is created by **start-process** is controlled by the variable **process-connection-type**—**nil** means use pipes, **t** means use ptys. Though it's a little baroque, it's a good idea always to wrap calls to **start-process** inside a **let** call where you temporarily set **process-connection-type** to the desired value, as in:

```
...
(let ((process-connection-type nil))
  (start-process "egrep"
                 buffer
                 crossword-egrep-program
                 "-i" regexp crossword-words-file))
...
```

Choosing Words

Now let's make it possible to select words from the `*Crossword words*` buffer and have them automatically inserted in the crossword grid.

The first thing we'll have to do is store some extra information in the `*Crossword words*` buffer—that is, in local variables in that buffer. If we expect to be able to press **RET** (say) on one of the words in that buffer and have it go in the right place in the Crossword buffer, then the `*Crossword words*` buffer will have to know which is the right Crossword buffer and where to place the word when it's selected.

Here's the information that must be communicated between buffers.

1. The value of `start + 1`—i.e., the place where the word may begin in the grid.

2. Whether the current word search is vertical or horizontal. As before, we'll restrict our examples to the horizontal case, but bear in mind the considerations arising from the two possible directions.

3. Information about the "core" of the regular expression. To explain why this is necessary, let's reconsider our earlier example: the crossword-grid line that looks like this:

   ```
   . . . . . . . a d a c . . . .
   ```

   The regular expression that `crossword-hwords` generates for this line is `^.?.?.?.?.?.?.?adac.?.?.?.?$`. The "core" is `adac`, with a "prefix" of `.?.?.?.?.?.?.?` and a "suffix" of `.?.?.?.?.`. When the user selects, for instance, the word `adactyl` from the `*Crossword words*` buffer, where in the line should it be placed? Should it be placed like this?

   ```
   a d a c t y l a d a c . . . .
   ```

   Of course not; it should be placed like this:

   ```
   . . . . . . . a d a c t y l .
   ```

   In order to place the word correctly within the line, it will help to know that the prefix is seven characters long, and that a match for the "core" of the regexp can be found at position zero in the word `adactyl`. In general, if the prefix is *p* characters long, and a match for the core can be found at position *m* in the chosen word, then we should skip *p* - *m* characters before beginning the word in the allotted space.

In order to store these variables locally in the `*Crossword words*` buffer, and in order to have a keybinding for **RET** that means "select the word that the cursor is on," let's define a little major mode for that buffer. Let's call it `crossword-words-mode`. Here it is:

```
(defvar crossword-words-mode-map nil
  "Keymap for crossword-words mode.")

(defvar crossword-words-crossword-buffer nil
  "The associated crossword buffer.")
(defvar crossword-words-core nil
  "The core of the regexp.")
(defvar crossword-words-prefix-len nil
  "Length of the regexp prefix.")
(defvar crossword-words-row nil
  "Row number where the word can start.")
(defvar crossword-words-column nil
  "Column number where the word can start.")
(defvar crossword-words-vertical-p nil
  "Whether the current search is vertical.")

(if crossword-words-mode-map
    nil
  (setq crossword-words-mode-map (make-sparse-keymap))
  (define-key crossword-words-mode-map "\r" 'crossword-words-select))
```

The return key is written `"\r"` in strings.

```
(defun crossword-words-mode ()
  "Major mode for Crossword word-list buffer."
  (interactive)
  (kill-all-local-variables)
  (setq major-mode 'crossword-words-mode)
  (setq mode-name "Crossword-words")
  (use-local-map crossword-words-mode-map)
  (make-local-variable 'crossword-words-crossword-buffer)
  (make-local-variable 'crossword-words-core)
  (make-local-variable 'crossword-words-prefix-len)
  (make-local-variable 'crossword-words-row)
  (make-local-variable 'crossword-words-column)
  (make-local-variable 'crossword-words-vertical-p)
  (run-hooks 'crossword-words-mode-hook))
```

We haven't yet defined `crossword-words-select`. We'll get to that in a moment. First, let's rewrite `crossword-hwords` to do two things:

- It must preserve information about the core of the regexp and the length of the prefix. To keep things simple, let's call it an error if there is no core, and abort the operation.

- When it creates the word-list buffer, it must place it in Crossword-words mode and set the various local variables.

Here it is:

```
(defun crossword-hwords ()
  "Pop up a buffer listing horizontal words for current cell."
  (interactive)
  (let ((coords (crossword-cursor-coords)))
    (if (eq (crossword-ref crossword-grid
                           (car coords)
                           (cdr coords))
            'block)
        (error "Cannot use this command on a block"))
    (let ((start (- (cdr coords) 1))
          (end (+ (cdr coords) 1)))
      (while (not (crossword-block-p crossword-grid
                                     (car coords)
                                     start))
        (setq start (- start 1)))
      (while (not (crossword-block-p crossword-grid
                                     (car coords)
                                     end))
        (setq end (+ end 1)))
      (let ((corestart (+ start 1))
            (coreend (- end 1)))
        (while (null (crossword-ref crossword-grid
                                    (car coords)
                                    corestart))
          (setq corestart (+ corestart 1)))
```

So far, same as before.

```
        (if (= corestart end)
            (error "No core for regexp"))
```

This time, if there is no core, abort with an error.

```
        (while (null (crossword-ref crossword-grid
                                    (car coords)
                                    coreend))
          (setq coreend (- coreend 1)))
        (let ((core "")
              (column corestart)
              (regexp "^"))
```

We're going to construct **regexp** from the inside out this time, starting by separately computing the core:

```
          (while (<= column coreend)
            (let ((cell (crossword-ref crossword-grid
                                       (car coords)
                                       column)))
              (if (numberp cell)
                  (setq core (concat core
```

```
                                         (char-to-string cell)))
                       (setq core (concat core "."))))
            (setq column (+ column 1)))
```

Now `core` holds the core of the regexp.

This constructs the prefix for the regexp:

```
            (setq column (+ start 1))
            (while (< column corestart)
              (setq regexp (concat regexp ".?"))
              (setq column (+ column 1)))
```

...This appends the core to the prefix:

```
            (setq regexp (concat regexp core))
```

...and this appends the suffix:

```
            (setq column (+ coreend 1))
            (while (< column end)
              (setq regexp (concat regexp ".?"))
              (setq column (+ column 1)))
            (setq regexp (concat regexp "$"))
```

Now let's move to the word-list buffer, but this time let's memorize the current buffer in `crossword-buffer` so we can easily refer to it later:

```
            (let ((buffer (get-buffer-create "*Crossword words*"))
                  (crossword-buffer (current-buffer)))
              (set-buffer buffer)
```

Now let's put `*Crossword words*` in Crossword-words mode:

```
            (crossword-words-mode)
```

and set its buffer-local variables:

```
              (setq crossword-words-crossword-buffer
                    crossword-buffer)
              (setq crossword-words-core core)
              (setq crossword-words-prefix-len (- corestart
                                                  (+ start 1)))
              (setq crossword-words-row (car coords))
              (setq crossword-words-column (+ start 1))
              (setq crossword-words-vertical-p nil)
```

The rest is the same as we've already seen.

```
              (erase-buffer)
              (let ((process
                      (let ((process-connection-type nil))
                        (start-process "egrep"
                                       buffer
                                       crossword-egrep-program
                                       "-i" regexp
                                       crossword-words-file))))
```

```
          (set-process-filter process
                              'crossword--egrep-filter)
          (set-process-sentinel process
                              'crossword--egrep-sentinel)))))))))
```

Now all that remains is to define **crossword-words-select**. Its purpose is to figure out the word that point is on, find a match for the core within that word, then figure out where in the crossword grid the word belongs, and put it there.

```
(defun crossword-words-select ()
  (interactive)
  (beginning-of-line)
  (let* ((wordstart (point))
         (word (progn (end-of-line)
                      (buffer-substring wordstart
                                        (point)))))
```

Now **word** contains the word from the selected line.

Next we find a match for the core in **word** using **string-match**:

```
         (corematch (string-match crossword-words-core
                                  word))
```

Now **corematch** contains the position within **word** of a match for the core.

```
         (vertical-p crossword-words-vertical-p)
```

This copies the buffer-local variable **crossword-words-vertical-p** into the temporary variable **vertical-p**, since we'll need to refer to it back in the Crossword buffer (where **crossword-words-vertical-p** isn't defined).

```
         (window (selected-window)))
```

This memorizes the window that contains the word-list buffer. Later in this function, we'll delete that window (but not the buffer) since the user is presumably finished with it after selecting a word.

```
    (if (not corematch)
        (error "This word does not fit"))
```

This shouldn't be possible—unless the user has altered the contents of the word-list buffer, so it's a good idea to test for it.

```
    (let ((row (if vertical-p
                   (+ crossword-words-row
                      (- crossword-words-prefix-len corematch))
                 crossword-words-row))
          (column (if vertical-p
                      crossword-words-column
                    (+ crossword-words-column
                       (- crossword-words-prefix-len corematch)))))
```

Now **row** and **column** designate the position in the crossword grid where we should begin placing the word.

```
(i 0))
```

We'll use i to iterate over the characters of **word**, adding them to the grid one at a time.

```
(switch-to-buffer crossword-words-crossword-buffer)
```

This switches to the Crossword buffer using **switch-to-buffer**, not **set-buffer**. This means that the Crossword buffer will still be selected after this command finishes.

```
(while (< i (length word))
  (crossword-store-letter crossword-grid
                          row
                          column
                          (aref word i))
  (crossword-update-display crossword-grid
                            row
                            column)
  (setq i (+ i 1))
  (if vertical-p
      (setq row (+ row 1))
    (setq column (+ column 1))))))
```

This stores each letter in the grid, moving horizontally or vertically as appropriate. After updating the data structure with **crossword-store-letter**, keep the display in sync by calling **crossword-update-display**.

When we call **crossword-update-display**, we don't want to update the cell that contains the cursor; we want to update the cell at **row** and **column** where we've just stored a letter. So let's pretend, for now, that **crossword-update-display** takes grid coordinates as optional arguments, and uses those instead of the cursor position if they're given. We'll revise **crossword-update-display** below.

Finally, let's delete the Crossword-words window so the user can concentrate on the Crossword buffer:

```
(delete-window window)))
```

Here's a version of **crossword-update-display** that takes optional grid coordinates, using the cursor position if the optional arguments are not specified.

```
(defun crossword-update-display (crossword &optional row column)
  "Called after a change, keeps the display up to date."
  (crossword-authorize
   (if (or (null row)
           (null column))
       (let ((coords (crossword-cursor-coords)))
         (setq row (car coords)
               column (cdr coords))))
   (let ((cousin-coords (crossword-cousin-position crossword
                                                   row
```

```
                                                column))))
    (save-excursion
      (crossword-place-cursor row
                              column)
      (delete-char 2)
      (crossword-insert-cell (crossword-ref crossword
                                            row
                                            column))
      (crossword-place-cursor (car cousin-coords)
                              (cdr cousin-coords))
      (delete-char 2)
      (crossword-insert-cell (crossword-ref crossword
                                            (car cousin-coords)
                                            (cdr cousin-coords)))))))))
```

There's just one more thing we have to adjust in this code: we have to solve the problem of ambiguous alignment of selected words.

Ambiguous Alignment

Imagine you have a section of a crossword line that looks like this:

```
# . . . f . #
```

and you press **C-c h** somewhere in that line. The regexp that **crossword-hwords** generates is ^.?.?.?f.?$; its core is **f**.

The word-list buffer fills up with lots of words containing "f". You choose "fluff". What happens?

When you select "fluff", **crossword-words-select** finds a match for the core, "f", at position zero in the word "fluff". This means that it will try to line up the first letter of "fluff" with the "f" that's already in the puzzle, running off the end like so:

```
# . . . f l #
```

In this case, we can't use the first match for the core. But we can't use the last match either, because that will cause the last letter of "fluff" to line up with the "f" in the puzzle, which places one too many letters to the left:

```
# l u f f . #
```

We must align the second "f" in "fluff" with the "f" already in the grid. How can we make the word line up correctly?

The answer is to choose the *rightmost match for the core that begins within the prefix-length*. This ensures that the string to the left of the match is short enough to fit in the prefix, while minimizing the number of characters to the right of the match.

For example, the word "fluff" contains three matches for the core regexp, `f`. The first is at position 0, the second is at position 3, and the third is at position 4. The length of the prefix of the regexp is 3. So the rightmost match for `f` in 'fluff' that begins at or before position 3 is the second one.

Choosing the rightmost match that isn't too far to the right ensures that we fill up at much of the prefix as possible when placing the word in the grid. That, in turn, will ensure that we don't run off the end on the right.

We should therefore replace the following part of **`crossword-words-select`**.

```
(let* (...
        (corematch (string-match crossword-words-core
                          word))
      ...
```

with this:

```
(let* (...
        (corematch
         (let ((bestmatch nil)
               (index 0))
           (while (and index (<= index
                              crossword-words-prefix-len))
             (let ((match (string-match crossword-words-core
                                   word
                                   index)))
               (if (and match
                       (<= match crossword-words-prefix-len))
                   (setq bestmatch match
                         index (+ match 1))
                 (setq index nil))))
           bestmatch))
      ...
```

Here's how that works:

```
(let ((bestmatch nil)
      (index 0))
```

We use **`bestmatch`** to hold the rightmost match so far and **`index`** to denote where to begin the next search. The loop terminates when **`index`** becomes **`nil`** (which is not the same as its initial value of 0).

```
(while (and index (<= index
                   crossword-words-prefix-len))
```

This keeps the **`while`** loop going until we've gone too far to the right (i.e., until we start searching for matches beyond the position **`crossword-words-prefix-len`**).

```
(let ((match (string-match crossword-words-core
                      word
                      index)))
```

Here we use the optional third argument to `string-match`, which is the position in `word` where the search should begin.

```
(if (and match
         (<= match crossword-words-prefix-len))
```

We must make sure `match` is non-`nil` before passing it to `<=`, which accepts only numbers.

If there was a match suitably early, memorize it and begin the next iteration one position to the right; otherwise, escape the loop by setting `index` to `nil`:

```
      (setq bestmatch match
            index (+ match 1))
  (setq index nil))))
```

Finally, return `bestmatch` as the value for `corematch`.

```
  bestmatch)
```

Last Word

We could add features to Crossword mode from now until the cows come home, and it's hard for me to resist the temptation to do just that. For example, once the grid is full, it would be nice to number the squares in the grid and generate lists of Across and Down words. It would also be nice to have cursor motion commands that move around the grid in units of words.

But this is as far as I've taken Crossword mode. I have a book deadline to meet, and besides, no one likes a programmer who doesn't know when to abandon a pet project.

Of course there's no limit to how far *you* can take Crossword mode—or to how far you can take Emacs, in whatever direction you choose.

Conclusion

You are now ready to embark on your Emacs Lisp programming career. The discussion of techniques and tools in this book should accomplish for you what it took me years of experimentation to learn.

As I wrote in the Preface, this book isn't exhaustive in its coverage of the language. There are many interesting areas of Emacs Lisp we haven't covered. We haven't made use of Emacs's "selective display" facility, for example. Selective display allows you to hide and reveal individual lines or portions thereof. We haven't used "text properties" either. Text properties allow you to associate things like colors and fonts and even Lisp actions with the text in a buffer. We haven't tried to customize a mode line. We barely touched on the minibuffer and the various prompting and completion routines. We didn't even *mention* timers, `apply`, or `funcall`. And we've skirted the whole subject of tailoring Emacs's "undo" mechanism.

What we *have* done is to learn what *kinds* of things are possible in Emacs Lisp and what they tend to look like. We've investigated the process of developing an Emacs Lisp solution to a wide variety of problems. We've gotten a good, solid feel for where to begin, how to proceed, where to seek information, and what pitfalls to avoid.

We learn by doing. Rather than belabor every aspect of Emacs Lisp, my goal has been to get you on the fast track to writing your own Lisp code and exploring the remaining expanse of Emacs on your own. If I've done my job, the existence of still-uncharted Emacs Lisp territory should no longer daunt you. It should whet your appetite.

Happy hacking.

Lisp Quick Reference

This appendix summarizes general Lisp syntax as used in Emacs, and some important Lisp functions. It does not summarize Emacs-specific features such as buffers, hook variables, keymaps, modes, and so on. For a complete Emacs Lisp reference, see *The GNU Emacs Lisp Reference Manual*. Details on obtaining it are in Appendix D, *Obtaining and Building Emacs*.

Basics

A *Lisp* expression is a unit of data that can be *evaluated*. The expression may be composed of *subexpressions*, as in the cases of *lists* and *vectors*.

Every Lisp expression has a way to produce a *value* when evaluated. Most kinds of expression are *self-evaluating*, which means that they are their own value.

A Lisp expression can be treated as *literal* data instead of being evaluated. Non-self-evaluating expressions must be *quoted* in order to use them as literals and prevent them from being evaluated.

The symbol `nil` denotes falsehood. It is exactly the same object as the empty list, `()`. Every other Lisp object denotes truth, but the symbol `t` is reserved to mean truth anyway.

Emacs Lisp (unlike some other dialects of Lisp) is case-sensitive.

Data Types

Numbers

Emacs Lisp supports integers and floating-point numbers. They're written in just the way you'd expect: as a string of base-10 digits with an optional leading minus sign and optional decimal point. Some functions that operate on numbers are:

(numberp *x*)
> Test whether *x* is a number.

(integerp *x*)
> Test whether *x* is an integer.

(zerop *x*)
> Test whether *x* is zero.

(= *a b*)
> Test whether two numbers are equal.

(+ *a b c* ...)
> Addition.

(- *a b c* ...)
> Subtraction.

Characters

Single characters can be written in Emacs Lisp by preceding them with a question mark. For instance, ?a denotes lowercase a. Some special characters, particularly those that can be used to begin other kinds of Lisp expression, must be preceded with question mark-backslash, such as ?\", ?\(, and ?\). Some special characters can be written by combining a backslash with a letter. For instance, ?\t is a tab character, and ?\n is a newline character.

The result of evaluating a character is its ASCII code. For instance, evaluating ?a yields 97. In fact, integers can be used wherever characters are expected; Emacs Lisp does not distinguish between the two, except to allow the more convenient form of denoting characters.

(char-equal *a b*)
> Test whether two characters are equal. Ignores case if the variable case-fold-search is non-nil.

(char-to-string *c*)
> Create a one-character string containing *c*.

Strings

A string is a sequence of characters, and is written by enclosing the characters in double-quotes, `"like this"`. If a double-quote or backslash appears in the string, it must be preceded with a backslash, `"\"Like this,\" he said."`. Strings are self-evaluating.

Emacs, being a text editor, has many functions for operating on strings. Here is a tiny sample:

(`stringp` *x*)
> Test whether *x* is a string.

(`string=` *s₁ s₂*)
> Test whether two strings are equal.

(`string-lessp` *s₁ s₂*)
> Test whether string *s₁* comes before string *s₂* according to ASCII sorting order.

(`concat` *a b c* ...)
> Create a new string by concatenating other strings.

(`length` *s*)
> Return the length in characters of string *s*.

(`aref` *s i*)
> Return the *i*th character of string *s*, counting from 0.

(`aset` *s i ch*)
> Set the *i*th character of string *s* to *ch*.

(`substring` *s from* [*to*])
> Extract the substring of *s* beginning at position *from* and extending to position *to* (or to the end of *s* if *to* is omitted).

Symbols

Symbols are names that can have certain kinds of data associated with them. The name of a symbol is a sequence of characters that must not look like a number, string, list, vector, or other Lisp data type.

Symbols can be used as variables, function names, or as atomic values themselves. The result of evaluating a symbol is its variable value.

(`symbolp` *x*)
> Test whether *x* is a symbol.

(`setq` *sym expr*)
> Use *sym* as a variable: assign the value of *expr* to *sym*.

sym

> A symbol evaluates to its value as a variable.

(defun *sym* . . .)

> Use *sym* as a function name.

(*sym* *arg₁* *arg₂* . . .)

> A list that starts with a symbol denotes a function call of the function named by *sym*.

Every symbol has a property list associated with it. The property list is a mapping where the keys are Lisp symbols and the values are arbitrary Lisp expressions.

(put *sym* *key* *value*)

> In *sym*'s property list, assign *value* to symbol *key*.

(get *sym* *key*)

> Get the value previously assigned to symbol *key* in *sym*'s property list, or nil if there was none.

Symbols are normally stored internally in a symbol table to prevent duplicate symbols from being created. It is possible to explicitly add entries to the symbol table or to create symbols that are not placed in the symbol table (and which may therefore duplicate the name of other symbols).

(intern *string*)

> Return a symbol from the internal symbol table whose name is *string*. If one didn't previously exist, one is created.

(make-symbol *string*)

> Return a brand-new symbol whose name is *string*. The symbol is not placed in the internal symbol table, and is distinct from all other objects, including identically named symbols.

Lists

Lists are the foundation of Lisp. A list is a sequence of zero or more other Lisp expressions (including, potentially, other lists). A list is written by writing its subexpressions, separated by whitespace; and then surrounding the whole sequence with a pair of parentheses.

Lists are used to denote function calls in Lisp. When evaluated, the function designated by the first element of the list is invoked, with the values of the remaining elements as arguments.

Internally, a list is implemented as a chain of cons cells. Accessing an item in the list therefore entails traversing the chain until the element is found.

(listp *x*)

Test whether *x* is a list.

(null *x*)

Test whether *x* is the empty list.

(consp *x*)

Test whether *x* is a non-empty list.

(car *list*)

Return the first element of *list* (or the first part of a cons cell).

(cdr *list*)

Return the remainder (all but the first element) of *list* (or the second part of a cons cell).

(list *a b c ...*)

Construct a new list, with the values of the given arguments as elements.

(cons *a b*)

Insert *a* at the beginning of list *b* (or create a new cons cell (*a . b*).

(append *list₁ list₂ ...*)

Create a new list by (effectively) stripping off each sublist's outer parentheses, sticking all the elements together, and surrounding the whole thing with a new pair of parentheses.

(nth *i list*)

Return the *i*th subexpression of *list*, counting from 0.

(nthcdr *i list*)

Return the result of calling cdr on *list* *i* times.

Lists are covered in detail in Chapter 6, *Lists*.

Vectors

Like a list, a vector is a sequence of zero or more subexpressions, written with square brackets instead of parentheses. Unlike a list, a vector's elements can be randomly accessed (without first traversing an internal data structure). Vectors are self-evaluating.

When you write a vector, its subexpressions are automatically quoted. To construct a vector from elements that are evaluated first, use the **vector** function.

(vectorp *x*)

Test whether *x* is a vector.

(vector *a b c ...*)

Construct a new vector, with the values of the given arguments as elements.

(`length` *vector*)
> Return the length of *vector*.

(`aref` *vector i*)
> Return the *i*th subexpression of *vector*, counting from zero.

(`aset` *vector i expr*)
> Set the *i*th element of *vector* to *expr*.

Sequences and Arrays

Some Emacs Lisp data types are related. Strings and vectors are both kinds of *arrays*. An *array* is a linear collection of data elements that permits random access to its elements. A *string* is an array of characters, while a vector is an array of arbitrary expressions. The functions `aref` and `aset` are for manipulating arrays, and work on vectors as well as strings.

A *sequence* is an even more general kind of data structure that includes arrays and lists. A sequence is a linear collection of data elements, period. The function `length` works on lists, strings, and arrays.

(`arrayp` *x*)
> Test whether *x* is an array.

(`sequencep` *x*)
> Test whether *x* is a sequence.

(`copy-sequence` *sequence*)
> Return a copy of the list, string, or vector *sequence*.

Control Structures

Variables

To reference a variable, simply use its name (a symbol). To assign a variable, use `setq`.

```
(setq x 17)          ; assign 17 to variable x
x ⇒ 17               ; value of variable x
```

To make temporary variables that are in effect only in a certain region of code, use `let`.

```
(let  (($var_1$  $value_1$)
       ($var_2$  $value_2$)
       ...)
   $body_1$  $body_2$  ...)
```

In a `let`, all the *values* are computed in an unspecified order before any of the *vars* are assigned. The variant `let*` (whose syntax is identical to `let`) evaluates *value_i* and assigns it to *var_i* before evaluating *value_{i+1}*.

Sequencing

To evaluate a sequence of expressions where only a single expression is allowed, use `progn`.

    (progn *expr_1* *expr_2* ...)

Evaluates each *expr* in turn. Returns the value of the last *expr*.

To evaluate a sequence of expressions and return the value of the *first* subexpression instead of the last, use `prog1`.

Conditionals

Emacs Lisp has two kinds of conditional expression: `if` and `cond`.

    (if *test*
        then
      else_1 *else_2* ...)

Evaluates *test*. If the result is non-`nil`, evaluates *then*. Otherwise, evaluates each *else* expression in turn. Returns the value of the last expression it evaluates.

    (cond ((*test_1* *body_{11}* *body_{12}* ...)
           (*test_2* *body_{21}* *body_{22}* ...)
           ...))

Evaluates *test_1*. If the result is non-`nil`, evaluates each *body_1* in turn. Otherwise evaluates *test_2*. If the result is non-`nil`, evaluates each *body_2*, and so on with each "cond clause." Returns the value of the last expression it evaluates.

A common practice is to place a catch-all clause at the end like this:

    (cond ((*test_1* *body_{11}* *body_{12}* ...)
           (*test_2* *body_{21}* *body_{22}* ...)
           ...
           (t *body_{n1}* *body_{n2}* ...)))

The logical operators `and`, `or`, and `not` are often used in conjunction with—and sometimes as substitutes for—conditionals.

    (and *expr_1* *expr_2* ...)

Evaluates each *expr* until one returns `nil` (or it runs out of subexpressions), then returns. The result is the value of the last expression evaluated. This is the logical operation "and" because `and` returns truth if and only if none of its subexpressions is false.

The expressions

```
(if expr1
   (if expr2
      ...
         (if expr_{n-1} expr_n)))
```

and

```
(if (and expr_1 expr_1 ... expr_{n-1})
    expr_n)
```

are frequently condensed to

```
(and expr_1 expr_2 ... expr_{n-1} expr_n)
```

The expression

```
(or expr_1 expr_2 ...)
```

evaluates each *expr* until one returns non-`nil` (or it runs out of subexpressions), then returns. The result is the value of the last expression evaluated. This is the logical operation "or" because **or** returns falsehood if and only if none of its subexpressions is true.

The expression

```
(if a a b)
```

is often condensed to

```
(or a b)
```

Finally,

```
(not expr)
```

returns the logical negation of *expr*. If *expr* evaluates true, return `nil`. If *expr* evaluates false, return `t`. (Interestingly, **not** is the same exact function as **null**.)

Looping

Emacs Lisp has one looping function, **while**.

```
(while test
   body_1 body_2 ...)
```

Evaluates *test*. If the result is non-`nil`, evaluates each *body* in turn. Then repeats. Returns when *test* yields `nil`.

Function Call

To call a function, write a list whose first element is the function name and whose remaining elements are the arguments to the function.

(*function arg₁ arg₂ ...*)

Calls *function* with the given arguments; returns the result of *function*.

Literal Data

To make a literal out of a control structure—i.e., to prevent an expression from being evaluated—*quote* it by preceding it with ´.

```
´ expr ⇒ expr
(quote expr) ⇒ expr        ; same thing
```

To make a literal list in which individual subexpressions can be evaluated, *backquote* it, then *unquote* the individual subexpressions.

```
`(a b c) ⇒ (a b c)
(backquote (a b c)) ⇒ (a b c)  ; same thing
`(a ,b c) ⇒ (a value-of-b c)
```

To unquote a list-valued expression and "splice" its elements into the containing backquote template, use the splicing unquote operator, ",@".

```
(setq b ´(x y z))
`(a ,@b c) ⇒ (a x y z c)
```

Code Objects

Functions

A function is a list in the following form:

```
(lambda (parameters ...)
   "documentation string"
   body₁ body₂ ...)
```

The *documentation string* is optional.

When the function is invoked, the actual arguments will be bound to the *parameters* listed in the parameter list. The keyword `&optional` appearing in the parameter list means the following parameters are optional. If the function is called without a value for an optional parameter, the parameter is assigned `nil`. The last parameter may be preceded by the keyword `&rest`, meaning that all remaining unused arguments are placed in a list and assigned to that parameter.

The result of invoking a function is the result of the last *body* expression.

To define a function with a name, use `defun`.

```
(defun name (parameters ...)
   "documentation string"
   body₁ body₂ ...)
```

This creates a `lambda` expression and assigns it to the *function value* of the symbol *name*. This is different from *name*'s variable value, so there is no conflict between function names and variable names.

Macro Functions

A macro function is a list like a `lambda` expression, but instead of `lambda`, `macro` is used. When a macro is invoked, its arguments are not evaluated. Instead, they are used in their literal form to compute a new Lisp expression. Then *that* is evaluated.

To define a macro with a name, use `defmacro` exactly like `defun`.

B

Debugging and Profiling

This appendix describes some facilities in Emacs for testing and debugging your Lisp programs.

Evaluation

A Lisp expression in any buffer can be evaluated by placing the cursor at the end of the expression and pressing **C-x C-e** (`eval-last-sexp`). The keystroke **M-:** (`eval-expression`) prompts for a Lisp expression to evaluate in the minibuffer. You can also use the commands `eval-region` and `eval-current-buffer`.

The `*scratch*` buffer is normally in Lisp Interaction mode (and if it isn't, it can be put in that mode with **M-x lisp-interaction-mode RET**). In that mode, **C-j** is normally `eval-print-last-sexp`, which is like `eval-last-sexp` except that it also inserts the result of evaluation into the buffer. Also in Lisp Interaction mode is **C-M-x**, `eval-defun`, which evaluates the "defun" that point is in. The meaning of "defun" in this context is broad; it means the enclosing Lisp expression (if there is one) that begins with an open-parenthesis at the left margin. Finally, Lisp Interaction mode allows you to type partial Lisp symbols and complete them with **M-TAB**.

Lisp expressions can also be placed in files and loaded with `load`, `load-file`, `load-library`, and `require`.

The Debugger

Emacs Lisp has a built-in debugging mode that can be invoked automatically under certain circumstances. Entering the debugger is controlled as follows.

`debug-on-entry`

This is a command. It prompts (with completion) for the name of a function. Whenever that function is invoked, Emacs will enter the debugger.

`debug-on-error`

This is a variable. If it is non-`nil`, then Emacs will enter the debugger whenever an error is signaled.

`debug-on-next-call`

This is a variable. If it is non-`nil`, Emacs will enter the debugger the very next time an expression is to be evaluated.

`debug-on-quit`

This is a variable. If it is non-`nil`, Emacs will enter the debugger whenever a "quit" is signaled (e.g., when the user presses **C-g**).

When the debugger is invoked, a window displaying the Lisp stack appears. In this buffer, called `*Backtrace*`, each line represents a pending function call, with the top lines representing more recent calls. You can see the pending Lisp expressions, test the values of variables and other expressions in different contexts, and force a function to return a certain value.

These are the useful debugging-mode commands.

`c`

Leave the debugger, continuing whatever code was interrupted by entering it. This isn't possible when the debugger was invoked because of an error.

`q`

Leave the debugger, aborting the pending computation.

`d`

Continue execution until the next function call, then reenter the debugger.

`e`

Prompt for a Lisp expression to evaluate in the context of the topmost stack "frame."

`b`

"Break" when returning from the current function. If the debugger is invoked when a function is called, then this command will continue execution until the same function is about to return, then will reenter the debugger.

`r`

When about to return from a function, prompt for a Lisp expression to be that function's return value (instead of whatever value it computed).

Edebug

Edebug is an elaborate debugging environment that is far more powerful than the debugging facilities described in the previous section. It allows you to step through the actual source code of a running Lisp program. Edebug is an amazing piece of work written entirely in Lisp; it's a testament both to the talents of its author, Daniel LaLiberte, and to the expressive power of Emacs Lisp, which provides enough access to its own internals to make such a tool possible.

This section is only a brief summary of Edebug. For complete information, refer to the Edebug section of *The GNU Emacs Lisp Reference Manual.* Details on obtaining it are in Appendix D, *Obtaining and Building Emacs.*

To use Edebug, you must select those functions that you specifically wish to be able to trace. Each function must be individually *instrumented*, which means evaluating it in a special way. The command `edebug-defun` performs this task, and is used like `eval-defun`. The variable `edebug-all-defs` (q.v.) controls whether loading Edebug should redefine the various `eval-` commands to do instrumenting as well.

After instrumenting the desired functions, leave their definitions available in some buffer. You can uninstrument functions by re-evaluating their definitions in the ordinary way.

Edebug is activated whenever any instrumented function is called. A window showing the function's definition appears, along with a little arrow in the left margin indicating on what line execution has stopped. The cursor will be placed at the beginning of the expression that is about to be invoked (but if you wish, you can move the cursor, or even hide the buffer, without affecting the operation of Edebug).

At this point, you're in Edebug mode and can execute the following commands:

c

> Continue execution.

q

> Abort execution and leave Edebug.

SPC

> Single-step. If Edebug is stopped at a variable or a constant, move past it and show its value. If Edebug is stopped at the beginning of a function call, move inside the function call. Subsequent single-steps will move over each argument, showing their values. If Edebug is stopped at a point where all the arguments to a function have been evaluated, then single-stepping calls that function with those arguments and displays the result. If that function is also

instrumented, single-stepping will descend into it. At each step, the cursor moves to the appropriate point in the source code.

n

Next. Like single-step, but evaluates nested, instrumented functions without descending into them.

e

Prompt for an expression to evaluate in the context of the stopped program.

h

"Continue to here." If you place the cursor in a spot in the source code where you'd like to stop, h will cause the program to continue execution until it reaches that spot.

d

Display a backtrace, similar in appearance to Emacs's `*Backtrace*` buffer (see the previous section) but without the functionality. (Edebug commands continue to work.)

b

Set a breakpoint at the location of the cursor. The program will stop any time it reaches that point.

u

Unset a breakpoint.

x

Set a conditional breakpoint. You'll be prompted for a Lisp expression. Each time this breakpoint is reached, if the expression is true, the program will stop.

Edebug has many more capabilities than the few listed here, but these are the most-often-used features.

The Profiler

Profiling a program is the process of figuring out how much time different parts of it take to run, presumably in a quest to make it more efficient. Barry Warsaw has written an ingenious package for profiling Emacs Lisp called ELP.

Like Edebug, ELP relies on functions being "instrumented." This is done with the command `elp-instrument-function`, which prompts for a function name. There's also `elp-instrument-package`, which prompts for a prefix. Any existing functions whose names begin with the given prefix will get instrumented.

Functions are uninstrumented with `elp-restore-function` and `elp-restore-all`.

To use ELP, simply run your program after instrumenting the functions you wish to profile. Profiling data will accumulate silently. When you're ready to see the results so far, run the command `elp-results`. A buffer will appear, showing, for each profiled function, the number of times it was called, the total time spent in the function, and the average time per call.

Use `elp-reset-function` to set a function's call-count and elapsed-time counters back to zero; `elp-reset-all` does this for all profiles functions.

C

In this appendix:
- *Preparing Source Files*
- *Documentation*
- *Copyright*
- *Posting*

Sharing Your Code

If you write a terrific new Emacs mode, or feature, or game, or whatever, it's in the spirit of free software for you to share it with others by posting it to the *gnu.emacs.sources* newsgroup. This appendix describes the conventions for sharing Emacs Lisp code.

Preparing Source Files

Before sharing your code with the world, it's considerate to first test it with reasonable thoroughness, fixing any bugs you happen to find. Learn more about testing and debugging in Appendix B, *Debugging and Profiling*.

Once the code is working the way you'd like it to, you should add a comment block to the beginning of each source file describing the file, its copyright (see below), its authorship, its version information, and other commentary. Here's a typical beginning:

```
;;; foretell.el -- predict what the user will do
;;; Copyright 1996 by Mortimer J. Hacker <mjh@mjh.net>

;;; Foretell is free software distributed under the terms
;;; of the GNU General Public License, version 2.  For details,
;;; see the file COPYING.

;;; This is version 1.7 of 5 August 1996.

;;; For more information about Foretell, subscribe to the
;;; Foretell mailing list by sending a message to
;;; <foretell-request@mjh.net>.
```

The file should end with a comment line like this:

```
;;; foretell.el ends here
```

which will help identify the file boundary if the file is sent through email (which might cause signature and other lines to be appended).

If your package includes more than one file, it's customary to create a file called *README* describing the package, the files in it, and how to install it; then to combine all the files into a single distribution file with the *shar* program. If you don't have *shar*, you can obtain the GNU version; refer to Appendix D, *Obtaining and Building Emacs*.

Documentation

At a minimum, your source files should contain enough commentary in the beginning comment block so that readers can understand what they're for. Ideally, your code will also be self-documenting—i.e., you will have made liberal and effective use of docstrings in all your function and variable definitions.

If you're ambitious about writing documentation, you might want to consider creating a Texinfo manual for your package. Texinfo is the standard documentation format of the GNU system. Texinfo files can be processed with the *makeinfo* program to produce Info files, which are browsable, tree-structured text files that can be viewed in Emacs's Info mode. Texinfo files can also be processed with the TEX typesetting system to produce nicely-formatted printed manuals.

An excellent Info manual on how to write Texinfo manuals accompanies the GNU *texinfo* package, which includes *makeinfo*. For information on obtaining it or TEX, see Appendix D.

Copyright

You are free to assign any copyright terms to your code you wish, within the law, of course. Most authors of Emacs Lisp packages choose to make their software "free" (in availability, not necessarily price) by assigning to it the terms of the GNU General Public License, a special kind of copyright invented by the Free Software Foundation. Software covered by the GPL is assured of remaining freely available, which isn't the case when, say, you release your software into the public domain. (In that case, someone can legally copy your software, make a change to it, call it their own, sell the binaries, and refuse to continue distributing the source code.)

If you wish to place your software under the GPL (a process humorously referred to as "copylefting" your software), you need to include the terms of the GPL either in your source files, or in a separate file (usually *COPYING*) that is referenced in the copyright notice of each source file (as in the example at the

beginning of this appendix). You can see the GPL from within Emacs by typing
M-x describe-copying RET.

Posting

Once you've assembled your *shar*'d, copyrighted, documented, tested and
debugged software, post it using your favorite newsreader to the
gnu.emacs.sources newsgroup. Be sure to provide a helpful one-line description
in the `Subject:` field of the post, and be sure that readers of the newsgroup
know how to contact you with questions or comments. Note well, it is considered
very bad form to post anything other than Emacs Lisp sources to
gnu.emacs.sources. For non-source posts, use *gnu.misc.discuss*.

Obtaining and Building Emacs

Availability of Packages

All the software packages described in this book, with the exception of TEX, are GNU software from the Free Software Foundation. Their software and other packages can be retrieved via anonymous FTP from the Internet site *ftp.gnu.ai.mit.edu* in the directory */pub/gnu*. There are numerous mirror sites, information about which is in *GNUinfo/FTP*.

If you cannot download the packages you want from the Internet, or if you wish an easier solution, you can order software distributions from the Free Software Foundation. They are available in diskette, tape, and CD-ROM form. You can also order printed, bound copies of many GNU manuals, including several about Emacs, plus the Texinfo manual mentioned in Appendix C, *Sharing Your Code*. For more information, including prices, contact the FSF:

> Free Software Foundation, Inc.
> 59 Temple Place – Suite 330
> Boston, MA 02111-1307 USA
> Telephone: +1-617-542-5942
> Fax: +1-617-542-2652
> Email: *gnu@prep.ai.mit.edu*

The packages mentioned in this book that are available from the FSF are:

Emacs
> The editor itself, plus a huge number of Lisp extensions. Available in source form as file *emacs-x.y.tar.gz*, where x and y are the major and minor version numbers of the latest version (presently 19.34).

Texinfo

> The GNU documentation system, including *makeinfo* and a manual on writing Texinfo documents. Requires TEX to make printed manuals. Available as *texinfo-*x.y.*gz*. The present version is 3.7.

Emacs Lisp Reference Manual

> The Texinfo document *The Emacs Lisp Reference Manual* is available in source form as *elisp-manual-19-*x.y.*tar.gz*. (The 19 refers to the major version of Emacs.) The present version of the manual is 2.4. An online copy of this manual, created from source with `makeinfo`, is indispensable for Emacs Lisp programmers.

Shar utilities

> Includes *shar* and *unshar*, for creating and unpacking software distributions. Available as *sharutils-*x.y.*gz*. The present version is 4.2. Note that *shar* files can be unpacked without *unshar*; just feed them to the standard UNIX *sh* command.

Gzip Compression and decompression package

> Available as *gzip-*x.y.*shar*. The present version is 1.2.4.

Tar—Another program for creating and unpacking software distributions

> Available as *tar-*x.y.*shar.gz*. The present version is 1.11.8. Note that GNU *tar*, unlike most other implementations, can intrinsically handle *.tar.gz* files without requiring the use of Gzip.

The Jargon File

> The *On-line Hacker Jargon File* (which was cited in the Introduction) is also available from the FSF as the file *jarg*version.*txt.gz*, where *version* is presently 400. There's also an Info format version, *jarg*version.*info.gz*. It's a treasure trove of hacker lore, and is periodically published in book form as *The New Hacker's Dictionary*.

You can obtain TEX from the TEX Users' Group:

> TEX Users Group
> 1850 Union Street—Suite 1637
> San Francisco, CA 94123 USA
> Home page: *http://www.tug.org/*
> Email: *tug@tug.org*
> Fax: +1-415-982-8559

Unpacking, Building, and Installing Emacs

Like most GNU software, Emacs is trivially easy to unpack, build, and install. In fact, the instructions that follow apply to nearly all GNU software packages, not merely Emacs.

Unpacking

If you have a compressed *tar* file (file name ending in *.tar.gz*, *.tar.Z*, or *.tgz* and you have GNU *tar*, run:

```
tar zxvf file
```

If you don't have GNU *tar*, use this:

```
zcat file | tar xvf -
```

(You'll find *zcat* in the Gzip package.) If you use the *tar* that comes with SVR4-derived variants of UNIX, you may need to use **xvof** in place of **xvf**. The **o** makes you the owner of the extracted files. (Otherwise, the owner is the *tar* file's originator—who probably isn't known on your computer.)

If you have a *shar* file (file name ending in *.sh* or *.shar*), run

```
unshar file
```

or simply

```
sh file
```

If the *shar* file is compressed (*.Z* or *.gz*), uncompress it first with *gzip -d*.

Building and Installing

First, in the top-level directory of the software package being built, configure the software by running the *configure* script.

Different software packages have different configuration options. See what the options are for a package with *./configure --help*. The options for Emacs are:

--with-gcc
　　Use the GNU C compiler to compile Emacs.

--with-pop
　　Compile in support for the Post Office Protocol (POP), sometimes used for retrieving email (for those who read email with Emacs).

--with-kerberos
　　Use the Kerberos authentication extension to POP.

--with-hesiod

> Use Hesiod for finding the POP server.

--with-x

> Build in X Window support.

--with-x-toolkit

> Fancier X Window support; uses toolkit widgets. The X Toolkit is used by default, but *--with-x-toolkit=motif* uses the Motif toolkit instead.

You may also want to watch what the *configure* script is doing while it runs—it can take a while—so you'll probably want to use the *--verbose* option, too. Here's how I always invoke *configure*:

```
./configure --verbose --with-x --with-x-toolkit
```

After configuring the package, run *make*. This will compile the program and can take a long time.

Next, run *make check*. This runs any self-tests that are included with the package.

Presuming that the software successfully compiled and passed its tests, install it with *make install*.

Index

Symbols

* (asterisk), 48–50
   in buffer names, 149
   in regular expressions, 58
@ in interactive declaration, 154
' (backquote), 114, 193
\ (backslash), 6, 58, 186
\\< and \\> metacharacters, 60
\\b and \\B metacharacters, 60
\\[...] construct, 49
\\(\\) metacharacters, 59
[ ] (brackets), 135, 189
   in regular expressions, 58
^ (caret) in regular expressions, 58
,@ (splicing operator), 115, 193
$ (dollar sign) in regular expressions, 59
- (hyphen) in regular expressions, 58
( ) (parentheses), 3
   in regular expressions, 59
. (period), 58
+ (plus sign) in regular expressions, 59
? (question mark), 186
   in regular expressions, 59
" (quotation mark), 7
' (single quote), 7, 193
/ (slash) function, 143

A

activate (keyword), 31
active keymaps, 128
add-hook function, 25

advice tool, 30–32
after (keyword), 30
after-change-functions variable, 67, 99, 157
after-save-hook variable, 51
aliases, function, 22
alist-replace function, 91
alt key, 5
anonymous functions, 26
append function, 82, 114, 189
apropos command, 10
aref function, 135, 187, 190
arguments, optional, 17
around (keyword), 31
ASCII codes for characters, 186
aset function, 135, 187, 190
assoc functions, 88
association lists, 85, 89, 91
assq function, 89
asterisk (*), 48–50
   in buffer names, 149
   in regular expressions, 58
asynchronous process objects, 169–173
atoms, 85
auto-save-mode, 97
auto-fill-mode, 96
autoload function, 75
autoloading files, 75

B

b (debugging command), 196, 198
backquote ('), 114, 193
backslash (\), 6, 58, 186

 # More Titles from O'Reilly

UNIX Basics

Learning the UNIX Operating System

By Grace Todino, John Strang & Jerry Peek
3rd Edition August 1993
108 pages, ISBN 1-56592-060-0

If you are new to UNIX, this concise introduction will tell you just what you need to get started and no more. Why wade through a 600-page book when you can begin working productively in a matter of minutes? It's an ideal primer for Mac and PC users of the Internet who need to know a little bit about UNIX on the systems they visit. This book is the most effective introduction to UNIX in print. The third edition has been updated and expanded to provide increased coverage of window systems and networking. It's a handy book for someone just starting with UNIX, as well as someone who encounters a UNIX system as a "visitor" via remote login over the Internet.

Learning GNU Emacs, 2nd Edition

By Debra Cameron, Bill Rosenblatt & Eric Raymond
2nd Edition September 1996
560 pages, ISBN 1-56592-152-6

Learning GNU Emacs is an introduction to Version 19.30 of the GNU Emacs editor, one of the most widely used and powerful editors available under UNIX. It provides a solid introduction to basic editing, a look at several important "editing modes" (special Emacs features for editing specific types of documents, including email, Usenet News, and the World Wide Web), and a brief introduction to customization and Emacs LISP programming. The book is aimed at new Emacs users, whether or not they are programmers. Includes quick-reference card.

Learning the bash Shell

By Cameron Newham & Bill Rosenblatt
1st Edition October 1995
310 pages, ISBN 1-56592-147-X

Whether you want to use *bash* for its programming features or its user interface, you'll find *Learning the bash Shell* a valuable guide. If you're new to shell programming, it provides an excellent introduction, covering everything from the most basic to the most advanced features, like signal handling and command line processing. If you've been writing shell scripts for years, it offers a great way to find out what the new shell offers.

Learning the Korn Shell

By Bill Rosenblatt
1st Edition June 1993
360 pages, ISBN 1-56592-054-6

This Nutshell Handbook is a thorough introduction to the Korn shell, both as a user interface and as a programming language. The Korn shell is a program that interprets UNIX commands. It has many features that aren't found in other shells, including command history. This book provides a clear and concise explanation of the Korn shell's features. It explains *ksh* string operations, co-processes, signals and signal handling, and command-line interpretation. The book also includes real-life programming examples and a Korn shell debugger called *kshdb*, the only known implementation of a shell debugger anywhere.

Using csh and tcsh

By Paul DuBois
1st Edition August 1995
242 pages, ISBN 1-56592-132-1

Using csh and tcsh describes from the beginning how to use these shells interactively to get your work done faster with less typing. You'll learn how to make your prompt tell you where you are (no more pwd); use what you've typed before (history); type long command lines with few keystrokes (command and filename completion); remind yourself of filenames when in the middle of typing a command; and edit a botched command without retyping it.

Learning the vi Editor

By Linda Lamb
5th Edition October 1990
192 pages, ISBN 0-937175-67-6

This book is a complete guide to text editing with *vi*, the editor available on nearly every UNIX system. Early chapters cover the basics; later chapters explain more advanced editing tools, such as *ex* commands and global search and replacement.

O'REILLY™

TO ORDER: **800-998-9938** • *order@oreilly.com* • *http://www.oreilly.com/*
OUR PRODUCTS ARE AVAILABLE AT A BOOKSTORE OR SOFTWARE STORE NEAR YOU.
FOR INFORMATION: **800-998-9938** • **707-829-0515** • *info@oreilly.com*

sed & awk, 2nd Edition

By Dale Dougherty & Arnold Robbins
2nd Edition Winter 1997
450 pages (est.), ISBN 1-56592-225-5

sed & awk, one of the most popular books in O'Reilly & Associates' Nutshell series, describes two text processing programs that are mainstays of the UNIX programmer's toolbox. The book lays a foundation for both programs by describing how they are used and by introducing the fundamental concepts of regular expressions and text matching. This new edition covers the *sed* and *awk* programs as they are now mandated by the POSIX standard. It also includes a discussion of the GNU versions of both programs, which have extensions beyond their UNIX counterparts. Many examples are used throughout the book to illustrate the concepts discussed.

SCO UNIX in a Nutshell

By Ellie Cutler & the staff of O'Reilly & Associates
1st Edition February 1994
590 pages, ISBN 1-56592-037-6

The desktop reference to SCO UNIX and Open Desktop®, this version of *UNIX in a Nutshell* shows you what's under the hood of your SCO system. It isn't a scaled-down quick reference of common commands, but a complete reference containing all user, programming, administration, and networking commands.

UNIX in a Nutshell: System V Edition

By Daniel Gilly & the staff of O'Reilly & Associates
2nd Edition June 1992
444 pages, ISBN 1-56592-001-5

You may have seen UNIX quick-reference guides, but you've never seen anything like *UNIX in a Nutshell.* Not a scaled-down quick reference of common commands, *UNIX in a Nutshell* is a complete reference containing all commands and options, along with generous descriptions and examples that put the commands in context. For all but the thorniest UNIX problems, this one reference should be all the documentation you need. Covers System V, Releases 3 and 4, and Solaris 2.0.

What You Need to Know: When You Can't Find Your UNIX System Administrator

By Linda Mui
1st Edition April 1995
156 pages, ISBN 1-56592-104-6

This book is written for UNIX users, who are often cast adrift in a confusing environment. It provides the background and practical solutions you need to solve problems you're likely to encounter—problems with logging in, printing, sharing files, running programs, managing space resources, etc. It also describes the kind of info to gather when you're asking for a diagnosis from a busy sys admin. And, it gives you a list of site-specific information that you should know, as well as a place to write it down.

Volume 3M: X Window System User's Guide, Motif Edition

By Valerie Quercia & Tim O'Reilly
2nd Edition January 1993
956 pages, ISBN 1-56592-015-5

The *X Window System User's Guide, Motif Edition* orients the new user to window system concepts and provides detailed tutorials for many client programs, including the xtermterminal emulator and the twm, uwm, and mwmwindow managers. Later chapters explain how to customize the X environment. Revised for Motif 1.2 and X11 Release 5.

What You Need to Know: Using Email Effectively

By Linda Lamb & Jerry Peek
1st Edition April 1995
160 pages, ISBN 1-56592-103-8

After using email for a few years, you learn from your own mistakes and from reading other people's mail. You learn how to include a message but leave in only the sections that make your point, how to recognize if a network address "looks right," how to successfully subscribe and unsubscribe to a mailing list, how to save mail so that you can find it again. This book shortens the learning-from-experience curve for all mailers, so you can quickly be productive and send email that looks intelligent to others.

O'REILLY™

TO ORDER: **800-998-9938** • **order@oreilly.com** • **http://www.oreilly.com/**
OUR PRODUCTS ARE AVAILABLE AT A BOOKSTORE OR SOFTWARE STORE NEAR YOU.
FOR INFORMATION: **800-998-9938** • **707-829-0515** • **info@oreilly.com**

How to stay in touch with O'Reilly

1. Visit Our Award-Winning Web Site

http://www.oreilly.com/

★ "Top 100 Sites on the Web" —*PC Magazine*
★ "Top 5% Web sites" —*Point Communications*
★ "3-Star site" —*The McKinley Group*

Our web site contains a library of comprehensiveproduct information (including book excerpts and tables of contents), downloadable software, background articles, interviews with technology leaders, links to relevant sites, book cover art, and more. File us in your Bookmarks or Hotlist!

2. Join Our Email Mailing Lists

New Product Releases
To receive automatic email with brief descriptions of all new O'Reilly products as they are released, send email to: **listproc@online.oreilly.com**
Put the following information in the first line of your message (*not* in the Subject field):
subscribe oreilly-news "Your Name" of "Your Organization" (for example: subscribe oreilly-news Kris Webber of Fine Enterprises)

O'Reilly Events
If you'd also like us to send information about trade show events, special promotions, and other O'Reilly events, send email to: **listproc@online.oreilly.com**
Put the following information in the first line of your message (*not* in the Subject field):
subscribe oreilly-events "Your Name" of "Your Organization"

3. Get Examples from Our Books via FTP

There are two ways to access an archive of example files from our books:

Regular FTP
- ftp to:
  ftp.oreilly.com
  (login: anonymous
  password: your email address)
- Point your web browser to:
  ftp://ftp.oreilly.com/

FTPMAIL
- Send an email message to:
  ftpmail@online.oreilly.com
  (Write "help" in the message body)

4. Visit Our Gopher Site
- Connect your gopher to:
  gopher.oreilly.com

- Point your web browser to:
  gopher://gopher.oreilly.com/

- Telnet to:
  gopher.oreilly.com
  login: gopher

5. Contact Us via Email

order@oreilly.com
To place a book or software order online. Good for North American and international customers.

subscriptions@oreilly.com
To place an order for any of our newsletters or periodicals.

books@oreilly.com
General questions about any of our books.

software@oreilly.com
For general questions and product information about our software. Check out O'Reilly Software Online at **http://software.oreilly.com/** for software and technical support information. Registered O'Reilly software users send your questions to: **website-support@oreilly.com**

cs@oreilly.com
For answers to problems regarding your order or our products.

booktech@oreilly.com
For book content technical questions or corrections.

proposals@oreilly.com
To submit new book or software proposals to our editors and product managers.

international@oreilly.com
For information about our international distributors or translation queries. For a list of our distributors outside of North America check out:
http://www.oreilly.com/www/order/country.html

O'Reilly & Associates, Inc.
101 Morris Street, Sebastopol, CA 95472 USA
TEL   707-829-0515 or 800-998-9938
         (6am to 5pm PST)
FAX   707-829-0104

O'REILLY™

Titles from O'Reilly

Please note that upcoming titles are displayed in italic.

WEB PROGRAMMING

Apache: The Definitive Guide
Building Your Own Web
   Conferences
Building Your Own Website
CGI Programming for the World
   Wide Web
Designing for the Web
HTML: The Definitive Guide,
   2nd Ed.
JavaScript: The Definitive Guide,
   2nd Ed.
Learning Perl
Programming Perl, 2nd Ed.
Mastering Regular Expressions
WebMaster in a Nutshell
Web Security & Commerce
Web Client Programming with
   Perl
World Wide Web Journal

USING THE INTERNET

Smileys
The Future Does Not Compute
The Whole Internet User's Guide
   & Catalog
The Whole Internet for Win 95
Using Email Effectively
Bandits on the Information
   Superhighway

JAVA SERIES

Exploring Java
Java AWT Reference
Java Fundamental Classes
   Reference
Java in a Nutshell
Java Language Reference, 2nd
   Edition
Java Network Programming
Java Threads
Java Virtual Machine

SOFTWARE

WebSite™ 1.1
WebSite Professional™
Building Your Own Web
   Conferences
WebBoard™
PolyForm™
Statisphere™

SONGLINE GUIDES

NetActivism   NetResearch
Net Law   NetSuccess
NetLearning   NetTravel
Net Lessons

SYSTEM ADMINISTRATION

Building Internet Firewalls
Computer Crime: A
   Crimefighter's Handbook
Computer Security Basics
DNS and BIND, 2nd Ed.
Essential System Administration,
   2nd Ed.
Getting Connected: The Internet
   at 56K and Up
Linux Network Administrator's
   Guide
Managing Internet Information
   Services
Managing NFS and NIS
Networking Personal Computers
   with TCP/IP
Practical UNIX & Internet
   Security, 2nd Ed.
PGP: Pretty Good Privacy
sendmail, 2nd Ed.
sendmail Desktop Reference
System Performance Tuning
TCP/IP Network Administration
termcap & terminfo
Using & Managing UUCP
Volume 8: X Window System
   Administrator's Guide
Web Security & Commerce

UNIX

Exploring Expect
Learning VBScript
Learning GNU Emacs, 2nd Ed.
Learning the bash Shell
Learning the Korn Shell
Learning the UNIX Operating
   System
Learning the vi Editor
Linux in a Nutshell
Making TeX Work
Linux Multimedia Guide
Running Linux, 2nd Ed.
SCO UNIX in a Nutshell
sed & awk, 2nd Edition
Tcl/Tk Tools
UNIX in a Nutshell: System V
   Edition
UNIX Power Tools
Using csh & tsch
When You Can't Find Your UNIX
   System Administrator
Writing GNU Emacs Extensions

WEB REVIEW STUDIO SERIES

Gif Animation Studio
Shockwave Studio

WINDOWS

Dictionary of PC Hardware and
   Data Communications Terms
Inside the Windows 95 Registry
Inside the Windows 95 File
   System
Windows Annoyances
Windows NT File System
   Internals
Windows NT in a Nutshell

PROGRAMMING

Advanced Oracle PL/SQL
   Programming
Applying RCS and SCCS
C++: The Core Language
Checking C Programs with lint
DCE Security Programming
Distributing Applications Across
   DCE & Windows NT
Encyclopedia of Graphics File
   Formats, 2nd Ed.
Guide to Writing DCE
   Applications
lex & yacc
Managing Projects with make
Mastering Oracle Power Objects
Oracle Design: The Definitive
   Guide
Oracle Performance Tuning, 2nd
   Ed.
Oracle PL/SQL Programming
Porting UNIX Software
POSIX Programmer's Guide
POSIX.4: Programming for the
   Real World
Power Programming with RPC
Practical C Programming
Practical C++ Programming
Programming Python
Programming with curses
Programming with GNU Software
Pthreads Programming
Software Portability with imake,
   2nd Ed.
Understanding DCE
Understanding Japanese
   Information Processing
UNIX Systems Programming for
   SVR4

BERKELEY 4.4 SOFTWARE DISTRIBUTION

4.4BSD System Manager's
   Manual
4.4BSD User's Reference Manual
4.4BSD User's Supplementary
   Documents
4.4BSD Programmer's Reference
   Manual
4.4BSD Programmer's
   Supplementary Documents
X Programming
Vol. 0: X Protocol Reference
   Manual
Vol. 1: Xlib Programming Manual
Vol. 2: Xlib Reference Manual
Vol. 3M: X Window System User's
   Guide, Motif Edition
Vol. 4M: X Toolkit Intrinsics
   Programming Manual, Motif
   Edition
Vol. 5: X Toolkit Intrinsics
   Reference Manual
Vol. 6A: Motif Programming
   Manual
Vol. 6B: Motif Reference Manual
Vol. 6C: Motif Tools
Vol. 8 : X Window System
   Administrator's Guide
Programmer's Supplement for
   Release 6
X User Tools
The X Window System in a
   Nutshell

CAREER & BUSINESS

Building a Successful Software
   Business
The Computer User's Survival
   Guide
Love Your Job!
Electronic Publishing on CD-
   ROM

TRAVEL

Travelers' Tales: Brazil
Travelers' Tales: Food
Travelers' Tales: France
Travelers' Tales: Gutsy Women
Travelers' Tales: India
Travelers' Tales: Mexico
Travelers' Tales: Paris
Travelers' Tales: San Francisco
Travelers' Tales: Spain
Travelers' Tales: Thailand
Travelers' Tales: A Woman's
   World

O'REILLY™

TO ORDER: **800-998-9938** • *order@oreilly.com* • *http://www.oreilly.com/*
OUR PRODUCTS ARE AVAILABLE AT A BOOKSTORE OR SOFTWARE STORE NEAR YOU.
FOR INFORMATION: **800-998-9938** • **707-829-0515** • *info@oreilly.com*

How to stay in touch with O'Reilly

1. Visit Our Award-Winning Web Site

http://www.ora.com/

★ "Top 100 Sites on the Web" —*PC Magazine*
★ "Top 5% Web sites" —*Point Communications*
★ "3-Star site" —*The McKinley Group*

Our web site contains a library of comprehensiveproduct information (including book excerpts and tables of contents), downloadable software, background articles, interviews with technology leaders, links to relevant sites, book cover art, and more. File us in your Bookmarks or Hotlist!

2. Join Our Email Mailing Lists

New Product Releases

To receive automatic email with brief descriptions of all new O'Reilly products as they are released, send email to:
listproc@online.ora.com
Put the following information in the first line of your message (*not* in the Subject field):
subscribe ora-news "Your Name"of "Your Organization" (for example: subscribe ora-news Kris Webber of Fine Enterprises)

O'Reilly Events

If you'd also like us to send information about trade show events, special promotions, and other O'Reilly events, send email to:
listproc@online.ora.com
Put the following information in the first line of your message (*not* in the Subject field):
subscribe ora-events "Your Name" of "Your Organization"

3. Get Examples from Our Books via FTP

There are two ways to access an archive of example files from our books:

Regular FTP
- ftp to:
  ftp.ora.com
  (login: anonymous
  password: your email address)
- Point your web browser to:
  ftp://ftp.ora.com/

FTPMAIL
- Send an email message to:
  ftpmail@online.ora.com
  (Write "help" in the message body)

4. Visit Our Gopher Site
- Connect your gopher to:
  gopher.ora.com

- Point your web browser to:
  gopher://gopher.ora.com/

- Telnet to:
  gopher.ora.com
  login: gopher

5. Contact Us via Email

order@ora.com
To place a book or software order online. Good for North American and international customers.

subscriptions@ora.com
To place an order for any of our newsletters or periodicals.

books@ora.com
General questions about any of our books.

software@ora.com
For general questions and product information about our software. Check out O'Reilly Software Online at **http://software.ora.com/** for software and technical support information. Registered O'Reilly software users send your questions to: **website-support@ora.com**

cs@ora.com
For answers to problems regarding your order or our products.

booktech@ora.com
For book content technical questions or corrections.

proposals@ora.com
To submit new book or software proposals to our editors and product managers.

international@ora.com
For information about our international distributors or translation queries. For a list of our distributors outside of North America check out:
http://www.ora.com/www/order/country.html

O'Reilly & Associates, Inc.
101 Morris Street, Sebastopol, CA 95472 USA
TEL   707-829-0515 or 800-998-9938
       (6am to 5pm PST)
FAX   707-829-0104

O'REILLY™

International Distributors

UK, Europe, Middle East and Northern Africa (except France, Germany, Switzerland, & Austria)

INQUIRIES
International Thomson Publishing Europe
Berkshire House
168-173 High Holborn
London WC1V 7AA, United Kingdom
Telephone: 44-171-497-1422
Fax: 44-171-497-1426
Email: itpint@itps.co.uk

ORDERS
International Thomson Publishing Services, Ltd.
Cheriton House, North Way
Andover, Hampshire SP10 5BE, United Kingdom
Telephone: 44-264-342-832
  (UK orders)
Telephone: 44-264-342-806
  (outside UK)
Fax: 44-264-364418 (UK orders)
Fax: 44-264-342761 (outside UK)
UK & Eire orders: itpuk@itps.co.uk
International orders: itpint@itps.co.uk

France

Editions Eyrolles
61 bd Saint-Germain
75240 Paris Cedex 05
France
Fax: 33-01-44-41-11-44

FRENCH LANGUAGE BOOKS
All countries except Canada
Phone: 33-01-44-41-46-16
Email: geodif@eyrolles.com

ENGLISH LANGUAGE BOOKS
Phone: 33-01-44-41-11-87
Email: distribution@eyrolles.com

Australia

WoodsLane Pty. Ltd.
7/5 Vuko Place, Warriewood NSW 2102
P.O. Box 935, Mona Vale NSW 2103
Australia
Telephone: 61-2-9970-5111
Fax: 61-2-9970-5002
Email: info@woodslane.com.au

Germany, Switzerland, and Austria

INQUIRIES
O'Reilly Verlag
Balthasarstr. 81
D-50670 Köln
Germany
Telephone: 49-221-97-31-60-0
Fax: 49-221-97-31-60-8
Email: anfragen@oreilly.de

ORDERS
International Thomson Publishing
Königswinterer Straße 418
53227 Bonn, Germany
Telephone: 49-228-97024 0
Fax: 49-228-441342
Email: order@oreilly.de

Asia (except Japan & India)

INQUIRIES
International Thomson Publishing Asia
60 Albert Street #15-01
Albert Complex
Singapore 189969
Telephone: 65-336-6411
Fax: 65-336-7411

ORDERS
Telephone: 65-336-6411
Fax: 65-334-1617
thomson@signet.com.sg

New Zealand

WoodsLane New Zealand Ltd.
21 Cooks Street (P.O. Box 575)
Wanganui, New Zealand
Telephone: 64-6-347-6543
Fax: 64-6-345-4840
Email: info@woodslane.com.au

Japan

O'Reilly Japan, Inc.
Kiyoshige Building 2F
12-Banchi, Sanei-cho
Shinjuku-ku
Tokyo 160 Japan
Telephone: 81-3-3356-5227
Fax: 81-3-3356-5261
Email: kenji@ora.com

India

Computer Bookshop (India) PVT. LTD.
190 Dr. D.N. Road, Fort
Bombay 400 001
India
Telephone: 91-22-207-0989
Fax: 91-22-262-3551
Email: cbsbom@giasbm01.vsnl.net.in

The Americas

O'Reilly & Associates, Inc.
101 Morris Street
Sebastopol, CA 95472 U.S.A.
Telephone: 707-829-0515
Telephone: 800-998-9938 (U.S. & Canada)
Fax: 707-829-0104
Email: order@ora.com

Southern Africa

International Thomson Publishing Southern Africa
Building 18, Constantia Park
240 Old Pretoria Road
P.O. Box 2459
Halfway House, 1685 South Africa
Telephone: 27-11-805-4819
Fax: 27-11-805-3648

O'REILLY™

TO ORDER: **800-998-9938** • **order@ora.com** • **http://www.ora.com/**
OUR PRODUCTS ARE AVAILABLE AT A BOOKSTORE OR SOFTWARE STORE NEAR YOU.
FOR INFORMATION: **800-998-9938** • **707-829-0515** • **info@ora.com**